I WANT YOU TO BE FREE

S. Nadja Zajdman

HOBART BOOKS

HOBART BOOKS

I WANT YOU TO BE FREE

ISBN 978-1-914322-09-9

First Published in 2022

by

Hobart Books, Oxfordshire, England

hobartbooks.com

Printed and bound in Great Britain

I WANT YOU
TO BE FREE

By S. Nadja Zajdman

with

Renata Skotnicka-Zajdman.

The story of Renata Skotnicka-Zajdman, an orphan of war who matured into a rescuer of Memory.

A remarkable woman. An extraordinary story.

Dedicated to the memory of

Dr Jean Liard

who also wanted me to be free.

ACKNOWLEDGEMENTS

A work as complex as this is difficult to produce without assistance. Many people have helped. Countless conversations and e-mail exchanges have taken place unrecorded. To all the unnamed individuals who have helped in some small yet significant way, I thank you.

Professor Dorota Glowacka at King's College in Halifax, Nova Scotia provided essential guidance on both Polish and German usage in the text. I am moved by her dedication to the memory of a woman she knew but briefly.

I salute Antonella Lalli and her ace team at the Eleanor London Library in Cote St. Luc, Quebec, both for their assistance with historical research and for their patience with me.

I bow to the Collections Department of the Montreal Holocaust Museum for scanning the images reproduced in this work, as well as for the gracious manner in which they did so.

I thank The Society of Authors Foundation in London for their monetary award. Above and beyond their financial assistance, the validation is priceless.

At the height of a pandemic, Adam Gardner had the courage and optimism to found Hobart Books. He has my deepest admiration and respect.

S. Nadja Zajdman
January 2022

LIST OF FIGURES

Cover image editorial credit (street scene): Everett Collection / Shutterstock.com

FOREWORD

Of all the grandparents I never got a chance to know, I feel closest to my mother's father Łucjan. Perhaps it was my mother's vivid storytelling that made him seem accessible. I've inherited his talents and temperament, so I was told. Sometimes I fantasise that I can time travel to Poland in the 1930s and meet my grandfather Łucjan. How would I introduce myself to him? How would I communicate with him? He didn't speak English, and I speak neither Polish, Russian, German, Italian – nor, for that matter, Latin. How would I make myself known to him? I'd have to bring photographs. On first seeing me would he gasp in shock, the way my Uncle Alek from Australia gasped, because I look so much like my grandmother Natalia.

As I write, Łucjan's image glows from a wall. Well into middle age, my mother discovered the one extant photograph of her father. It was a group photograph, and Łucjan is peering over a head from the third row in the back. My mother took the picture to a photographer, and Łucjan's face was enlarged and isolated. It now rests as a lamination on one of my walls, next to a profile of Natalia. On my wall, my grandparents are reunited. Natalia is gazing at Łucjan, while Łucjan is looking straight forward, and ahead. A dark cap covers his bald head, his mouth is sensuous, and heavy lids hood his eyes. If I look from a certain angle, it appears Łucjan is looking at me. What does he see? Łucjan was demanding. Would my grandfather like me? Would he approve of me? What a gift it would have been for him to see his first grandchild born on his birthday. With the grandfather I never knew, I share a birthday. What else do we share? What else might we have shared?

PART I

THE END IS IN THE BEGINNING

CHAPTER ONE

Łucjan Skotnicki, my grandfather, was born on 6 December 1889, on the outskirts of Warsaw, in what was then a rebellious area of Tsarist Russia. When he reached military age his father, a country doctor, injected him with the cholera bacterium in order to keep him from being conscripted into the Russian Army. As a side effect of the induced illness, Łucjan lost his luxuriant black hair. It never grew back. He would be bald for life.

As a financially struggling student, Łucjan marketed himself as a tutor. He was consequently hired by a wealthy Warsaw family to help their youngest daughter with her homework. Sixteen-year-old Natalia Młynek fell in love with the sensuous-lipped and prematurely bald young man, an idealistic youth who was passionate about politics and social justice. They promised themselves to each other and planned to marry. When Natalia's mother got wind of the romance she ordered the tutor out of her house. Natalia was the youngest of three unmarried sisters, and seeing the youngest marry first would shame the older siblings. Also, this tutor was from the provinces, the son of a country doctor who accepted payment in the form of produce from his patients' farms and fish from local streams. This near-peasant was considered completely unsuitable for the sophisticated, city-bred Natalia.

Łucjan retreated, and licked his wounds. Natalia was sent to Vienna, where she studied opera. Upon her return to Warsaw, she was married off to a second cousin and became

Natalia Młynek Młynek. The woman destined to become my grandmother was born into Jewish Warsaw's social elite. She was part of it. She was also its victim.

At the outset of the First World War, Natalia's thwarted suitor somewhere found the funds to travel and study at the University of Zürich. Life in Zürich during the First World War must have been an exhilarating experience for an intelligent and receptive young Pole. Neutral Switzerland served as a sanctuary, but along with being a safe haven, the city was also a centre of espionage.

In wartime Zürich, the cafés and cabarets were teeming with artists, pacifists, philosophers, and revolutionaries engaged in heated debates. Did Łucjan attend a Dadaist performance at the Café Voltaire? Did he cross paths with Lenin before the Bolsheviks set off to lead his country in revolution? What is known is that, while abroad, Łucjan discovered Italy and fell in love with all things Italian. This youthful affinity would have far-reaching effects.

Whatever his experiences Łucjan returned, post-war, to the newly formed republic of Poland, still a firebrand, but now a more cosmopolitan one, remaining both, for the rest of his tragically short life.

Setting up practice in Sochaczew, the newly minted attorney remained stubbornly single, though not celibate. He entered into an affair with a local beauty who was married and the mother of a young daughter. This scandalous liaison was an open secret that became the talk of the small town.

In the mid-1920s Łucjan's first love Natalia was suddenly widowed, and in an unknown fashion he found her again. Destiny had been delayed, but it could not be denied. The universe was offering them a second chance, and they seized it. The second time around, no overbearing mother could stop them. At the end of 1927, Łucjan and Natalia finally married. Before the end of 1928 Natalia gave birth to my mother, the only child they had together, a girl Łucjan named Renata, which is the Italian translation of 'reborn'. The name proved a fortunate one. During the course of her long life Renata would have to reinvent herself many, many times.

It seems Łucjan and Natalia were brought together only long enough to produce my mother.

At the height of The Great Depression, the furniture stores Natalia inherited from her father, were failing. In Sochaczew, in the triplex Natalia purchased for Łucjan and his parents, their toddler lay drifting into sleep. Natalia knelt beside the drowsy three-year-old. Renata felt her cheeks grow wet as her mother's tears fell upon them. She kissed her baby goodbye, left her in Łucjan's care, and returned to Warsaw to rebuild the family business. Renata would not see her mother again for the next two years. All the while, within earshot of the child, tongues wagged. The pack of relatives, whom Natalia supported financially, as well as Łucjan's relatives, hissed, 'Her mother abandoned her. Her mother abandoned her…' Family interference tore the marriage apart, and Łucjan and Natalia separated in 1935.

In the wake of their separation, an exhausting legal battle ensued. Łucjan agreed to a divorce on condition he be given sole custody of Renata. He reasoned it was only fair, since Natalia had two other children of her own. Natalia refused and argued that, as the mother, she had the right to sole custody of her child. The presiding judge placed the decision in the hands of seven-year-old Renata. Without hesitation, she chose to go with her father. Because of her half-sister's hostility to Łucjan and, by extension, to her, as the daughter of 'the man who took my mother away,' Renata felt like an outsider in her mother's home. Natalia was torn between her child with Łucjan and her two fatherless children. With Łucjan, Renata knew she came first. The judge then granted the couple joint custody and a legal separation. Łucjan and Natalia never divorced. Each year, for the few years left to them, they reunited on Renata's birthday. Every 23rd October tentatively they reached out to each other and shyly touched hands. Renata embraced her birthdays for no other reason than it gave her one day out of the year when she could have her parents back together. Each year, Natalia and Łucjan asked their daughter, 'What would like for your birthday?' Each year, Renata's answer was the same. 'I want the two of you to be my family again.'

Natalia remained in Warsaw. Łucjan returned to Sochaczew, and to his married mistress. In the late 1930s Łucjan's mistress gave birth to a second daughter who, it was rumoured, was not her husband's child, but Łucjan's. Debate over the girl's paternity is pointless. This child's life would end in Treblinka.

Ina Kenigstein, Łucjan's mistress, with her husband and their daughters, now lived on the top floor of the triplex that Natalia had purchased for him. His parents, and then his widowed mother, lived on the ground floor, and his divorced sister Sallah lived next door. Renata considered Ina's daughter Jadzia to be one of her two best friends.

Łucjan seemed to recognise that Renata would be his legacy. He treated his legitimate child as apprentice, successor and heir. As a hands-on parent, he was ahead of his time. In order to accelerate Renata's academic progress he had her home-schooled. By the time he decided to register her in the local elementary school, Renata was ready for second grade.

Łucjan supervised Renata's reading and academic studies, bringing in a tutor when she demonstrated a weakness in maths. He demanded her best, and got it. By the time Renata was ten years old, she was ready for high school. Sochaczew's high school, or *Gimnazjum*, was named for its most illustrious son, the composer Fryderyk Chopin.

Like her counterparts in North America, Renata was mesmerised by the magic of talking motion pictures. Conveniently, the father of Renata's other buddy owned the local *kino*. Renata and her friend Irena spent many enchanted hours in the darkened hall, sighing with Greta Garbo, swooning over Robert Taylor, and lustily singing along with Disney's seven dwarfs as they heigh-hoed off to work. Irena Draber was the eldest of five daughters born to a Catholic father and the daughter of the town rabbi. Both the Catholic and Jewish communities shunned the Drabers and their daughters, except for Łucjan, who set for his daughter an example in social acceptance. Consequently, Renata was the Draber sisters' only friend. Though Jewish students were exempt from catechism classes, Renata attended them. These classes were held on Saturdays, when Jewish students were out of school. A Jewish classmate must have informed her mother, because the woman complained to Łucjan. 'How can you allow your daughter to sit with the [1]*goyim* on Saturdays?!'

'Renata is free to study whatever she likes.' Łucjan responded. 'Knowledge will never hurt her.'

In catechism, as in all subjects except for maths, Renata excelled. Decades later, Irena Draber would remind her Jewish friend that she had fed her answers when she faltered in class. Besides going to the movies with Irena, with Łucjan's blessing, Renata also attended church.

Feeding her love of movies, Łucjan enrolled Renata in the international Shirley Temple fan club. He opened charge accounts for her at the town's ice cream parlour and its pastry shop. Renata could not only treat herself at will; she

---

[1] Gentiles

could also treat her prepubescent social set. There was
[2]*bomba* and [3]*ponchik* for everyone! Perched in a basket that
perched on the side of Łucjan's motorcycle, Renata raced
through Sochaczew with her [4]*tatusz*. She was his precious
cargo.

Łucjan submitted a photograph of his daughter to the
local newspaper, which was running a children's beauty
contest. Renata came in first runner-up.

Officially, at the age of four, she was pronounced the
second-most beautiful little girl in Sochaczew. Proudly,
Łucjan displayed the newspaper announcement and
photograph on his desk. How I wish that photograph had
survived, and I could have it now.

Before Renata could read, Łucjan read to her from the
children's newspaper created by the paediatrician and author
Janusz Korczak. In particular, Renata loved to listen to
articles submitted by an older cousin. As soon as she could
write well enough, she vowed she, too, would pen articles for
Dr Korczak's newspaper.

Once Renata could read, and she learned early, in Polish
translation she read David 'Kuperfeld,' which introduced her
to Charles Dickens whom, decades later, in the original
English, she would introduce to me. She read Anne of Green
Gables, which introduced her to the country that became her
adopted home. Most particularly, Renata read *Uncle Tom's
Cabin*. How she cried at the plight of Stowe's black slaves.
The lawyer's daughter had inherited her father's sense of
social justice.

---

[2] An ice cream dish

[3] Doughnuts, Polish-style

[4] Daddy

Łucjan was impatient, defiant, and appeared fearless. He built the town library, which he named *The Sholem Aleichem Library*. Because he was its founder, a life-size portrait of the lawyer greeted library members at the entrance. How proud Renata was when she entered the library and encountered the cinema-sized poster of her Dad.

Besides founding a library, Łucjan also created a drama circle and performed flamboyantly in its amateur theatricals. He wore knickerbockers, not only because this style of menswear made it easier for him to straddle his motorcycle, but also because it showed off his shapely legs. It was generally conceded that Łucjan's legs were more attractive than Natalia's but then, a bout of rickets in infancy had left Natalia bow-legged. Her mother Gustawa refused to breastfeed, in order to maintain the height and contour of her breasts. Instead she farmed out her baby to a wet nurse in the countryside. The poor peasant took the wealthy matron's money and fed Natalia milk diluted with water, in order to have enough milk left over to feed her own child.

It was understood, and accepted, that Renata would inherit her father's law practice. She sat beside him in the town courtroom as he pleaded for the marginalised and fought for the underdog. Since Renata read anything she could get her hands on, she would read a text on the Napoleonic code, if she found nothing else. Łucjan poured into his child his love of great literature and classical music, his passion for social justice, and his blazing contempt for prejudice, ignorance, and narrow-minded fools.

The lawyer was a maverick. Flaunting his disdain for organised religion, he sauntered in front of the rabbi's home on *Yom Kippur*, blatantly puffing on cigarettes. He revered Mahatma Ghandi and wept at the death of Marshal Pilsudski. He also quoted Oscar Wilde. Łucjan gave soaring orations denouncing the fascist government that followed in the later

1930s, a government taking its cues from the neighbouring Third Reich. He vociferously decried the renewed harassment of Jews. When warned to tone down the defender declared, 'I am not running in a popularity contest!' Łucjan was sophisticated, cosmopolitan, and stuck in a small town. He alienated both the Catholic and Jewish communities, and almost wilfully courted disaster. He made life harder on himself than it needed to be, but his painfully honest nature wouldn't allow him to live any other way. Who can judge whether isolation or conformity is harder? Łucjan refused to shift with prevailing winds.

Yet Renata considered her childhood in Sochaczew idyllic. The Skotnicki clan ran the town. Łucjan's sister Sallah was a midwife. His brother Herman was a dentist. His father Mauriczy was a general practitioner who never asked whether a patient attended synagogue or church. From local peasants Dr Skotnicki often accepted produce from their farms or fish they caught in the river in lieu of cash payment, which infuriated his wife Rosalia. His youngest granddaughter Renata was his special pet. Renata adored her grandfather. She considered him a friendly giant. She accompanied him on his [5]*droshky* as he made his round of house calls. On Sundays he accompanied her to concerts conducted at Żelazowa Wola, Fryderyk Chopin's birthplace, on the outskirts of town. Renata's grandfather always had a muffin on hand, because he knew that the little girl loved muffins. Indeed, Renata's passion for muffins was so pronounced that her grandfather came to call her Miss Muffin.

***

It was in April of 1936, during the period of Passover (which the Skotnickis did not observe), that Mauriczy was called

---

[5]A buggy, usually attached to a horse

away. While Renata sat at breakfast with her grandparents, chewing on her morning muffin, there was an agitated pounding on the door. Sorry to disturb so early, but please, would Dr Skotnicki come and attend to a man who had taken ill? Without hesitation, Renata's grandfather left the table, pulled on his boots, and set out on his *droshky*.

Half an hour later, while Renata was scooping up muffin crumbs, there was another knock at the door. The messenger burdened with delivering this message was ashen-faced. Dr Skotnicki had arrived at the sick man's home, knocked on the door, announced himself, and when the door was opened he fell across the threshold and onto the floor. The town doctor was felled by a massive coronary. He died – with his boots on. At the time of his death Mauriczy Skotnicki was seventy-five years old.

His funeral was held the following day. Jews and Gentiles lined the streets. Local peasants doffed their caps and crossed themselves as the Jewish doctor's coffin passed. The mayor of Sochaczew and city councillors served as pallbearers.

Bizarrely, for a Jewish funeral, a marching band was part of the procession. The fire brigade had asked to be included. The suddenly-widowed Rosalia allowed them to march but refused to allow them to play, so the members of Sochaczew's fire brigade marched silently with instruments in hand.

Natalia, separated from Łucjan and estranged from his family, did not attend the funeral. To bid farewell to her father-in-law, discreetly she slipped in from Warsaw the following day. On her own, she visited the Jewish cemetery and laid a bouquet of flowers at his grave. Of all her in-laws, it was only Łucjan's father who had treated the beleaguered Natalia with kindness and respect. She loved him for it, and sincerely grieved his passing.

Natalia assumed her graveside visit had gone unnoticed. But a small town has spying eyes. When a neighbourhood gossip informed Rosalia that her daughter-in-law had placed flowers at Mauriczy's grave, the doctor's widow ordered that the floral tribute be thrown away.

***

In 1937, the enemies Łucjan made found a way of having him disbarred. It didn't deter him. He hired a young lawyer from Warsaw, Artur Wlodawsky, to front for him, while he continued working behind the scenes and appeared in court as 'legal counsel.' At the same time he went to work as an agent for an Italian insurance company. Along with a copy of Jules Verne's *Around The World in 80 Days,* Łucjan bought an insurance policy for Renata, telling her, 'When you're twenty-one, this policy will pay off and you'll have money to travel the world.' The Italian insurance company refused to honour the policy when Renata filed a claim belatedly in 1954. She was again refused when she tried once more in 2004, yet before she was twenty-one Renata travelled in ways Łucjan could never have dreamed.

CHAPTER TWO

In April of 1939, Łucjan was in the middle of one of his regular card games with the town mayor and his cronies, and he was winning. In recent years the mayor had joined the ruling fascist party. He instructed Łucjan to donate his winnings to the party. Łucjan refused. The mayor accused him of a dangerous lack of patriotism. Łucjan retorted, 'I'm a better patriot than you, you son-of-a-bitch mayor!' The mayor's response was to have Łucjan arrested on charges of insulting the majesty of the government. A trial was held on the afternoon of 27 April. Łucjan was found guilty and sentenced to internment at *Bereza Kartuska,* a concentration camp already established. The Polish fascist party was anticipating what was to come.

In the evening, in his apartment, while she slept in an adjoining room Renata later surmised that her father, who suffered from angina, felt the first stirrings of a heart attack. Perhaps he gasped and reached for the drawer that held his medication, but it was too late. The sound of a commotion woke the ten-year-old. She ran into his room and discovered her *tatus* in bed, writhing and gasping for breath. Renata threw herself onto the bed and cradled him in her arms. Four months before the outbreak of war, Łucjan died in his bed, in the arms of his beloved child.

In old age, confronting her own end, Renata questioned the circumstances surrounding her father's death. Through her work with a Jewish genealogy group, she discovered documents in her father's handwriting. With Natalia's money

13

he built and owned the triplex they lived in on Warszawska 13. Apartments not occupied by family or the Kenigsteins were rented. There was a janitor living on the premises. In an atmosphere when and where anti-Semitism was exploited and rewarded, the janitor's disrespect and insubordination led Łucjan to fire him. When the janitor refused to accept his dismissal, Łucjan resorted to legal measures in order to have him evicted. The janitor's offences must have been egregious, because a Gentile judge ruled in Łucjan's favour. The eviction was scheduled for 28 April. Renata remembered being wakened by the sound of 'a commotion'. Can a man dying and alone cause a commotion? Unless her memory was playing tricks on her, she began to believe she heard the scuffle of feet. By the time she reached her father's room, he was dying. When Renata realised that her *tatuś* had stopped breathing, she fled the apartment and screamed for help.

Her cries were answered by Aunt Sallah, who raced in from next door, and Łucjan's mistress Ina, who came running down the stairs. Renata then telephoned her mother in Warsaw. Łucjan was one of the privileged few in Sochaczew who owned a phone.

Aunt Sallah and Ina stayed up with the distraught child throughout a terror-ridden night. Łucjan's body was wrapped in a white sheet and laid on the floor. A candle was lit. Jewish male neighbours sat vigil and over the dead body took turns keening and wailing until dawn. Come morning, Łucjan's corpse was lifted into a plain narrow box and driven by a large *drosky* to the Jewish cemetery.

Natalia rushed in, by bus, from Warsaw, with her young adult son Alek. Ania did not deign to join them. Natalia held Renata's hand while Alek fought off anti-Semitic hooligans who jeered and threw stones at Łucjan's passing coffin. Among the children shouting curses, Renata recognised some of the classmates she treated to ice cream and pastry on a charge account paid for by her father. Even in death, the defender was under attack. Gripping her mother's hand, in a haze of horror, ten-year-old Renata somnambulated behind her father's coffin.

Now half-orphaned, Renata returned to Warsaw with her mother and brother, but briefly. In their mother's home Ania greeted her. 'I'm glad your father dropped dead!' Renata was locked inside the shock and numbness of the newly bereaved. So was Natalia, who said nothing. Not then, not ever. She neither censored Ania nor supported Renata, not even privately, after her two fatherless girls, separately, went to bed. Natalia's silence was as cruel as it was incomprehensible. Because of her hasty remarriage, perhaps she recognised her part in the creation of the vengeful creature Ania became. Perhaps she accepted Ania's viciousness as a form of punishment. Still, she might have gone to her grieving child after the fact and explained her cowardice, but she didn't. There's no way around it. Natalia sacrificed her stronger child for her tougher one.

'Nobody put their arms around me!' Seventy-three years later, on a cancer ward, Renata wailed into a cassette recorder. 'Nobody!' She was then in the last stages of her life.

Setting a template, Renata rescued herself through resourcefulness and wit. She insisted on completing the school year in her father's hometown. Her education mustn't be interrupted. Already the girl was honouring her father's memory. From the time of Łucjan's death until the end of June, Renata lived in the apartment she had shared with him, seeing no one, speaking to no one. The housekeeper, who stayed on to look after her, prepared her meals. Her aunt kept an eye on her from next door, and her father's mistress looked down from upstairs. The girl grew thin and wasted, but her grades did not suffer. If anything, they were even better than before. Each afternoon after school she headed to the Jewish cemetery, spread her textbooks and notebooks and pens and pencils on the grass, and spent the rest of the day doing homework at the site of Łucjan's grave.

***

Renata Skotnicka was born in a fashionable medical clinic in Warsaw on 23 October, 1928. Her older half-sister Ania needled her about it, as she needled Renata about everything else. 'Oh, you were an expensive baby! Me and Alek were made at home!' Ania bitterly resented the presence of a new man in her mother's life, and bitterly resented their baby. Aleksander, almost sixteen years Renata's senior, welcomed the presence of a new life, and treated his baby sister like a living doll.

Natalia and Łucjan's delayed union altered their destinies. Łucjan's first love and one wife were the same, yet not the same. He had fallen in love with a sixteen-year-old schoolgirl, yet married a thirty-three-year-old widow with two grieving children. Aleksander was indifferent to his stepfather. Ania detested him. The slew of relatives left behind by Natalia's first husband, who were financially supported by Natalia, grew anxious and ultimately ugly over issues of inheritance.

For the harassed Natalia it would be her housekeeper Janina, called Janka, who became her lifelong confidante and companion. While Natalia went into the wider world to provide for her children and a small army of extended relatives, it was Janka who pushed Renata's perambulator in the Saski Gardens, it was Janka who spoon-fed her *kefir*, and it was Janka who made her laugh and dried her tears.

For Janka, Renata may have filled the space left by the child she was forced to deny. A little girl wove in and out of Natalia's household, born in the same year as Renata. She was introduced as Janka's niece, and raised by Janka's sister.

In fact, the girl, Alicia, was Janka's daughter, the issue of a rape by her bestial brother-in-law.

Ewa Janina Wojcicka was born in the slums of Warsaw on Christmas Eve, 1908. She was the daughter of manual labourers, and had an older sister. She had been in Natalia's employ since she was a teenager. She was a doll-like young woman, perfectly formed, who seemed to have been created in miniature. She was so petite that those who knew her called her 'Lilliput.' She had a wide and open face, wore her ash blonde hair in a page boy cut, dressed in children's clothes because they came in the only sizes that fitted, and wrapped her slender torso in an ornately patterned peasant's shawl.

When school let out in June, Renata was compelled to return to her mother's home in Warsaw. She discovered that her nanny was large and swollen with child. Janka had spent the previous Christmas with those who passed for family and returned to Natalia's apartment in the New Year carrying another issue of another rape.

In the last summer of precarious peace Alek took Janka for daily walks, until he was mobilised into the reserves. At that point, Natalia and Janka disappeared into the countryside. When they returned, Janka's silhouette was slim once more.

CHAPTER THREE

In the spring of 1939, Ania and Alek were both engaged to be married. Natalia set up Ania in an apartment with a studio in Praga, across the River Bug. Ania had a fine eye for colour and form, along with the skill and talent to realise her visions. She began by designing and producing hand-made comforters and bed linens intended for sale in her mother's furniture stores. Ania was setting out to become a designer.

Alek's engagement party took place in his mother's home on 5 March 1939. It was his fiancée's twenty-first birthday. Renata came to call it 'the last good day of my childhood'.

Marysia Zilberstein, by all accounts a gentle young woman from a loving family of modest means, was beloved not only by Alek, but also by Natalia and Renata. Even Ania had nothing negative to say about her. For Renata, Marysia seemed the sympathetic older sister Ania wouldn't, or couldn't, be.

During the siege of Warsaw, in what was likely the last attack, the *Luftwaffe* targeted the city's Jewish district on *Rosh Hashonah,* which is the Jewish New Year. It was rumoured that this final bombardment was led by Herman Goering. Abramek Rosenbaum, one of Renata's cousins, found her at an aunt's home, where the family had sought shelter. Abramek was carrying a shovel. 'It got Marysia and her parents.' He whispered. Fourteen-year-old Abramek and not-quite-eleven year old Renata crossed Warsaw to the site

Figure 1: Uncle Alek (right) and the only surviving photo of his fiancée, Marysia (pictured here with her father in August 1939)

where the demolished apartment block had stood. The two children hauled Marysia's body out of the ruins and dragged it to a nearby garden square. Abramek dug out the earth in a patch of grass, and together the children buried the bride that would never be. When Renata returned to her aunt's apartment, it fell to her to inform Natalia.

Marysia was considered the family's first wartime victim. Her almost-mother-in-law was grief-stricken.

***

I remember the last week of August 1939 as if it were yesterday, when thousands of Poles of all ages, both Jews and non-Jews, dug trenches, vowing to fight the Nazis to the very end. People put away their differences and worked together.

I remember sirens, shelters, gas masks and daily drills. Poles and Jews were working side by side. The use of poison gas was expected and school children were instructed in making makeshift gas masks. There were daily air-raid alarms and frequent runs to the hastily built shelters. We learned to administer first aid and to go to the shelters quietly and in order. Instead of calming us, these activities increased our anxiety.

We were given gas masks, which we wore during air-raid drill. They smelled almost as bad as the gas they were meant to protect us from. Public bomb shelters, in cellars, were designated in each neighbourhood...

September first, 1939. As I tunnel through the years to that distant day, I feel a quickening of the heart...'

From the private memoir of Renata Skotnicka-Zajdman.

It was the first morning of September. Renata lazed in bed. With her eyes still shut she wondered about the upcoming school year, and what she would like to have for her birthday come October. Renata's eleventh birthday would be the first without her cherished *Tatus*.

Sunshine beckoned. Languidly Renata rose to meet it. Outside her bedroom window, the sky was a solid block of blue. On this first day of September, Renata had a special mission. With Ania, she had bought a broach and a bouquet of flowers. This first day of September was Natalia's birthday, and her daughters hoped the gesture would cheer her. Since Renata's return from Sochaczew, the atmosphere in her mother's apartment was steeped in gloom. Natalia was constantly in tears. Renata believed her mother was crying for her father, which may have been partly true. Though they hadn't been able to live together, Natalia's refusal to grant Łucjan the divorce whose proceedings she initiated, as well as tell-tale comments, led Łucjan's only child to believe that her Mum still carried a torch for her Dad. But Natalia was also frightened by the increasingly alarming news. Since the *Anschluss* in Austria and the November pogroms in the neighbouring Third Reich, Austrian Jews and Polish Jews who had lived in Germany were streaming across the border. Overnight they became homeless and stateless. Often, they were ejected from their homes in the middle of the night. For these displaced and desperate people Natalia opened her door, her closets, her pantry and her heart. Nightly she invited them to dinners she knew they needed. She pulled coats out of closets and blankets out of drawers. No one in need left Natalia's apartment empty-handed. At her dinner table she listened to accounts of outrages and abuse perpetrated by the Nazi regime. These shocking stories left her despondent. 'We're trapped.' She kept repeating, as she moped about the apartment. 'It's the beginning of the end.' Obsessively, Natalia kept repeating. 'It's the beginning of the end.'

On the first morning of September, Renata and Ania entered their mother's bedroom. *'Sto lat! Sto lat!'* They chimed, in the Polish version of Happy Birthday. Translated loosely, *Sto lat* means 'May we live one hundred years.' Natalia was still in bed. Her daughters approached, bearing gifts. As they hugged and cuddled, an ominous drone was heard outside the wide windows. Renata's ears perked up. Could a storm be brewing on such a lovely day? Within minutes, German bomber planes invaded the peace and sanctity of a clear blue sky. Within minutes, the wide windows of Natalia's luxury apartment rattled. Several minutes more, and they smashed. Fortunately Natalia's bed wasn't set against a window. Before breakfast Natalia was huddling against a wall with her daughters cowering in her arms.

What had begun as a day of celebration devolved into a day of terror. Natalia's forty-sixth birthday would be her last birthday. World War II had begun.

For the next forty-eight hours, German bombs rained on Warsaw and German panzer divisions raced through Poland's flat rural landscape, machine-gunning anyone who attempted to get in their way. Would Prime Minister Chamberlain keep his pledge to support Poland, or would he betray them as he had betrayed Czechoslovakia?

On Sunday afternoon, the 3rd of September, among a euphoric crowd, Renata marched with her mother to the British Embassy. Tens of thousands of Varsovians wept, whooped, danced in the bomb-battered streets waving homemade Union Jacks, sang the Polish national anthem, and attempted to sing God Save The King. On the balcony of the embassy Ambassador Kennard roared like a British lion, 'Long live Poland! We will fight side by side against aggression and injustice!' Not only Britain, but also France pledged to help defend the east European state.

'You see, *Mamusia.*[6] Not-quite-eleven-year-old Renata attempted to console Natalia. 'It will be alright now. England will fight with us. The English will rescue us. The English will save us. You don't need to cry anymore. Nothing worse is going to happen.' Natalia held her youngest child close, and sighed.

In the crowd Natalia spied a prominent citizen. Indeed, the gentleman was considered a national treasure. She pointed him out to her younger daughter. 'Look, Renusia. It's Dr Korczak.' Excitedly, Renata peered over the heads of

---

[6] Mummy

the throng and saw, in the flesh, her literary hero. Korczak's bald head shone in the sunshine and his goatee jutted forward as he listened intently to the British ambassador. Renata would see Janusz Korczak once more on what was, likely, the last day of his life.

The week that Renata was slated to resume school, Warsaw was under siege. In his raspy voice President Starzynski proclaimed over national radio, 'We will not succumb.' Repeatedly Poland's leader appealed to England and France for help. The Poles continued to deceive themselves, believing those who called themselves allies would keep their word and come to their aid. While Chamberlain's government demonstrated its solidarity by having the RAF drop propaganda leaflets on Berlin, Varsovians built barricades in the streets. They carried out of their homes tables and chairs, and overturned streetcars in a naïve effort to thwart the Nazi onslaught.

Bombardment was ceaseless. The sophisticated metropolis known as 'Paris of the East' became a terror-ridden fortress of smoke and fire. The bodies of the injured, the dying and the dead were strewn in courtyards and along wide boulevards. Those still on their feet were struck and buried by falling debris. With her mother, sister and relatives, Renata slept in hallways, far from windows and close to doorframes. It was commonly believed that if a house collapsed, the doorframes were the last of its structure to fall. By mid-September Warsaw resembled a grotesque stage set; its elegant apartment buildings were blasted open and three-sided rooms stood revealed.

Yet, through it all, Renata's sister Ania and her older cousins organised soup kitchens for the homeless and the refugees. Because German bombardment was incessant, the Polish authorities dispensed with air-raid warnings, and hourly Natalia and her daughters were forced into basements. The day they were staying with Natalia's older sister Anna, who lived at Plac Grzybowski 7, this distinctive work of architecture caught fire and Anna's son Bronek led them to the shelter next door, under All Saints' Church. When this round of bombardment stopped, they surfaced. What confronted the family were deep craters in the pavements filled with dead horses encircled by flies. Survivors of the most recent bombardment had emerged with knives and hatchets and were hacking away at horseflesh. They tossed the carcasses into the Vistula river, which polluted its waters. A typhoid epidemic broke out.

Figure 2: Full circle: line drawing of Plac Grzybowski 7, Renata's birthplace, overlain by her business card from her later activism

By the second half of September, hunger reached epidemic proportions. The carcass of a horse or a dog killed in the streets would attract rabid humans.

By the fourth week of the siege, the shops were empty. Food transports had ceased. German bombers attacked the filtration plants. Now there was no water. Power plants were hit. There was no electricity. Within a month, Natalia and her daughters had gone from living as members of a social and cultural elite to living in the dark.

Then the Russians invaded.

On 28 September, Warsaw capitulated. The air stilled. During the first week of October, Hitler rode triumphantly through the *Ujadowski Alee*. Natalia and her daughters returned to their luxury apartment, which was damaged, but not destroyed. During the siege Janka had returned to the slums, to her sister and brother-in-law. Now she came back to her employer's apartment. Within days of Hitler's visit, ethnic Germans, or Poles claiming to be ethnic Germans, stormed up to Natalia's door and demanded she hand over her apartment. Like the rest of the city, Natalia conceded defeat and vacated her sumptuous apartment, with Renata and Janka in tow. They congregated in Ania's small apartment across the River Bug. That is where Alek found them. He was in the air force and the air force, along with the rest of the military, was in disarray. In the general mêlée Alek bolted, burying his uniform, but keeping his gun. He stole a horse and acquired ill-fitting clothes from a peasant in a manner that can only be guessed at. He rode bareback to the outskirts of Warsaw, where he traded the horse for a bottle of water and a loaf of bread. He had heard that Warsaw was starving. Though Natalia had the foresight to stock up on food, she no longer had access to it. Her food reserves were stored in the apartment she had been ejected from.

Alek limped his way into the arms of his mother. For a week he lay in bed belly-down, while Natalia applied balm to his bare and bruised behind.

Ultimately Alek had to be informed of Marysia's death. When his mother told him, he went berserk. He grabbed his gun and lunged for the door, determined to murder every German in sight. The women wrestled the weapon out of his hands, and Natalia instructed Janka to get rid of it. Most likely Janka sold the gun, the way she later sold Natalia's possessions in order to keep Natalia's children from starving.

The skies were now quiet, but the streets held a new kind of danger. Under the German occupation, only trade schools and courses for factory workers were allowed to resume. In their campaign to reduce the Poles to serfdom, the new German masters banned higher education. Renata spent school hours inside her sister's apartment, reading works of literature her mother had managed to salvage from their original apartment, while Natalia and Ania braved the line-ups for bread. Only bakeries were allowed to re-open, under the supervision of the Germans. Sometimes women began lining up while it was still dark in order to reach the bakery doors before the bakers ran out of bread.

Queues formed in front of Warsaw's bakeries. One queue was allowed for Catholics, the other for the Jews. Ten Poles to one Jew were permitted to stand in these queues. On occasion patrolling German soldiers threw chunks of bread into the lines of hungry women in order to film them, for propaganda purposes, while they fought for the scraps.

Natalia insisted on standing in the queue for Catholics. She believed she could pass, and she was right. Natalia had fair skin, Slavic features, blue eyes and auburn hair. When German soldiers and Polish policemen stared into her face to check for tell-tale signs of Jewishness, Natalia defiantly stared back. She was never asked to produce her identity card, which stated her religion as the Faith of Moses. Other hungry Jewish women who braved the Polish queue were not so fortunate. Dark eyes or a trace of fear could lead to discovery and a merciless beating with nightsticks and rifle butts. As they patrolled these line-ups, German soldiers were assisted in identifying their victims by Polish collaborators who, at this early stage, were mostly teenage hoodlums heedless of the long-term consequences of their actions.

It was an inefficient way of removing the Jews, and the Germans prided themselves on their efficiency. In late autumn, posters plastered across the city, reinforced by radio broadcasts, decreed that, as of 1 December, all Jews over the age of twelve were obliged to wear white armbands illustrated with a blue Star of David. That is when Natalia announced, 'We're getting out of here.'

While Natalia and Ania spent the days acquiring bread and lard and coal, Janka developed business contacts. Semi-literate, under her mattress she hid the salary she received from Natalia. As Natalia's resources dwindled, Janka handed her employer money, as needed. With her own seed money Janka began buying from desperate Jews, and selling to savvy farmers. Even savvier, Janka bartered with the farmers, and pocketed her profits from the Jews. Quickly establishing a reputation as a black market racketeer, Janka used her increasing wealth to keep her adopted family alive. She brought in coal to heat the apartment for the coming winter, along with hefty sacks of potatoes and flour, while Natalia planned the escape of her children, and then, her own.

CHAPTER FOUR

On 1 December 1939, Ania and Renata crossed into Białystok. Local farmers, who found a new source of income leading Jews across the border into the Soviet sector, extorted more money from Ania than had been agreed upon. Natalia and Janka took the precaution to equip Ania for such an event and, once the farmers' greed was satisfied, the sisters were able to join Alek in a ramshackle farmhouse on the outskirts of town, filled with fellow refugees.

When Natalia received word that her daughters were safe, she embarked on her own escape. Janka stayed behind in the apartment. It was more wished for, than expected, that the war would be brief, and Natalia and her children could soon return to a home maintained by Janka.

By the time Natalia began her journey in early December of 1939, more and more escape routes were being discovered and becoming sealed. She had to take a roundabout route, and reached Białystok more than a week after her departure.

Ania, always restless, always reckless, could not endure the wait. She decided to cross back and retrieve her mother. Alek pleaded with her to have patience, and stay put. Generally irrational, Ania could not be reasoned with. She believed she knew the route and did not require the assistance of the farmer/smugglers. Going it alone, Ania attempted to re-enter the German zone. She was caught, arrested, beaten, and raped. The only reason she survived was because she was able to pass as Catholic. She was allowed to return to her home, only to discover that her mother was no longer there.

By the time she arrived in Białystok, Natalia was running a fever. A doctor was summoned. Natalia had contracted typhus. She was one of its first victims in the first of many wartime epidemics to come.

Natalia was removed to hospital, not so much for her own sake, but in order to spare the refugee shelter from coming under quarantine. There was no medication available. The doctors and Natalia's children could only watch and wait. The stricken woman survived the disease's first crisis, but succumbed to the second. My grandmother died at the dawn of 1940. At precisely six p.m. on New Year's Night.

After Natalia was buried, Alek decided that he and Renata must return to Warsaw and be with Ania. Renata was terrified of returning. Alek joined a band of refugees who had decided to go back. Some could not tolerate life in exile. Some could not bear separation from their families.

These frightened people were further frightened by the prospect of having a child in their midst. Alek pleaded with them to accept Renata, as he had pleaded with Ania not to attempt a return. The group relented, but Renata did not. Brother and sister had a violent argument. In frustration, Alek hit her and dragged her to the meeting point. As the adults climbed over fences, passing a point of no return, Renata made a split-second decision to run. In the other direction. Alek stared in horror at his fleeing sister, but it was too late to turn back. It was not so much the Germans Renata was terrified of returning to as Ania.

In Warsaw, without Renata, it fell to Alek to break the news of Natalia's death to Janka and, most traumatically, to Ania. In her frequent fits of hysteria, Ania taunted Alek for 'losing the child.' Alek finally slipped on the blue and white armband. This act of capitulation would have horrified his mother. Ania continued to defy the order and rely on her ability to pass as Catholic. Despite her dark, slanted eyes and luxuriant dark hair, Ania, chameleon-like, slipped easily out of her Jewish skin and into the persona of a Polish peasant. She could blend and weave in and out of crowds undetected as surely and swiftly as Janka. Together Janka and Ania bought and sold and bartered and bribed, keeping each other, and Alek, alive.

On 15 November 1940, Ania and Alek were compelled, under the new law, to enter the ghetto established for Jews in Warsaw. On that same date Janka moved out of Natalia's apartment and back into the slums, with her sister and bestial brother-in-law. She arranged to have Natalia's furniture moved to various safe houses, and then began selling it off. With the proceeds she bought food and smuggled it into the Ghetto, keeping Alek and Ania alive.

CHAPTER FIVE

In the winter of 1940, alone in Soviet-occupied Białystok, adult refugees from Warsaw took pity on orphaned Renata, and enrolled her in a state-run boarding school.

'How old are you, child?' The headmistress asked.

'Fifteen.' Renata lied.

'What did your father do?' The headmistress continued.

'He was a worker.' Again, the girl was lying.

Renata was tall and well-developed for her age. She had two long chestnut-coloured braids running down her back. She wore a maroon-coloured beret on her head, a maroon-coloured scarf around her neck, carried a full knapsack on her back, and was dressed in layers, like an onion.

The adults relinquished Renata to the care of the headmistress. From a corner in the reception hall, a girl who really was fifteen stood, watching. She had dark, saucer-shaped eyes that sparkled. She had a high forehead topped by ash blond hair. She was pretty. She was Polish.

With her new charge in tow, the headmistress approached the girl. 'We have a new student with us. She is Polish, too. You can show her to the dormitory.' The headmistress returned to her office.

'Good morning. My name is Irena. What's yours?'

'Renata.' Renata looked down, and shuffled her feet.

'Renata!' Oh! What a beautiful name! Do you know that, in Latin, 'Renata' means 'reborn?' I'm very good in Latin!' Irena bragged. Almost against her will, Renata smiled.

In front of the Białystok boarding school hung a shingle which read, in Russian and Polish: TEACHERS' JUNIOR COLLEGE. All the teachers in this teachers' college were Russian. All subjects were taught in Russian, except for one class in world geography. Political meetings, led by *Politruks* sent by Moscow, were held after regular school hours, in the classrooms. Mass rallies were held in the auditorium. There were portraits of Stalin and Lenin in every classroom, and photographs of students who entered the privileged ranks of the [7]*Komsomol* lined corridor walls. Another row of photographs underlined the first. These were images of those 'resistant' and in need of 're-education.' The student body came from different backgrounds. Some, like Renata, were Polish Jewish refugees. Most were Byelorussian peasants between the ages of sixteen and twenty-five. They entered this teachers' college illiterate, grateful for the educational opportunity provided by the Soviet state, and eager to repay it.

Irena led Renata into the students' dormitory. It resembled a military barrack. There were long wooden tables in the centre, lined with hard-backed chairs. This was the study area. Along the walls ran two rows of cots, and next to each, a box was provided as a personal storage bin.

'You can sleep here, next to me. This box is for your things.' Irena led Renata through a form of orientation. Quietly, Renata unpacked the few possessions she still had.

---

[7] The *Komsomol* was a political youth organisation in the Soviet Union

From the moment of their meeting, Renata and Irena bonded. They sat beside each other in class. They studied together in the library. In the corridors and the schoolyard they giggled in high-spirited conspiracy. In the dormitory they fell asleep next to each other, and took their meals together three times a day.

At breakfast, each student was given a large white bun, and a glass of milk diluted with water. Lunch and supper consisted of black bread, potatoes, and cabbage. Renata and Irena ate at a long table with peasants short on table manners. Irena's table manners were good. Renata's table manners were impeccable. Irena studied her new friend. And wondered.

Irena and Renata sat beside each other, listening to the daily lecture: 'We do not believe in God! All religion is superstition! Children, you must remember that the wealthy class is defended by the priests! We Soviets have no choice but to become chauvinist in order to free the enslaved peoples of Poland. In order to strengthen internationalism, we must stress the right of nations to unite! And the right to unite implies the right to secede! Your parents have been brainwashed by their masters, and may resist the new ways. If some of your parents, or your [8]*tavarischi*, have difficulty understanding the urgency of our message, you must inform us so that we will be able to re-educate them. It is for their own good, as well as for the good of all who desire to be free. Freedom before individualism! Redemption exists for those who repent! Children! Let us give thanks and bless *Batiuschka* Stalin, our Little Father, who has liberated you from your corrupt capitalist oppressors!' A collective roar rose and swept the auditorium. The members of the

---

[8] Comrades

Komsomol were ecstatic. Renata was bewildered. Irena applauded wildly, and nudged her buddy to do the same.

> *'My uncle, a most worthy gentleman,*
> *When he fell seriously ill,*
> *By snuffing it made us all respect him.*
> *Couldn't have done it better if he tried.*
> *His behaviour was a lesson to us all.*
> *But God above, what crushing boredom*
> *To sit with the malingerer night and day,*
> *Not moving even one footstep away.*
>
> *What demeaning hypocrisy to amuse the half-dead codger,*
> *To fluff up his pillows, and then,*
> *Mournfully to bring him his medicine;*
> *To think to oneself and to sigh:*
> *When will the old rascal die?'*

As Renata ended her spirited rendition of Pushkin's poem *Yevgeny Onegin,* the class cheered. Beaming, Renata bowed. A bell rang. The class dispersed. Irena and Renata gathered their books and headed to the library.

'You speak Russian really well. Where did you learn it?'

Flushed by her triumph, Renata slipped. 'I learnt it from my nanny.' Irena's eyes flashed and darted to the photographs on the walls. Protectively she gripped Renata's arm, and pulled her into the library.

When the frozen ground began to thaw and light lasted a little longer, Irena and Renata would wander into the surrounding fields and climb to the steeple of an unfinished church, open to the air, looking out over the few flickering lights of Białystok. Gazing out over the neighbouring villages, they told each of their lost homes and absent families. They imagined a future together. They dreamt that when the war ended and they graduated they would find work in a village school and live together and never be parted. Not ever.

While their classmates returned to families during holidays, Irena and Renata hiked through the woods and roamed the halls of the deserted school building, sharing secrets and telling each other of their own families, which they had lost. In eighteen months they learned so much about each other that one could take on the other's identity. Sooner than could be imagined this, Renata came to do.

As the weather warmed and grew hot, and final exams were completed, Irena returned to her grandmother's farm near Łomża. Renata got a job in the countryside, ten kilometres from the Soviet-German border, in a summer camp for and called Young Pioneers. Her instructions were clear.

'Your daily quota is eighteen floors, six verandas, and two outhouses. They must all be cleaned and spotless by the end of the day. You will take your meals with the rest of the staff, and sleep with the laundresses in Lapy.'

'*Da, tavarisch* Anya Alexandrowna.' Each blazing summer day Renata filled her quota, while Soviet campers cavorted on the grounds. Each evening she returned to the straw litter in a bare room, in the village of Lapy. The laundresses had strung up a bed sheet, to separate their space from hers. On the other side of the sheet, they supplemented their income by entertaining Russian soldiers. Renata couldn't sleep. On one such occasion, a drunken private stumbled towards the partition and began to unbuckle his belt. One of the women pulled him back. 'No,

Aloysha. Leave her alone. She's just a kid. I'll take care of you.' Aloysha belched, unzipped his pants, and turned away from the sheet. Renata lay rigid. On those steamy summer

35

nights the twelve-year-old orphan listened to, and learnt, the language of carnality.

***

Come September, the students in the dormitory were settling in for the new semester. Renata sat outside on the stoop, watching and waiting. In the distance, she saw Irena saunter up the path, a basket balanced on her hip. The basket was bulging with bread, cheese and *⁹kielbasa*. Renata raced towards her. 'Irena!'

'I have to talk to you.' Furtively, Irena glanced about. 'But not here.'

Irena and Renata were perched on a plank in the open-air steeple, chewing on bread and cheese, and cutting into the log of *kielbasa*.

'Basia. She was at school. She was playing. I don't know why she did it – she must've heard something.' Irena hesitated. Then she whispered, 'Basia scratched out Stalin's eyes!'

'What?!'

'The portrait. The portrait in class. Stalin's portrait. She took a pen and she scratched out Stalin's eyes with the nib. Her teacher denounced her and they took them away – Basia, Junia, my stepmother – everyone, except me and my grandmother. They didn't come at night, the way they usually do. We were at the market when they came.'

'To – Siberia?' Renata whispered the word that implied a dreadful fate. In response, all Irena could manage was a nod.

---

⁹ Polish meat sausage

'But why didn't they just 're-educate' Basia?' Renata asked, reasonably.

Apologetically, Irena explained. 'My father's family had property. A lot of it. My father was a nobleman. Before the war, the Podbielskis were rich.' Irena and Renata huddled in the open-air steeple, two guilt-ridden children from the wrong side of the tracks.

***

Throughout the autumn and winter of 1940 and into 1941 Renata, as a blood donor, paid regular visits to the hospital where her mother had died. In return for her donation she received a hot meal and five roubles, which she deposited in Irena's box. Once she was even given candy, which she hid under her blouse until, in the sanctuary of the steeple, she could share it with her friend. When a nurse at the hospital recognised the increasingly pale girl she was thrown out, and this source of income stopped. Her strength and concentration returned, and Renata was able to audition for the school's spring production, in which she landed a principal role.

The director of the production, Grisha Segalovich, was a Polish Jewish refugee who had been a filmmaker in Warsaw. Alina, who played the lead, was sixteen, Polish, and distantly related to Irena. She had genuine talent – she would become a professional actress after the war. Renata was good, too – she would make use of her acting ability during the war. The teachers' college production of Gorky's *Vassa Zheleznova* was cast with Poles, and with Polish-Jewish refugees.

'We'll try it again. Remember, Alina, you are a strong and powerful woman, a matriarch; you are used to having your own way. Renata, you are young, vulnerable, insecure, and a stranger in the house of your mother-in-law. Nevertheless, you hold your ground. Now girls, let's try it again…'

Irena helped with sewing the costumes, and she helped steady Renata's nerves. A professional theatre critic came from a local newspaper and reviewed the play.

'Children. Wait! I'll find it!' [10]*Pan* Segalovich, surrounded by his impatient drama circle, scanned the columns of the arts page. '*Tavarisch* Hoynacki says Alina shows great promise. And listen to this! 'Renata Lucianowna, as the Jewish revolutionary Rachel, is more convincing as a mother than she is as a revolutionary.'

The cast members laughed. *Pan* Segalovich chucked Renata under the chin. 'Eh, Renata, what do you think of that?!' Renata was perplexed and a bit jittery for a while, after such a review. Would she be arrested and deported to Siberia for being an unconvincing comrade? Nonetheless, the production was so well received that the student cast was invited to perform at the Summer Drama Festival in Moscow. Before attending that event, however, Renata was invited to spend time with her older cousin Rafal. She planned to join him on 22 June, right after her final exam. Rafal was stationed in Rovno. Renata already had her train ticket in hand.

Dr Rafal Skotnicki, son of Uncle Hermann, the town dentist, was born in Sochaczew on 6 December 1911. He was a surgeon serving in the medical corps of the Red Army. Whether he was recruited or press-ganged is open to debate. He seems to have been a Jewish Dr Zhivago. The handsome young doctor was last seen strolling through the streets of Rovno on 21 June 1941. Literally, he disappeared off the face of the earth.

***

---

[10] *Pan* is the honorific for 'Mr'. *Pani* is the equivalent for 'Mrs'

'The interests of the liberation of a number of big and very big nations stands higher than the interests of the movement for liberation of small nations..."

'Enough. You know it.'

'Are you sure?' Renata and Irena were propped up on their cots. Irena, with notebook in hand, was prompting Renata for a last exam. The dormitory was half-empty. Students who had finished their finals were already on summer holidays.

'Sure I'm sure.'

'But the exam's in the morning!'

'Yes, it is. And we should be rested for it, so let's get some sleep.' Irena stretched and rolled over. Renata continued muttering quotations from Lenin. Irena erupted, 'You know it!'

'Alright!' Renata submitted to her friend's request and finally fell asleep.

It was Sunday morning. It was the second day of summer. The sun crawled over the horizon. Daylight beamed, unaware of the looming darkness. A screech ripped the air. It blasted Renata into consciousness. She leapt into Irena's bed, cowering under the blanket.

'Irka! Wake up! They're bombing!'

A dazed Irena opened her eyes. 'Oh stop it. It's just a loud storm.'

'Irka! I know this sound! I remember it. It must be the Germans! They're bombing!' Irena contemplated the noise and tried to identify its source, as if it came from a neighbouring apartment. Human cries transformed into unearthly howls as dorm-mates and teachers and students from other parts of the school stampeded through the corridors and out the exits. Renata tossed her few possessions into a pillowcase, slipped into her shoes, and slid her winter coat over her nightgown. As the bombs exploded and shrieks of hysteria rent the walls, Irena conceded. 'Hmmm. I guess you're right. I have to go and get my grandmother.'

Renata grabbed her and screamed, 'There's no time to go back! We have to run!'

'But I can't leave without my grandmother!' Renata was no longer listening. She grabbed her bundle and dashed out, running with a mob of panic-stricken children. Wave after wave of diving *Messerschmitts* and *Stukas* spit death. Renata could see the black and white markings on the underside of their wings. The airplanes howled and the bombs they dropped whistled before exploding. Upon impact, the earth quaked and suddenly there were craters in the roads. Fleeing humanity and Russian military convoys dropped into them. Horses dropped dead and the wagons they were pulling overturned. The injured screamed for assistance or reflexively wailed in pain.

Renata raced across roads strewn with corpses, the carcasses of horses, scattered bundles and burnt-out vehicles. She dashed into a corn field and threw herself among its young stalks, averting her gaze from the suddenly dead, who littered the field like twisted rag dolls. Renata hugged the quivering earth in an attempt to melt into it. Through a veil of smoke the terrified child saw, or thought she saw her schoolhouse on fire. As she clung to the earth, guilt engulfed her. Oh God. Renata addressed the deity she would have a running argument with for the rest of her surprisingly long life. What have I done? I've abandoned my best friend. I left Irena alone to die.

***

Homesickness proved stronger than fear. Renata attempted to flee west, back to Warsaw and what was left of her family. Her dress was in tatters and she had lost her bundle. She made her way to a tiny village and sneaked into a barn at nightfall. In the middle of the night, the village was attacked and seemed to burst into flames. Renata ran with an escaping crowd and found herself heading south. On occasion she hitched a ride with a peasant on his cart, but mostly she hiked through woods and fields.

In the town of Bielsk, Renata found her way to the home of one of her classmates. Out of twenty-four classmates, besides Renata, only Haim and Haya survived the first day of Operation Barbarossa. At least, it seemed that way. Haim was lost on the road. Haya reached her family in Bielsk before Renata did.

Haya's male cousins had been hauled out of their homes and shot, though by whom, isn't clear. They were many ethnic Germans and Nazi sympathisers in Bielsk. Those robbing Jewish homes and pushing Jews out of breadlines were clearly Polish peasants.

Renata lasted less than a week in Haya's home. During those few days she and her former classmate went to work cleaning German army barracks in exchange for food.

In Bielsk, Renata saw the [11]*Einsatzgruppen* at work. She never spoke of it and in her private memoir made only a cryptic reference to these atrocities, but decades later she would sum up that time by saying, 'My eyes saw things no human eyes should ever see.'

There was no longer a German-Soviet border. The winner had taken all.

---

[11] German task forces of mobile killing units

Still, Renata was determined to reach Warsaw. She left Haya's home in Bielsk and made it as far as the outskirts of Białystok. Back to Białystok, where her latest odyssey had begun. Even fiercely stubborn Renata could not outrun the Germans. Hunger compelled her to stop and beg for food at a German army canteen. The weakened youngster watched, in envy, as German soldiers tossed chunks of meat to their dogs.

'If you want to eat,' a German private barked at the famished child, 'You have to work! You can peel potatoes for us!'

Renata was directed to a field kitchen. Was it only two years since she had been a poor little rich girl being served by housekeepers in her mother and her father's homes? In the Soviet youth camp Renata learned to scrub floors and toilets. Now she taught herself to peel potatoes. She also learned that she could pass as a Slav.

At the end of the first workday, the Germans gave Renata a bowl of hot soup. At the end of the second workday, the Germans gave Renata a bowl of hot soup.

Before the end of the third workday Renata walked away – carrying a bundle filled with potatoes. It was sunset, likely mid-July, when Renata reached Białystok. She saw German guards standing around a barbed wire fence. Penned inside the fence were exhausted human beings bearing yellow patches on the backs and fronts of their shirts and blouses. Honing her persona as a primitive Polish peasant, Renata tested a German guard.

'Let me in. I want to trade my potatoes for Jew-gold.'

'Get lost.' The German guard talked tough, yet he smiled. 'This place is for the Jew vermin, not for a pretty girl like you.'

'But I'm hungry! Potatoes aren't enough! I want to eat meat! *(like German dogs,* Renata thought.) Those Jewish scum are desperate. They'll take my potatoes and give me good money for it!'

'Oh do what you want.' The German guard let the girl pass. She's pretty, but an idiot, the look on his face seemed to say.

Renata entered the penned area and found family relatives whom, like many, were refugees from Warsaw. Natalia's cousin Stefania refused to let her into their apartment, but Stefania's husband Wladek welcomed her and gave her a pair of his own shoes to cover her bare and swollen feet. He replaced her torn and tattered dress with one of Stefania's nightgowns, which was powder blue, with a floral design. He also supplied her with a cord that served as a belt to secure the nightgown around her emaciated waist.

***

Renata arrived in Białystok on 28 June, a day after the Germans herded two thousand Jewish men into its Great Synagogue and set both the synagogue and the men on fire. The new arrival and the surviving Jews in what was now Białystok's Ghetto could see the still-smouldering ruins and smell its stench. Stefania was wild and forbidding with hysteria and grief, but Wladek allowed Renata to sleep in the antechamber of their apartment.

On orders from their German masters, the local *Judenrat*, the Jewish council, recruited young and strong workers to fix potholes on the roads. Wladek had a contact in the *Judenrat* who was in charge of the work battalions. Renata was placed in one of the battalions that the Germans selected each morning in front of the Judenrat office and escorted to different locations outside the Ghetto. Each morning Renata had to report to the *Judenrat* in order to register for a chain gang without chains. Work began at dawn and ended at dusk. In summer.

At the age of twelve, Renata became a slave of the Third Reich. Seven days a week, under armed guard, in blistering heat at the height of summer, Renata set out with other incarcerated youngsters to fix potholes on the roads. They wore yellow patches on their chests and upper backs, as a mark of shame.

Their workdays began and ended with severe beatings. Should they grow tired and slow down, they were beaten again. SS officers were frequent visitors. The Jewish youngsters kept their heads down when the SS officers came.

Each day that their work progressed, they had to walk further to begin it. Each day they passed the Ghetto gates to the taunts and jeers of local Poles, and each evening they re-entered to the sound of the same obscenities.

The Jewish children's payment for their labour was handfuls of dried fish that had been found in a warehouse abandoned by the fleeing Soviets. On occasion the ration of fish was augmented by a fistful of *kasha* or some other grain. Renata handed over the food to Stefania and Wladek. Like many Jewish children trapped on a planet gone mad, Renata took grim pride in keeping adults alive.

Relentlessly, the sun beat down. The dreaded days ended, if not early, than less late. On one of these evenings, as Renata marched towards the gates of the Ghetto along a gangplank flanked by hate-filled faces and vicious mouths shouting curses she heard, among them, the echo of a familiar voice calling a name only few people knew. 'Renusia! Renusia!' It was the diminutive used by family. 'Renusia! Renusia!' The voice grew louder and more insistent. Renata, who had learned to avert her gaze from the sight of the nightly mobs, turned to follow the call. A pint-sized woman with luminous blue eyes and a sleek ash-blond pageboy, her tiny torso wrapped in its signature peasant shawl, was calling to her. It was Janka. Renata gaped. Janka slipped through the crowd to Renata's side, and with her through the Ghetto gates. In the hope that she might find Renata alive Janka had brought, in a lid-less basket, a five-dollar U.S. bill, in case someone needed to be bribed, a tin medallion engraved with the image of the Virgin Mary, and the Jewish armband worn in Warsaw. The presence of the armband proved a grievous mistake.

'I came as soon as I could.' Janka's understatement was masterful. Renata, stunned and overwhelmed with grief and gratitude, led Janka to the apartment she had access to, where she was allowed to sleep in the hallway. Janka gave another young girl the five-dollar U.S. bill in exchange for two yellow patches and her place in the work detail. She quickly stitched the patches onto the front and back of her blouse, and cradled Renata to sleep in her arms on the mat in the hallway where they were allowed to lie.

In the morning Janka clipped the medallion around Renata's neck, under the light nightgown Renata wore, which doubled as a dress, and then marched through the gate with her and the other youngsters along the hot and dusty road. The parting from Stefania and particularly, from Wladek, had been wrenching. Renata knew that, without her, they would starve.

At noontime, which signalled lunchtime for the German guards and continued work for the Jewish youths, the guards retreated under the shade of scattered trees, enjoying the meals brought in on rolling canteens. Satiated and lulled by beer, the guards grew drowsy. Janka nudged Renata. 'Move and keep moving.' Gently Janka coaxed Renata into a ditch, dropping down beside her. They crawled on their bellies over the stones and hard grey earth, and then Janka stopped to pull the stitches out of the yellow patches on Renata's makeshift dress, and on her own blouse. She wrapped Renata's neck in a kerchief in order to camouflage the holes in the material left by the torn stitches, and then she wrapped her own shoulders in her colourful shawl, to do the same.

When Janka surmised that they had gained sufficient distance, she instructed Renata to rise. Janka was four feet five inches, and twelve-year-old Renata had grown to her full height of five feet four. 'Walk slowly. Keep calm.' In broad daylight, in blistering heat, the woman-child and the child-woman ambled down country lanes. As they nodded to passing peasants they were hailed with the traditional greeting, 'Praise the Lord.' Without irony, the Catholic nanny and her Jewish charge responded in the same way.

It took Janka and Renata two weeks to reach Warsaw. They sustained themselves by sneaking into barns in the evenings and sleeping there during the nights. Janka would wake Renata before dawn, which was when they stole eggs from under squatting chickens, cracked their shells, and drank the contents raw. Janka's lid-less basket, covered with a cloth, held a small cup and cans she picked up along the road. She taught Renata to milk cows and they drank the milk, along with the raw eggs, before the farmers were up and able to catch them at it. On their odyssey to Warsaw, they supplemented their diet from the farm fields by stealing carrots and cucumbers and potatoes. They ate the vegetables raw and enjoyed them; even the potatoes.

***

In downtown Warsaw, Janka and Renata boarded the tramway that ran through the streets of the Ghetto, and back. Police agents patrolled the platforms to make sure no one dared get on or off until the tramway returned to the Aryan Side. A socialist union with connections to the Polish underground resistance movement controlled Warsaw's transit system. Should an inmate of the Ghetto manage to board at one end and escape at the other, the drivers turned a blind eye. Often the drivers tossed loaves of bread out the window, as they rode through the Ghetto. Sometimes their passengers did the same.

Before boarding the tramway, Janka slipped the armband into Renata's pocket. A sharp curve was coming up on one of the Ghetto streets. The driver would be compelled to slow down. Janka instructed Renata to jump when the driver approached the curve. Renata positioned herself on the back platform, while the patrolling agent spied her from the front. After a summer of hard labour Renata was physically strong and deeply tanned, yet there was tell-tale terror in her eyes. Renata had the look and feel and scent of a hunted animal. The agent was trained to hunt.

Janka caught the agent eyeing his quarry. Her instructions to Renata changed. 'Renusia,' Janka whispered. 'Stay put.' She felt they had no choice but to continue riding the tramway full circle and finally, they disembarked at its starting point, on the Aryan Side.

The agent disembarked with them, grabbed Renata, frisked her, and found the armband. He struck her, and declared her under arrest. Renata protested that she had been trying to get into the Ghetto, not out. Though it was true, it was also unbelievable. The agent struck her again, and dragged her off. Janka pleaded with the agent to let the girl go. He shoved Janka out of his way.

'You Jewish whore!' The epithet was addressed to Janka. 'Stay out of this, or I'll arrest you too!' Helplessly, Janka could do no more than watch and follow from a distance.

Renata was hauled to a downtown prison and tossed into a cell with a gang of hardened prostitutes. The sight of their Virgin's image on the body of a Jewish girl enraged them.

For three days and three nights they taunted and tormented and beat Renata. They denied her access to the pail in the cell used as a toilet and the terrorised child grew incontinent, which is when they mocked and kicked her and spit into the thin broth served to all inmates. Warsaw's true whores were given free reign with someone they could feel superior to.

At the end of three days Renata was released into the custody of another policeman. 'Say hello to the Gestapo!' The prostitutes waved her off.

I'm taking you to your people,' the Polish policeman blandly informed the filthy, stinking and terrified child. At one of the Ghetto's several gated entrances the policeman stopped, unzipped his pants, and relieved himself again the Ghetto wall. The hunted animal became an alert animal. Renata spotted a hole in the wall. On their odyssey through the countryside Janka had updated Renata on current conditions in the outdoor prison penning in the Jews. While the cop's pants were still down Renata leapt through the hole dug by children on the other side, knowing no adult could follow her there.

CHAPTER SIX

'I saw streets filled with the smell of poverty and despair. Children sitting or lying lethargically on sidewalks, their little faces like masks of death. Parents, often dying themselves, watched their children's bodies wither. Gaunt, shrivelled babies in their arms, too weak even to cry. Those were the children of hunger, the most wretched, and devoid of hope. Some were still crying; others lacked the strength even to speak. Children with distended bellies. Limbs thin and lifeless, bones protruding through their sunken cheeks. Crawling skeletons, like spiders, dragging themselves along the sidewalks and collapsing in order to die there. I saw things no human eyes should ever see.'

From the private memoir of Renata Skotnicka-Zajdman

Escaping the Catholic cop, on the other side of the Ghetto wall, Renata was snatched and tossed into a holding pen by a Jewish cop, along with a horde of whining children who had attempted exiting to the Aryan side. Children small enough crawled through holes created by dislodged bricks in order to beg, steal, or barter for bread that might keep them and their parents, if they still had parents, alive for one more day. Children became the Ghetto's lifeline, daily risking their lives. For their efforts to feed and sustain their families, these kids were called ghetto rats.

Once more protesting that she had been trying to get into the Ghetto and not out, Renata was savagely thrashed. Her resulting cries were so loud that a clerk in a neighbouring room, working in what passed for the post office, shouted from the other side of the wall, 'Make that kid shut up! I can't concentrate!'

'Ignatz!' Renata shrieked. She recognised the voice belonging to a relative. 'It's me! Renata!'

The postal worker dashed next door. His little cousin was barely recognizable beneath the filth and grime accumulated over three days in a prison cell. She continued to scream in terror and pain as the Jewish policeman beat her repeatedly with his truncheon.

'Stop it!' Ignatz screamed at the cop. 'It's Alek's sister!'

Instantly, the cop dropped his stick. He had known Alek socially, at a time when social life existed.

'Your family has been frantic!' In shock, with relief, Ignatz roared at Renata. 'Janka is desperate. She had to tell Alek – worse, she had to tell Ania – that she found you, and then she lost you!'

Alek was contacted. Telephones still worked. In the Ghetto, the telephones functioned until the end.

Besides the public tramway, in the Ghetto the only form of transport in service were pricey rickshaws, since private motor vehicles had been confiscated by the Germans and horses were either eaten or traded. Alek was repulsed by the idea of a human being hauling other human beings on chairs with wheels, as though they were beasts of burden, but on this occasion he went against principle and took a rickshaw to fetch Renata and bring her to what now passed for home. The pen filled with ghetto rats devoid of family connections, accused of the crime of smuggling, remained at the mercy of the Jewish cop.

During that same month, October of 1941, German gendarmes publicly drowned thirty Jewish children in water-filled clay pits, as a warning and supposedly as a deterrent. On 1 November, the German occupation decreed that any child caught 'smuggling' would be immediately shot. On 10 November this new law was enforced, when the Germans removed from jail six girls and two boys who, on their orders, were summarily executed by Polish police. On 15 November, fifteen children were machine-gunned for this same crime of smuggling. Yet children small enough to crawl through holes in the Ghetto walls continued to do so.

One of the gates was guarded by a German who ghetto inhabitants nicknamed Frankenstein, a sadistic gendarme who amused himself by taking pot shots at children as though they were sparrows. After begging for bread on the Aryan side, kids had to crawl through the wall's holes one at a time. Frankenstein would wait until several leapt back onto the Jewish side, closely grouped together. Then he would gun then down, all in one go. It was rumoured that 'Frankenstein' set himself the goal of killing at least one little Jew before breakfast. Yet the children kept going and coming back. The prospect of being quickly dispatched by bullets proved preferable to death by slow and agonizing starvation.

The German occupiers felt no need to justify the killing of adults. When in the mood for murder, German gendarmes piled into a black Mercedes and rode through the Ghetto streets, gunning down pedestrians at random and at will.

On 7 December, Japanese forces attacked the American naval base at Pearl Harbor. The United States entered the war, and all aid in the form of packages sent by American Jewish charity organisations came to a halt. If only the great and good American president Roosevelt knew how badly they were being abused, Ghetto inhabitants assumed, he would surely intervene. Now that America had entered the fight, Ghetto inhabitants reasoned, the Germans would ultimately be vanquished. But when? How long would it take? Would any of them live to see it?

At Christmas of 1941 General Hans Frank issued an order decreeing that, within forty-eight hours, all Ghetto inhabitants were to deliver to the *Judenrat* all furs. This order applied not only to full fur coats, but also to collars and trimmings, down to the smallest pieces. The German occupiers plastered posters across the Ghetto. Any material that was hairy or contained the hide of an animal or rodent had to be relinquished. Failure to comply meant death, or more precisely, murder.

There was no heat or electricity with which to endure the winter of 1942. Now there would be no fur. In an attempt to keep warm, Ghetto inhabitants took to their beds. If they had beds.

Natalia's children considered themselves fortunate to be allowed to shelter in a small room in a relative's large apartment in Karmelicka 5. These relatives were able to keep their apartment because it was located within the confines of what became the Ghetto. Natalia's three children slept on folding beds, next to each other. They didn't feel cramped. In the kitchen they could boil water and wash. They even had an acetylene lamp. They considered themselves lucky. Too many Ghetto inhabitants were spending the frigid winter nights in courtyards, alleyways, basements, attics, warehouses, and hallways. Daily, and nightly, they died by the thousands. In the middle of the night corpses were laid out on the pavements for collection by Pinkerton's staff of undertakers, who deposited them in a common grave. These corpses joined the ragged skeletons expiring on the sidewalks and dying babies sucking futilely on their dying mothers' empty breasts. Their families (if they still had families), and communal leaders tried to keep their identities secret so their ration cards could be passed on to those still living. A Ghetto inhabitant was given just 185 calories a day on which to live.

The only Ghetto inhabitants able to decently bury and mourn their dead were converts who, under Nazi law, were still considered Jewish. They attended church and prayed to Jesus while wearing an armband marked with the Star of David. While alive, they were imprisoned in the Ghetto. Upon death they became free, when a hearse came to collect them and drive them to a Christian cemetery. Two family members were allowed to accompany their dead. They entered the hearse bearing a painted cross, with the Star of David gripping their arms.

In this grotesque atmosphere, culture and education flourished. While hunger, typhus and terror dominated daily existence, a counter culture percolated just below the radar. Education for Jews was illegal, so Ghetto inhabitants who were teachers before the war set up clandestine classes. Lectures were held in private apartments and, for safety, in small groups. No textbooks were used, in case the Germans should stage a raid. Texts were duplicated by typewriter. There were no discipline problems. Children hungered for knowledge almost as much as they hungered for food. Renata's education never stopped. In this nightmarish landscape she was tutored in history, geography, Latin and literature. Through donations, an underground library was formed. Renata became a courier in what became known as 'a walking library.' Lists of available titles were collected, along with lists of interested readers, and couriers would deliver them, one book at a time, hidden under their cloth coats. As a tip Renata sometimes received a piece of bread, but gaining access to the classics was considered priceless. Literature, always loved, became her weapon against despair. In the ghetto Renata read Tolstoy's *War and Peace*. Eerily, she read Franz Werfel's *Forty Days of Musa Dagh,* his account of the Armenian genocide. Crouched in a corner of the room she shared with Alek and Ania, Renata began reading Emile Zola's *Nana,* the story of a French prostitute who is the ruin of every man who pursues her. Alek pulled the novel out of her hands. 'You're too young to read this. You can read it when you're eighteen.' Matter-of-factly the hollow-eyed youngster replied, 'I won't live to be eighteen.'

In the winter of 1942, Renata fell victim to the latest typhus epidemic. Once more Janka rescued her, by smuggling into the Ghetto the new wonder drug penicillin. Renata also developed a low-grade form of tuberculosis and, without medication, in the worst conditions, survived it.

The brutal cold and recurring epidemics kept German killing sprees at bay. With the advent of spring, murder became more organised. In April, in one night, fifty-one men were dragged out of their beds and shot. There was no reason given. For people without rights, there doesn't need to be. These night-time raids escalated until summer, as a more efficient and final solution was being set in place.

In Hell on Earth, Renata found romance. With Ryszard Szwager. When Ryszard was eighteen, Renata was thirteen, but she no longer considered herself a child. Renata met Ryszard through her brother Alek. The Szwager family were part of Natalia's social set pre-war, but since Renata spent most of her time in Sochaczew with Łucjan, she wasn't aware of them.

Ryszard's twenty-year-old sister Danuta was in love with Renata's brother. Though Alek was fond of her, he resisted becoming involved. Alek couldn't see a future with Danuta. Alek couldn't see a future. How does one allow love when there is no Tomorrow?

Renata remembered Ryszard as tall and thin, with owl-shaped framed glasses. Before the war the Szwager parents were working chemists. Ryszard wanted to become a doctor. Since formal education was illegal, he pursued his studies under the guise of a workshop purporting to teach the containment of infectious disease. Terrified of contagion, the German masters allowed this workshop on condition that it be held outside the confines of the Ghetto, so at the start of each day, equipped with a special permit, Ryszard braved the armed sentries at Ghetto gates in order to attend Professor Ludwig Hirschfeld's clandestine class in medicine. At the end of each day Renata waited for him by the gates, never knowing whether or not he would come back alive. Ryszard could not be caught with textbooks, but he lugged a skeleton in an opaque bag. Renata tagged along beside him. His mother would not allow the bag of bones into their flat, so Ryszard kept trying to discard the cadaver in the streets, while obliging passers-by kept trying to return it to him.

On the one birthday they were able to share, Ryszard gave Renata an entire white bun and a brooch which lit up in the dark. How he acquired these treasures is unknown and unknowable. Ryszard also gave Renata her first kiss. Theirs was a chaste romance, like the romance between Peter van Pels and Anne Frank, who were hiding in an Amsterdam attic.

Ryszard's sister Danuta was sensitive, observant, and a gifted scholar. She took Renata seriously, speaking to her of literature and philosophy. The solemn youngster looked up to the young woman. She considered Danuta a role model and mentor. Stoically, the young woman also spoke of what appeared to be their impending collective fate. 'We are marked for murder. We're like prisoners on Death Row. If one of us survives they must tell the world what was done to us.' Danuta issued an injunction which reverberated down the decades. 'IF YOU LIVE, YOU MUST TELL'.

During one of the daily dragnets Renata, Danuta and her mother hid inside a false wall, in the attic of their apartment building on Orla 10. Ryszard built the false wall and supplied bread and water. After shepherding them in, the resourceful young man camouflaged the wall's exterior with heavy oak furniture. He also smeared it with naphtha, in order to confuse inquisitive dogs. He then sought refuge elsewhere. If he hadn't come back for them, the three women, including the little woman Renata, would've been entombed.

Inside the wall, mother, daughter and Renata lay motionless. The heat was intense. So was the quiet, though it wasn't quiet for long. An old woman who lived on the ground floor was discovered, pulled out and shot. The voices of soldiers yelling in German, Ukrainian and Latvian echoed in the halls. A raid was on. The hunt was on. The screams of captured Jews and carbine rifle shots resounded. There was the thud of heavy boots thumping up the stairs, followed by the ear-piercing shock of locks being smashed and doors being flung open. In the apartment building opposite, Rottweilers, trained for this purpose, sniffed out Jews attempting to evade deportation. The Jews were shot, and the dogs made a meal of them. In the flat below, the hunters took their time. They were looting. In the attic, inside the wall, their quarry lay paralysed and waiting.

Then came the shriek of a long, sharp whistle and a command shouted in German. The hunt was over. For the day.

Ryszard lived long enough to return to the attic and rescue the women he loved but soon he, too, met a lonely and gruesome death. During another dragnet, he hid in a lumber yard. Rottweilers sniffed him out. A Ukrainian henchman killed him. One prays the teenager was dead before the dogs tore him apart.

Danuta and her mother were permitted to live a little longer. They served as slave labourers in a Ghetto workshop. When their services were no longer required, mother and daughter were shipped to Treblinka and gassed.

The father of the family, Henryk Szwager, along with his youngest child Alfred, survived because they were hidden, fed and protected by the Catholic woman who served the family as housekeeper before the war. At war's end Henryk Szwager married his Catholic housekeeper, and the reconstituted family emigrated to Australia.

Safe among Melbourne's sub-tropical gardens, one wishes Alfred Szwager could know that the brother and sister he barely knew were not only loved, but remembered.

CHAPTER SEVEN

It was a cool and cloudy day in August of 1942. The Ghetto was being culled of its old, its sick, its homeless, and its orphaned. Renata was hiding on a roof as she watched the director of the Ghetto's ever-expanding orphanage march through its streets with 200 of his charges. The Polish Underground offered to rescue Janusz Korczak but he refused, stating, 'You don't leave a sick child alone in the night. You don't abandon children at a time like this.' It was rumoured that even an SS officer, familiar with Korczak's literary works, offered to let him escape, but still, the doctor refused. He told the children, some as young as two years old, that they were going for a picnic in the countryside. They would escape the stale air and grimy walls of the Ghetto. They would pick berries in open meadows, he lied, and in the woods they would find the season's first mushrooms. For the younger children, the nightmare landscape of the Warsaw Ghetto was the only world they had ever known, or would know. They had never frolicked freely in an open meadow. They had never tasted the juice of a sun-kissed berry, and never would.

Renata prepared her knapsack. She strapped it on and was about to join Korczak and his charges when Alek entered the room. 'What are you doing?'

'I'm going with Korczak and the children.'

'What?!'

'I'm going with Dr Korczak. They say they will give us jam and bread at the [12]*Umschlagplatz*. He and the children are going to work in the East. I've been to the East. I've worked there.'

Violently Alek grabbed Renata, pulled the knapsack off her back and flung her against a wall.

'You're not going anywhere! Promise me! You're not going anywhere! Whatever happens you run and hide! Don't ever let them catch you! You run and hide, run and hide, run and hide! You hear me?! Promise!'

'But I don't understand! Why are people talking about letting Korczak escape when the children are going? Of course Dr Korczak would go with the children. He takes care of them. Why would Dr Korczak want to escape? Escape from what?!'

Alek stared at his little sister. Renata's question was answered by the look of horror in his eyes. In Alek's haunted eyes Renata perceived the true nature of the transports. She shuddered. She said nothing. What she did was to climb onto the roof. From this vantage point she became an eyewitness to what would become an iconic moment in Holocaust history.

The gentle paediatrician had his charges dress in their best clothes, such as they were. He held a tender babe under his arm and a toddler by the hand, while a macabre band of doomed children followed quietly behind. Their blue knapsacks were strapped to their backs and each carried a favourite book, or a favoured toy. Their protector, wittingly sharing their fate, kept them calm, ignorant, and free of fear,

---

[12] Transfer site and terminal: in this context: the gathering point for Jews destined for deportation to the Treblinka death camp

as he marched them to the cattle trains that would carry them to their mass murder at Treblinka.

When Korczak and the children were removed from view, Renata climbed down from the roof.

Renata's response to the departure of Dr Korczak and the deportation of the Ghetto's orphans galvanised Alek into action. A few days later he issued non-negotiable orders.

'I've got you into a work detail that will be leaving the Ghetto. Once you're on The Outside, a Polish policeman will approach you. He is going to arrest you. Don't try to resist him, and don't be afraid. He's on our side.'

Renata followed her brother's instructions without protest, and was arrested without incident. The policeman winked at her, and led her to his home. Hovering in the background, like a guardian angel, was Janka.

***

On the evening of 1 September, the Russians sprang a surprise bombing raid on Warsaw. They tossed flares from the sky to identify their targets. The policeman's family, which included his brother-in-law Janek, along with his wife, hastened to the basement of their apartment building.

The policeman, Pawel Golombek, and his family sheltered another Jewish girl whom the Golombek's sister-in-law claimed, to nosy neighbours, to be her illegitimate daughter by a Roma. Ten-year-old Isabella was taken to the basement shelter, but Renata was instructed to remain upstairs for fear she'd be recognised as a Jewess and betrayed by neighbours. Feeling abandoned in the safe house during the bombardment on the anniversary of her dead mother's birthday, the traumatised teenager snapped. She went to the bathroom, found a razor knife, and lifted it to her wrist. On the verge of opening a vein,, Renata hesitated. Instead, she began to scream. Her uncontrollable cries were so loud that they could be heard in the basement, even through the din of bombardment. Janek, the policeman's brother-in-law, dashed towards the stairs.

'No!' His sister cautioned. Janek disregarded his sister's warning, raced up to the apartment, and barged through the bathroom door. He was horrified by what he saw. 'No!' Janek yelled, echoing his sister, and knocked the razor knife out of Renata's hand before she fully yielded to despair. He darted to his bedroom, grabbed a blanket off his bed, pulled Renata out of the bathroom, enveloped her in the blanket and then into his warm, strong arms. While the flares flashed and bombs exploded Janek stroked Renata's trembling head, rocking her and soothing her with visions of survival and a new world at peace and free from humiliation, violence, and pain. He sang lullabies to the quivering child, who felt like a wounded bird cupped in his hands, until she finally fell asleep.

While Renata resided in the sanctuary provided by the policeman and his family, Janka went to work arranging false identity documents, and another safe house. When the policeman's neighbours grew suspicious, Renata was removed. As Janka kept watch, detecting the questioning looks and wagging of tongues, Renata was removed from another safe house, and moved again. Running out of available safe houses, Janka resorted to locking up Renata in her brother-in-law's rat-infested tool shed. His job as a bricklayer kept him away during the day. In the evenings Janka plied him with vodka and his wife went to bed with him so that he would be unable, or too indifferent, to inform on them. These were desperate measures, and couldn't be kept up for long. In the next apartment Renata was moved to she was spotted, denounced and arrested so quickly that even Janka was unable to save her. It was Ania who came to the rescue then.

The policeman who arrested Renata beat her and she broke, confessing the crime of her Jewish identity. While languishing in the prison cell, expecting to be taken to the Gestapo, a dark-haired woman with dark, slanted eyes and high, wide cheekbones, a brazen young woman with a manner of the streets, barged through the doors of the station and strode up to the policeman on duty. From behind bars, Renata gasped. It was her sister Ania. 'Let her out!' Ania ordered the policeman.

'Have you taken leave of your senses, woman?! Do want me to arrest you too?!'

'Let her go.' Ania confronted the policeman like Moses confronting Pharaoh. 'I used to work for the family. They were good to me. I promised her mother I'd take care of her.' That last part was true. 'Look,' Ania began to negotiate. 'If you hand her over to the Germans you'll get nothing. I'll pay you for her. How much do you want?'

The cop considered the offer. 'Fifteen thousand *zlotys*.'

Ania opened her purse. 'I don't have that much on me. I'll give you what I've got and bring the rest tomorrow, but you've got to give me the girl now.' The corrupt cop accepted Ania's offer. He released Renata, and the two Jewish sisters, stone-faced, walked out of the police station, free.

Ania kept her word to the cop. The next day she returned to the station and paid the balance owing on Renata's life. The money came from Ania and Janka's contacts in The Underground.

A time came when the cop would pay for his ill-gotten gains. Ultimately he was executed by the Underground for collaborating with the Germans, if not for blackmailing captured Jews.

After this electrifyingly narrow escape, Janka kept Renata close. Natalia's former employee chose homelessness, rather than abandon Natalia's child. The nanny and her charge slept side by side on the platforms of train stations, pretending they were waiting for the train. On cold nights Janka and Renata snuck into cellars and attics and slept there, creeping out again before morning light. When the weather was clement they curled up in ditches, or huddled together in open fields. They stole potatoes and carrots to keep from starving. They also stole coal from stationary freight cars on the outskirts of town. Anticipating winter, in the autumn of 1942 coal became as valuable as gold. Janka and Renata took turns scrambling up the ladders attached to the sides of the open cars, and tossed down heavy black lumps to each other. Then they returned to the city and sold their booty. Janka and Renata had to fight for the fuel with street toughs, who had clambered up the freight cars for the same purpose.

Janka taught Renata the language of the streets. She insisted the Jewish girl learn to swear and curse like a hardened hoodlum. Renata was a quick study, but not quick enough. Janka goaded and provoked until, exasperated, Renata blasted, 'Oh, fuck off!'

'Bravo!' Janka applauded like a demented professor. 'Now you've got it!'

Winter was coming, and Warsaw was unreasonably dangerous for Jews. They could not continue living in the streets. Janka sent out feelers to farmers she bartered with. By November, in a hamlet located between Radzymin and Wołomin, Janka and Renata had farmed themselves out as hired hands.

Janka and Renata slept in the farmer's barn. The farmer, his wife, his toddler, and his mother-in-law resided in the main house. The farmer had a city cousin. Henryk, a young man in his early twenties, had joined a cell of partisans hiding in the forest. He used his cousin's farm as a base, coming to eat and to bring food to his gang. When Henryk was in residence, he, too, slept in the barn. Henryk seemed a quiet young man.

During the first week of their employment, Janka trained Renata. Under Janka's tutelage Renata learned to milk the cows, feed the pigs, spread manure, and harvest potatoes. Henryk kept a watchful eye. When Renata made a mistake and hurt her hands, and when her palms became calloused from the unaccustomed work Renata felt compelled to hide them. Their employer believed he had hired experienced hands.

After the first week on the farm, seeing that Renata could hold her own and believing her charge was safe, Janka decided to return to Warsaw. 'I want to get Alek out. If I can find a safe house for him, maybe I can convince him to escape. As soon as I can, Renusia, I will come back for you.'

When Janka left, the assaults began. At night, in the barn, Henryk crossed over from his pile of hay and grabbed Renata. 'Rebecca!' He hit her.

'What?! My name is Krystyna!' Krystyna was Renata's Catholic pseudonym; the name registered on her false identity documents.

'I know who and what you are, Rebecca,' Henryk smirked. 'If you want to live, you'll do what I want and what I say.'

Renata was barely fourteen and sexually illiterate. She didn't understand what was happening until it happened. Throughout the ordeal she clung to the tin medallion around her neck and prayed vociferously to the Virgin Mary. Renata cried and Henryk laughed.

For the next five weeks Renata laboured in the fields by day, and nightly returned to the barn and the relentless rapes. Malnutrition had suppressed her menses, so Renata was spared pregnancy. She was spared nothing else.

On Sunday morning Renata attended the local church with the farmer and his family. Henryk was not in attendance. On one Sunday, Renata recognised a girl in a neighbouring pew. Before the war, they went to school together. Renata's former classmate smiled at her. The next morning, on the farm, a forester from the adjacent town came to arrest Renata.

'You've got a Jew on your premises,' the policeman informed the farmer.

'What?! That's impossible. Krystyna can't be Jewish! She prays with us in church! If that girl is Jewish I'll run her through with my pitchfork! I'll kill her myself!'

The catechism classes at *Gimnazjum* Frydryk Chopin were paying off. Not only did Renata pray and sing in the church choir, but she also went to confession. Though she got the impression that the priest would have kept her secret, Renata did not admit to the sin of being Jewish.

The hamlet was so small and the adjacent towns so ill-equipped, that a co-operative group of farmers and foresters with horses and buggies worked with the police when transportation was required. It would be inefficient to bring in a sole Jew, so a forester was sent to pick up Renata after picking up three partisans who were being brought into the police station for questioning.

It was December. Snow blanketed the farm and covered the fields. It wasn't late, but it was already dark. Renata was ordered onto the front seat of the buggy, next to the forester. Three strapping young men, clearly non-Jews, sat sullenly in the back. Henryk decided to come along for the ride. The arrested men were his comrades. What they didn't say, they signalled with their eyes.

A full moon hung in the frigid air, like a lamp. The snow was high and the forest was still, except for the clip-clop of the horses' hooves. The young men, seated behind the forester, began to negotiate, offering Renata's sexual services in exchange for their freedom. Growing tense and nervous, the forester snapped at his passengers to shut up. Renata sensed sudden movement behind her back. There was a skirmish. One of the men leapt on the forester. The forester had no gun, but he had a knife. Instinctively he lashed out, and cut Renata's throat.

'Scram!' Henryk screamed at Renata, who seemed stunned into paralysis. 'Beat it!' The partisan shrieked, as he and his buddies laid in, murderously, upon the trapped forester. 'Run!' Henryk howled at the girl, and at the baleful moon. Renata's rapist was saving her life.

Henryk's wails shocked Renata into action. She ran through the woods, in the opposite direction to where the forester had been heading, in snow sometimes waist-high, her path lighted by a benevolent moon. Red drops splattered onto the plush white carpet of snow. Renata realised she was bleeding. She wrapped her peasant's shawl tightly around her neck, as a tourniquet. The bare black trees bore silent witness to the wounded girl's dash for life and freedom. The full bright moon beamed over her until relieved of its post, at dawn.

Reaching the adjacent town and its train station in early morning, Renata edged her way onto the crowded commuter line, and arrived in Warsaw before the conductor had time to ask for her ticket. Pale, weakened, and in stinging pain, Renata dragged herself to the flat where her sister roomed with an old laundress. Ania had staged her own escape from the doomed Jewish ghetto. She gasped at the sight of her wounded sister. Ania hid Renata in her room and staunched the gash with vodka. The right side of Renata's neck was infected.

For the first time that Renata had seen, Ania broke down. She wept and answered Renata's unasked question. 'Janka is dead.' On that frosty December morning, while dressing the wound on Renata's neck, Ania invented a story. She told her little sister that Janka had been caught in a round-up in the countryside and shot there. It would be decades before Ania could bring herself to reveal the truth. Janka was making one of her regular forays into the Ghetto, this time to bring Alek food. She was hoping to convince him to allow her to help him escape. Diminutive Janka, with her loaded, unlidded basket, was negotiating with a sentry at one of the Ghetto gates. Usually Janka knew who could be bribed and whom it was best to avoid. Perhaps this sentry was a new recruit. Perhaps it was simply that Janka's luck ran out that day.

Ania was an eyewitness. She had been standing across the street watching, in helpless horror, the pantomime of Janka's wild gesticulations. In 1942, Germans soldiers didn't engage in protracted debates with Polish women. The sentry ended the discussion by shooting the pest dead.

Janka's corpse lay in the street, in the snow, until a work squad pushing wheelbarrows for just this purpose tossed it into the barrow, and wheeled it away. No one claimed Janka's corpse. Except for those helpless to act, no one cared. If Janka had lived to Christmas Eve, she would've seen her thirty-fourth birthday.

Somewhere in the landscape of the Polish countryside there were two lost children, unknown even to each other who, even if they survived, would never learn that a saintly smuggler and Christ-like thief, martyred and murdered at the age of thirty-three, was none other than their mother.

CHAPTER EIGHT

The death of Janka drove Natalia's children to despair. 'We won't make it,' Ania stated, and she believed it. 'We can't survive without Janka.'

Renata knew she couldn't impose on her sister for long. Ania had a hard enough time inventing a plausible explanation to the laundress she roomed with why a wounded girl turned up at her door. For her part, Renata wanted nothing more to do with the world. It was horrifyingly clear that there was no room for her in it. A quick and lethal bullet, whenever it came, was preferable to a brutal existence filled with violence, hunger, humiliation, and pain.

I can no longer ask her, so I don't know how Renata managed to re-enter the Warsaw Ghetto one final time. Unlike Janka's attempt, Renata's attempt succeeded, and she found her way to her brother.

By the end of 1942, the Warsaw Ghetto resembled a ghost town. The old, the sick, the children and babies were dead and gone. Only strong young people remained, toiling as slaves in workshops the Germans maintained because it served the war effort. While the Christian world celebrated the birth of a Jew, Renata hid in an abandoned building.

Each evening, under cover of darkness, her brother brought her half his ration of bread.

During this holiday season there was no peace on earth nor goodwill towards men. Under a cold moon, Renata thought she saw snow falling. What she saw were flurries of feathers flying out of broken windows, as German soldiers ransacked empty apartments. They were ripping open pillows and shaking out their contents, searching for what might be hidden in them. Now that they had murdered the human beings, the Germans were searching for what they considered of value.

There was almost no one left, and nothing left to lose. With a pistol supplied by the Underground movement, Alek shot and killed a German soldier for the first time, but not for the last. That same night, the night of 18 January, he shoved Renata into the manhole of a sewer, issuing one injunction: LIVE. Then he quickly turned, vanishing into the darkness. Before Renata could cry out, an arm reached up and pulled her into the bowels of Warsaw. Then Renata, as one of a group of Ghetto Jews guided by a naturally blond, Aryan-looking leader, waded up to her knees in slime and polluted water through the dank, cave-like sewers. Each escapee clutched the arm or belt of the escapee in front of them, so as not to get lost in the darkness. When directly under manholes, they maintained a resounding silence. Rats and the corpses of those who had tried to make this trip, and failed, floated past them. In sections where unexploded grenades tossed in by the Germans dangled, the group was compelled to crawl. As they inched their way through the wet and congested alleys they could decipher the sounds of the city at night, at street level. They caught snatches of conversations between soldiers on patrol. Intermittently the sewer walls were pierced by the howl of a vicious bark, and the shock of a pistol shot. There was no curfew for the Germans, nor for their dogs.

At the exit under the Aryan side the exhausted escapees, one at a time, hauled themselves up a flight of iron ladder steps leading to another manhole, and dragged themselves out of it.

Their underground journey had lasted all night. The escapees stretched and blinked in the light of the coming dawn. Each scurried off, separately, to previously arranged safe houses. It was the dead of winter. It was 1943.

***

The top of the Ghetto Wall had crushed glass and barbed wire embedded in its cement surface. The Germans removed bricks from the Wall, and were using holes as observation points. They raised the water level in the sewers, and threw gas into the manholes. The streets were swarming with gendarmes, secret police, and blackmailers, all on the lookout for Ghetto escapees. Machine guns were firing from the balconies and the windows of apartments surrounding the Ghetto. Behind the Wall, there was steady artillery fire. Tanks were rolling in and planes were flying low, dropping incendiary bombs that scorched the Ghetto confines scarlet. In downtown Warsaw, thousands climbed onto roofs or perched on balconies to watch the spectacle of trapped Jews leaping, like human torches, off the tops of burning buildings. In Krasinski Square, children rode the merry-go-round, and couples on the carousel flew high while a calliope played a carnival tune. The melody blended with the sound of salvoes from behind the Ghetto Wall. Dark kites of smoke billowed by as church bells rang. Pious Poles were leaving Easter Sunday services accompanied by their offspring. They paraded through the streets in their finery. Approaching the Wall, fathers hoisted sons onto their shoulders for a better view. The children clapped their hands in glee. 'Look! Look! The Jews are burning!' A young man wiped away what appeared to be tears. *'Psiakrew!* I've got smoke in my eyes!' At the foot of the Wall, an old woman was on her knees, praying for the souls of the tormented Jews. Behind the old woman stood Renata. Her hair was bleached blonde. Still, she kept a beret on her head. She watched, and heard everything: the adults, the children, the fire that must be consuming her brother; the old Catholic woman praying for the Jews. The Ghetto flames seared a silence into her soul that lasted for decades. Her eyes bore a haunted look that would, in time, in a very long time, diminish, but never leave her.

Renata walked away from the Wall and into a German dragnet. Deliberately. Along with other young captives, she was shoved into the back of an open truck and hauled off to a transit camp. Threading through the Easter Sunday crowd, members of the Polish Underground trailed her there.

***

In the gymnasium of a former school now serving as a transit camp, Poles marked and labelled for shipment to Germany were examined for lice and checked for disease. Women and girls were forced to strip naked. A German doctor inserted his fingers into their scalps and into their vaginas while German guards leered.

The men were ordered to drop their pants. Their scrotums were lifted with large pliers, and their genitals were inspected for tell-tale circumcision. Perhaps a Jew might attempt to evade murder by volunteering to work in the Third Reich.

There was no way to detect a Jewess through physical examination, though a Polish Catholic woman, a harridan of the streets slated for slave labour, thought she had when she caught the haunted look of the hunted in Renata's sorrowful eyes.

'That one.' The shrew exclaimed, calling to their German captors. 'That one over there!' She shouted, pointing to Renata. 'She's a Jew! I know them. I can smell them.'

The guards cocked their pistols and moved towards Renata. Her would-be rescuers, peering through the windows, were helpless to act. It was dead Janka's training which rescued Renata.

'You cock-sucking motherfucker!' She suddenly screamed, startling everyone, including herself. 'I'll kill you for calling me that!' The fourteen-year-old Ghetto escapee leapt at her accuser, and smacked her across the face. 'You scumbag! You cockroach! Who dares call me a Jew?! I hate those vermin and if I found one I'd hand her over myself!' Renata raised her fists, and the Catholic woman raised her arms to fend her off, to no avail. Ferociously Renata grabbed fistfuls of hair on the woman's head, using it as a ballast. Then she kneed her in the gut.

The woman howled and doubled over. Renata wasn't finished with her yet. 'I'll kill you for calling me a Jew!' Inflamed, Renata feigned insult. 'To make up such a vicious lie, YOU must be a Jew!' Renata pounced furiously on the hapless Catholic, pummelling her to the ground. She threw herself on top of the woman, slapping her and spitting into her face. 'Meeeow!' Renata purred sarcastically. 'Alley cat.' Renata taunted, as she had been taunted. 'Jewish cat. There must be cracks in the Ghetto wall!'

Both the German guards and their captured quarry were struck dumb. Renata's savage reaction whisked everyone's breath away.

'Kill this Jewish cunt!' Renata roared, smacking the Catholic woman one last time, for good measure. 'Take her away!' She continued to rage. 'Take her away!' She shrieked at the guards. Renata was fighting for her life.

Taken off guard, the German guards obeyed. The Catholic woman was taken away under suspicion of being a

Jew. If she survived the ensuing interrogation, one can assume she never again dared to denounce anyone.

Members of the Polish Underground infiltrated the camp with the intention of rescuing Renata, but Renata refused to be rescued. In her mind and heart she heard the voice of her father. 'It's safest in the lion's den.' Łucjan's spirit advised, and guided. It turned out that Łucjan was right.

CHAPTER NINE

'Giving up my identity meant playing a part, becoming someone else. The better I played the role, the safer I was. My natural acting ability helped me. Sometimes I was so caught up in the part that I actually forgot who I really was. Perhaps if I were an adult during those dark years it would've been easier for me to make the distinction. As it was, I became my double. I felt ashamed for giving up what was cherished by my parents, by those I loved. But being Jewish meant being hunted, and being Christian meant being safe. Who was I?'

Renata Skotnicka-Zajdman, in a public address.

Renata's reputation as a rabid anti-Semite followed her into the Third Reich. It was the best cover she could have. The Poles who passed inspection in the transit camp and rode with Renata recognised it was best not to mess with her.

It took several hours to load the human cargo from Warsaw. Several hundred people were riding on this transport. It was early evening before the train began to move. Its passengers were destined for slave labour on farms, in factories, and wherever else there was a need and demand for their bodies, their backs, and their hands.

At first, the passengers were silent and subdued. There was an occasional, tentative smile offered as eyes met, and a common fate created a momentary bond.

As the train chugged into the blackness of night, the captured quarry from Warsaw began to question themselves, and each other. Would it not be better to work on a farm, rather than in a factory? At least, on a farm, there was enough food. Renata held herself aloof from the questions and conversations. She did not share her recent experience as a field hand, nor inform her fellow passengers that one can starve working on a farm just as easily as labouring in a factory.

As dark turned to dawn the train stopped, and a large portion of its passengers were led off. It proved a long stop, and those destined to travel further into Germany were allowed to disembark, but they were not allowed to enter the waiting room. Renata stood on the platform, surveying the scene. For the first time, she saw German civilians. With intense loneliness she watched loving mothers and fathers doting on their children. She could not reconcile these images with the terrifying monsters who had terrorised her at home.

After a two-hour break, those not removed reboarded the train. They gazed out the windows, and at each other, in anxiety and wonder. Their final destination was unknown.

Renata sat quietly by a window with a rising and surprising sense of adventure. During her few years of formal schooling, geography and history were her favourite subjects. Łucjan, who had been lucky enough to study and travel abroad, instilled in his daughter a desire for travel and curiosity of the wider world.

Before the cataclysm that destroyed her childhood, her parents, and dispossessed her of everything she trusted and knew, Renata imagined the Germans as benign. Now, on a pleasant spring day, riding deeper into southern Germany, she could almost forget the reason she was on this train, and admire the loveliness of the Alpine landscape beckoning at the window. Could Łucjan have imagined his daughter travelling as a captive?

It was night when the slave train reached its destination. Its passengers discovered they were in the industrial city of Mannheim. The atmosphere was unremittingly dark. A full black-out was in force. The group of captives were bunked in army barracks overnight and in the morning Renata, along with other enslaved women and girls, were led under armed guard to the Daimler-Benz branch of Mannheim's Mercedes-Benz factory. In wartime, Daimler-Benz was producing undercarriages for German submarines. In the factory Renata encountered slave labourers from across the occupied countries of eastern and western Europe, though the majority came from Poland. Those who arrived in 1940 and 1941 were volunteers. Living under occupation in diminished conditions, their occupiers seduced them into volunteering by promising good wages, decent housing, paid vacations, and annual leaves to visit their homes and families. Upon arrival in The Reich, they found themselves harnessed to work like horses. There would be no home leave, and paid vacations, or any other kind of pay, was fantasy. It was [13]*verboten* to go to the movies. It was *verboten* to quaff a glass of beer in a tavern. It was *verboten* to ride on a train. When the Allies' bombing raids began, it would be *verboten* to enter German bomb shelters. In the meantime, the discovery of an affair with a German *fraulein* was punishable by immediate hanging.

The social status of these unlikely slaves matched their working conditions. They were labelled, collectively, *Untermenschen* – subhuman. They were also labelled in terms of country of origin. Like the Jews, the slave labourers were compelled to wear patches. The Poles were tagged with a purple P, which they wore on their chests. The Russians were tagged with a white patch and OST, marked in blue, upon their backs. These patches made them easily identifiable to

---

[13] Forbidden

German civilians, who understood that these creatures could be abused, and even murdered, with impunity.

Once word got back to the occupied lands as to the true conditions of employment in The Reich, the Germans' appeal for volunteers went unanswered, so they took to raiding movie theatres, train stations, parks and heavily populated streets, press-ganging young men and women into slavery.

While Germany's youth stormed across Europe in conquest, Europe's youth toiled in the farms, factories and private homes of The Reich. No occupied country could protect its youth from being abducted and degraded as slave labour.

After a brief stint working for *Herr* Benz and his daughter Mercedes (it would be decades before Renata allowed herself to ride in a Mercedes Benz, and when she did, it would be with an American rabbi, in Poland!), she was taken to *Arbeitsamt*, the manpower office, where another form of selection took place. Prosperous German civilians bribed employment agency clerks into giving them first dibs on fresh batches of the slave labourers, which is how Renata was chosen by an obese butcher to work as a cleaning lady in his home and shop, as well as a helper in his slaughterhouse, which was located behind the shop. Renata was taken to Viernheim, on the outskirts of Mannheim, and assigned a cubicle-sized room in the attic of the butcher's large and lovely home. It was in Viernheim that she received her first piece of mail from Poland.

For a Jew to successfully pass as Catholic in the Nazi Reich, the masquerade entailed more than assuming a different name. It involved creating a new identity, which not only meant becoming someone else, but also proving to the audience you were attempting to convince that the character you played was not alone in the world. A biography had to be invented and populated with family and relatives. The member of the Underground resistance who acted as liaison and go-between in forging false identity documents, and who trailed and watched over Renata in the transit camp, now found a way of reaching her through what passed for post. Through several couriers, a letter wound its way from Warsaw to Mannheim, to Viernheim. It was addressed to 'Irena Krystyna Podbielska', because that is who Renata had become. In code, its author gave the newly created Krystyna a wondrous piece of news. Her brother Alek was alive! Sitting on her cot in the tiny attic room, Renata trembled as her eyes devoured the words on the page. After the war, she would learn the details of his survival.

Alek fought in wartime Europe's first urban uprising, the doomed Warsaw Ghetto rebellion, to the last. Near the end, he hid in a mountainous pile of excrement. Though German bloodhounds sniffed him out, their masters refused to approach because they couldn't bear to sully their boots. Alek then made a mad dash for freedom through the Ghetto gates. The Germans didn't chase him because they couldn't stand his stink. He made his way to Ania, still rooming with an old laundress. After cleaning him up, Ania steered him to one Irena Bobinska, a Catholic woman who, because she could read and speak German, was working in Warsaw's *Arbeitsamt,* the German-run manpower office. Irena was a member of the underground resistance movement.

Alek was slated to stay with Irena for a few days, before joining a group of partisans in the outlying forests. When several of the partisans came to collect him, Irena barred the door.

'He's not leaving.' She dismissed them. 'He's staying with me.' The partisans caught sight of the one bed in the one room, sized up the situation, and left. Alek would stay with

Irena for the next thirty-five years. They would produce four children.

Renata did not know, could not know, any of this at the time. All she knew was that her brother was alive, and a renewed determination to survive surged within her.

Soon Renata, or rather, Krystyna, for that, for the foreseeable future, is how she would be known, began receiving lyrical love letters from Poland, signed by one 'Marion.' Alek wrote them. His intention was to discourage unwanted sexual advances by establishing the existence of a male protector. The Poles were romantic people. A Jewish girl hiding on a farm could be taken by force, without consequences, but the Poles' sense of honour prevented them from poaching another man's property.

Renata had it good, for a slave in The Reich. The work was hard and the hours were long, but she was neither beaten nor abused, and she didn't go hungry. Living outside the city distanced her from the immediate war zone and the increasingly frequent Allied bombing attacks. She might have waited out the war in the small German town. Still, even among slaves, or especially among slaves, there is a grapevine. Word spread of Krystyna's working conditions. Her fellow travellers on the slave train began to visit and pressured her into supplying extra food for one of their number, a tubercular victim being worked to death in a factory. The young man from the slums of Warsaw was starving.

Pressure upon Krystyna grew intense. On Sundays, their one day off, if they got a day off, foreign labourers gathered in Mannheim's parks, because parks were the only public places accessible to them. Coerced into proving her solidarity with fellow Poles, and also feeling sorry for the guy, Krystyna took to pilfering bits of sausage meat from the butcher's kitchen pantry. They were paltry amounts, only as much as she could slip into a pocket of her overalls.

Over time, the butcher's wife began noticing the gaps in the pantry. She confronted her slave. 'Empty your pockets.' Krystyna had no choice but to obey. Shamefaced, she withdrew a slice of sausage the size of her thumb. The butcher's wife smacked her across the face.

'Thief! Ingrate! I take you in, give you food and shelter, and this is how you repay me?! Our *Führer* told us you Slavs were good for nothing, and couldn't be trusted. He was right! I don't want you in my house! I'm taking you back to *Arbeitsamt*! They can send you to the Gestapo, for all I care!'

Krystyna neither tried to explain, nor defend herself. She was developing the mentality of a slave.

CHAPTER TEN

In Mannheim's manpower office, the butcher's wife dragged in her fourteen-year-old slave.

'Take her back! I don't want her! She's a thief! She's been stealing sausage meat from me!' The employment agents were perplexed. What does one do with unwanted slave labour?

The slave and her labour were rerouted to the Rosol cleansing powder factory. Krystyna was assigned the task of unloading sacks of ammonium salts and soda from off the back of transport trucks. Some of the sacks weighed as much as fifty pounds. The first time Krystyna attempted to lift a sack, she felt as though her waist would crack. Gradually her muscles toughened and she learned to swing a sack like a professional porter. Krystyna's focus and determination caught the eye of the woman who ran the factory.

Before the war, Paula Duplessis and her business partner Gertrude Hammer were secretaries in the employ of the Jewish manufacturer Ganz who, with his family, escaped to England. *Frau* Duplessis and *Fraulein* Hammer were now running *Herr* Ganz's factory. Impressed with the Polish girl, *Frau* Duplessis had her transferred to the factory floor. When chemicals burnt off Krystyna's eyebrows and eyelashes, *Frau* Duplessis gave her extra milk. Then she invited Krystyna to come to her home on Sundays, and help her clean it.

Frau Duplessis was a childless woman who lived with her elderly mother. Her husband, a highly educated man, had refused an officer's commission and was a simple and older soldier on the Russian front. His family was from Alsace-Lorraine, which is how he came to inherit a French name. In her own old age Renata would describe *Frau* Duplessis's old mother as 'a gem'. She knitted Krystyna a sweater. She fed her extra rations. She slipped money into her pocket.

Frau Duplessis found herself drawn to the young Polish slave who postured as a tough from the slums. Using harsh peroxide, Krystyna dyed her hair a straw-coloured blonde. She swore like a stevedore and badmouthed the Jews, yet *Frau* Duplessis was not convinced by the show. The girl was exceptionally bright. That was obvious. There was something different, something special about her. *Frau* Duplessis began taking Krystyna to the opera and theatre.

Frau Duplessis lent Krystyna stylish dresses to wear on their cultural outings. *Frau* Duplessis's mother adorned the dresses with a broach. *Frau* Duplessis enjoyed Krystyna's enjoyment of these events. Secretly, Krystyna's enjoyment was enhanced by the irony of sitting next to S.S. officers who nodded to her politely. Should conversation be required, *Frau* Duplessis claimed her young companion was a visiting relative and ethnic German. At the height of the war Krystyna attended a stage production of *The Jew Suss,* the distorted and viciously anti-Semitic version of the Feuchtwanger play and novel, sitting among an audience of Nazi brass.

One Sunday afternoon, as Krystyna was cleaning in a back room, she sensed movement outside the window. At the far end of *Frau* Duplessis's garden there was a shed that contained more than tools. Several pairs of large, dark and frightened eyes peered from behind its small window pane. Spying Krystyna spying on them, the shadowy figures inhabiting these eyes quickly receded from view. Instantly, Krystyna understood. *Frau* Duplessis was hiding Jews.

Waves of loneliness engulfed Krystyna – or was it Renata? Her true identity and false identity were beginning to merge. How she longed to reveal herself to the sympathetic *Frau* Duplessis! She didn't dare. At war's end, she finally confessed. *Frau* Duplessis's reaction was mild, and subdued. 'I'm not surprised,' she stated simply. 'I knew there was something different and special about you.'

They would bid farewell, but not goodbye. Through the chaos and upheaval of displacement and immigration, Renata kept in touch with Paula Duplessis. Before I came to learn of her, she came to learn of me. Before dying of cancer in the late 1950s, Paula Duplessis knew that her wartime protégée settled in Canada, married happily, and had a baby. The baby was me.

***

In wartime Germany, in the factory, Renata made a friend. He was a fellow slave labourer. His name was Roger Briand. He was a prisoner of war, originally from Paris. Roger was in his early thirties, physically strong, athletic, and single. Before the war he was a member of France's national rugby team. He had a sister who met a French Canadian tourist, married him and moved with him to Montreal. Before the war, Roger visited his sister in Montreal. During work breaks and black-outs Roger would tell Renata about the beautiful North American city where his sister now lived.

'C'est le Paris d'Amerique du nord!' Like Paula Duplessis, Briand sensed something different about this teenager who postured as a tough from a Warsaw slum. Instinctively, he took a liking to her. He recognised her intelligence, but derided her anti-Semitic outbursts.

83

'Ce n'est pas bon, Krystyna.' Unwittingly, Roger chided a Jewish girl for badmouthing Jews. *'Ce n'est pas bon!'*

As with Paula Duplessis, Renata longed to reveal her true identity to Roger, but didn't dare. She intended to tell him at war's end, but the Parisian was repatriated so quickly that she never got the chance. Forever after, Renata was haunted by a sense of unfinished business with this sympathetic Frenchman.

'How I wish I had been able to tell him. He was such a good and kind man.' Mum smiled fondly, in remembrance. 'And I slapped his face.'

'He was a good and kind man and you slapped his face?' There must have been a method to Mum's madness.

'It was during a bombing raid.' Mum began, by way of explanation. 'The factory was in blackout. In French, Roger appealed to me. *'Krystyna, donne-moi un bougie.'* I didn't understand French then.'

In the wartime Reich slave labourers from occupied Europe, deported and displaced, constituted a veritable Tower of Babel.

'In Polish,' Renata continued, *'daj buzi'* means 'give me a kiss', and that's what I heard. I thought Roger was taking advantage of the blackout to start up with me, so I slapped his face.' The elderly Renata grinned. 'We got it straightened out later.' Then my mother grew melancholy. 'I hate the idea that he would remember me as a vulgar and foulmouthed Jew hater! How I wish I'd had the chance to tell him who I really was. Who I really am.'

In the late 1940s, when Renata was given the choice of immigrating to either Toronto or Montreal, she chose Montreal because of Briand's lyrical descriptions of the city. 'I wish he could know that.'

Figure 3: A blonde with dark roots: Renata's fifteenth birthday, 23 October 1943, as a slave labourer in Mannheim

In the late 1990s, on an extended stay in Paris, my mother Renata and I tried to trace Briand and/or his descendants, but to no avail. When we came home I wrote to the administration of France's rugby association, but they didn't answer. It was only in the last stages of my mother's life, on the cancer ward, listening to and recording her wartime tales, that I erupted, 'He had a sister in Montreal! He might have visited her again after the war! We might've placed an ad in *La Presse* looking for the sister! Sure, she'd have another name because she was married, but Briand didn't! You could've looked for the sister of Roger Briand! *Cherchez la femme!'*

'Oh Shaaaaron!' Renata wailed, in a corridor of the cancer ward. 'Why didn't you think of this before?!'

***

On 23 October 1943, Renata went to a photographer's studio and, paying with money slipped to her by Frau Duplessis's mother, had her picture taken. Her hair was bleached blonde, she wore a gash of scarlet lipstick in order to look older, and sported a bonnet on her head, tied with a string, under her neck. She tried to smile, but failed. There was a haunted quality about her eyes, which the photographer captured. She sent this photograph to her contact in Warsaw with an inscription of friendship, and the date X/23/43. Upon leaving the photographer's studio Renata sneaked down a side street into an alley, pulling from a pocket of her overalls a chunk of bread, a candle and a match. She inserted the bottom of the candle into the softest part of the bread, struck the match, and lit the candle. Crying quietly, she sang, to herself, the Polish version of Happy Birthday. Krystyna celebrated her saint's day as well as her eighteenth birthday publicly, in spring. This nippy autumn day was Renata's birthday. She was fifteen years old.

CHAPTER ELEVEN

When Leska, the contact in Warsaw, received news that Renata had been booted out of the butcher's home in Viernheim and was re-located in the front line of fire, she notified Ania. Ania went to *Arbeitsamt*, to Irena Bobinska, who was now her common law sister-in-law.

'Get me to Mannheim.' Ania did not ask. She commanded. Irena registered Ania as Catholic, and as a volunteer.

Unlike those who were press-ganged, at this later stage, those who volunteered for work in The Reich could choose their destination. Though still considered *Untermenschen*, their status was deemed a tad higher than that of scum and accordingly, their documents were marked with a diagonal red line.

In a letter written in code, Renata was alerted to her sister's arrival, and it was arranged that they would meet on a Sunday, in a park, near the Neckar River. Natalia's eldest daughter, the budding designer, was now washing dishes in a restaurant kitchen. Renata and her sister would meet in a park by the river on Sundays, but never let on that they were related, in case one might be captured and tortured into revealing the identity of the other.

When the seemingly invincible German army was defeated at Stalingrad in the winter of 1943, the bombing assaults on Mannheim intensified. From the front entrance of the Rosol cleansing powder factory, one could look out and see across the Rhine River, the chimneys of I.G. Farben Industries spewing smoke full blast, as it manufactured the lethal chemical Zyklon B. A direct hit from an Allied bomber exploded a boiler at I.G. Farben Industries. It also killed 200 slave labourers. The bomb and the boiler exploded at precisely six p.m. on an evening in early winter. The Allies arrived several minutes too early, the community of slave labourers mused. A paid German work force was scheduled to take over the night shift.

Since they had no money with which to outfit themselves for winter, the slave labourers were sent to *Winterhilfe*, a government-sponsored charity centre where social workers distributed warm clothing confiscated from Jews just before they were gassed or shot into pits in Poland.

Fully into 1943, the Americans were carpet-bombing Mannheim during the day, while British bombers handled the night shift. The downtown core, where Ania worked, was reduced to rubble. When a siren signalled the All Clear, Renata raced to the site. An entire block of buildings had collapsed, and people were trapped beneath its ruins. Fortunately there was no fire, and after several hours, which seemed like an eternity, Ania emerged unscathed.

Now that she was out of a job, Ania had to report to the *Arbeitsamt*, the manpower office. Renata asked *Frau* Duplessis to intervene. Ania was accepted for work in the factory and moved into the army barracks where Renata lodged with eight women.

Ania's cot lay next to Renata's. After their first night together Ania cautioned Renata, quietly, that she mumbled and cried out in her sleep. Loudly, Ania complained that Krystyna was snoring and disturbing HER sleep. She suggested Krystyna tie a scarf around her mouth so as not to disturb the others. The others applauded the idea, and henceforth Krystyna lay on her cot at night with a scarf tied over her mouth. Krystyna became afraid to fall asleep in front of her co-workers, but it was Renata who would develop and suffer chronic insomnia.

Lack of adequate sleep at night made the day's hard labour even harder. The two sisters were put to work at the furnace mixing soda, ammonia and liquid soap in a huge cauldron, and then boiling the mixture. They had to stoke the furnace and shovel the hot mixture into barrels. Once the mixture cooled, at a separate machine they poured portions into small containers and then sealed the final product with metal covers. Ania kept prodding Renata, as exhaustion and the heat of the furnace threatened to put her to sleep. Falling asleep on the job could be interpreted as negligence, and even as sabotage. Supported by the steely presence of her sister, and encouraged by the increasingly strong presence of the Allies in the skies, despite her diminishing physical resistance, Renata determined to survive.

In Mannheim, there was also an army of male slaves recruited from across occupied Europe. Camille Hoyos hailed from Belgium. He had volunteered to work in The Reich soon after his country was occupied.

Camille may once have had aspirations of a kind. He came from the Belgian countryside, left and moved to a larger town, where he joined the Communist Party. During The Occupation, his political activities got him into trouble with local authorities. In order to evade arrest, he escaped into The Reich. As a volunteer and western European, Camille's work and living conditions were slightly superior to those of the Slav slave labourers. He wooed and seduced Ania with food, and there were nights when Ania did not return to the cot that lay beside her sister's in the barracks.

It may have been during a post-coital embrace that Camille's lulled lover betrayed not only her true identity, but also the identity of Renata. From that moment on, Camille had the two Jewish sisters in his power.

***

All the slave labourers in the Rosol factory were in the power of the sadistic Nazi foreman, *Herr* Phenning. When Renata turned from the furnace to answer a question from a fellow slave, Phenning tossed a metal canister at her head. The metal struck her skull and cracked it. Renata raised her arms to the side of her head and screamed. Rushing to her side, Ania screamed for *Frau* Duplessis. The screams of the two women she didn't know were sisters sent Paula Duplessis running from an outer office, onto the factory floor. Ania could not leave her post and accompany Renata to hospital, because neither of them dared acknowledge that they were kin. It was Paula Duplessis who helped Renata into hospital and held her hand. *'Schweinhund!' Frau* Duplessis muttered repeatedly, as the young Polish slave girl moaned and gripped her hand. *'Schweinhund!'*. Paula Duplessis was only a trustee, managing the factory in the absence of her Jewish employer. It was the foreman Pfenning, as a Nazi party member, who held real power and everyone, including Paula Duplessis, knew he could abuse his position with impunity.

Renata's head wound healed, but she never made a full recovery. She would lose hearing in the ear located below the original injury, and sustain permanent nerve damage that led to life-long tinnitus.

***

Close to Christmas of 1944, the Polish slave Irena Krystyna Podbielska received a summons ordering her to report to Gestapo headquarters. She was to bring her identification documents with her. From Roger Briand, Renata learnt that

Łomża was now under Soviet control. She knew her documents could not be checked against church or municipal records.

On the appointed day, at the appointed hour, Renata went to meet the Gestapo. It was raining. There were no festive lights. The red of the swastika banners that draped the edifice housing Gestapo headquarters was the cityscape's only colour. Inside the grey building, along the long tall corridors, there were more draped banners and opulent stretches of carpet. Jittery citizens of the Reich were seated along the side walls, waiting to be called in for what might be an interview, or an interrogation. After presenting herself at a reception desk, *Fraulein* Podbielska was ushered into a plush office. As she entered, Renata willed her nerves to steady and her heart to slow its painful and rapid beat.

Inside the office, several SS officers, a medical doctor, and a Polish-speaking interpreter confronted the Jewish teenager. In a cordial manner, she was questioned about her background. The interpreter, misinterpreting Renata's sketchy knowledge of her ancestry, insisted on suggesting that she must have German blood. From a desk drawer an SS officer withdrew a set of instruments and handed them to the doctor. They were not instruments of torture. With these instruments the doctor took measurements of Renata's forehead, earlobes, and profile.

'Such a fine, intelligent forehead.' The Gestapo lackey concluded, in admiration of Renata's features. In an almost fatherly way he queried, 'Are you sure you don't have German blood?'

'Not that I know of.'

'Are you absolutely sure?' The SS officers so much wanted to believe that *Fraulein* Podbielska was German, so Renata thought it best not to disappoint them.

'Absolutely not! My grandmother's maiden name was Schmidt! Everybody in the family knew that!'

'Ha!' The doctor and the officers exulted. [14]*Da liegt der hund begraben!'*

Renata, along with her alter ego, left Gestapo headquarters unmolested. On the factory floor, word circulated of her interview – because Renata made sure that it did. Among the Polish slave labourers, the results of Renata's interview with the Gestapo gave her a reputation as a 'German bitch.' It was precisely the impression the Jewish teenager wanted to give.

For decades, Renata remained mystified by her bizarre brush with the Gestapo. In middle age she discovered that there had been a nineteenth century aristocrat named von Podbielski who was a general in the Prussian army and subsequently a minister in Bismarck's government. Did the SS hope to discover a Podbielski descendant among their slaves on a wartime factory floor? It is a logical explanation. It is the only explanation.

---

[14] Literally, *'the dog is buried there',* but a more apposite translation is *'there lies the heart of the matter'.*

CHAPTER TWELVE

'Hide and seek was reality, not a game. For the most part I lived in hunger. Under constant terror of discovery. I was a witness to evil and bestiality. I was a witness to wholesale murder and the imminence of my own death was pervasive. I had to grow up overnight and assume the adult responsibility of caring for myself. I was old before I was young.'

Renata Skotnicka-Zajdman, delivering a public address.

It was the cusp of spring on the planet Earth, a spring millions did not survive to see. Renata stretched and leaned against a pillar supporting the span of a small bridge in an industrial park on the River Rhine. Cones of light swept the night sky. Markers burst, like fireworks. Renata listened to the drone of bombers and then heard the staccato of a direct hit in Mannheim, across the river. The ground beneath the girl trembled, yet she remained calm. Each time an Allied bomber struck its target, hope swelled in her heart.

Allied bombing destroyed the Rosol factory and its barracks. Its slave labourers were on the loose. Renata considered fleeing to the mountains, to Heidelberg. It seemed everyone, including German civilians, had the same idea and the roads were congested with refugees so Renata, along with Ania and Camille, decided to take their chances in the front line of fire.

'*Chodź,* Krystyna.' The shadows tossed by distant fires outlined Ania's silhouette. Ania called her sister by her pseudonym at all times, in order to avoid an inadvertent slip.

'Get back into the cylinder.' Denied access to Mannheim's bomb shelters by German air raid wardens, the slave labourers sought sanctuary in the long and tall metal cylinders dotting the banks of the river. In these cylinders they couldn't stand and stretch to their full heights, but they could sit, and lie down. From the remains of the factory the slaves had the foresight to lug containers of water with them.

'Oh Ania, isn't it beautiful!' Renata was mesmerised by the sight of The Reich's destruction, as if she were watching a fireworks display. 'They're finishing it. The Americans are finishing it. We're going to live. We're going to be free!'

'*Tak, kochana.* We have a good chance, but we mustn't get caught in last-minute crossfire.' Gently, Ania tugged on her sister's arm. Never letting her eyes off the wondrous display of light and sound, Renata allowed herself to be led back to the cramped quarters of the sewage cylinder pipe system, situated directly opposite Ludwigshafen and the infamous I.G. Farben factory, which was now destroyed.

It was in the atmosphere. Renata was too scared to believe it, but she could feel it, and even breathe it. The air was still. The environment was silent.

In the stillness of an early morning in late March, the trio huddling in the cylinder felt the pressure of a heavy vehicle rumbling overhead. They heard young and gruff male voices commiserating in a language they were familiar with from pre-war movies.

'*Amerikanskis.*' Ania said it, for all of them. Renata peeked out and saw a white five-pointed star painted on an olive green-coloured tank. She retreated into the cylinder and the trio sat silent for several hours more, still too frightened to stir. Was hunger inducing hallucinations? Might this one harbinger of freedom still be forced back?

More olive green-coloured tanks joined the first olive green-coloured tank. Their reassuring rumble encouraged Renata to enquire, 'Have you got something white?'

Ania, the would-be designer, wriggled out of her overalls and removed her panties (in which she hid a small photograph of their mother Natalia), fashioning the underwear into a makeshift flag. The trio crawled out of the cylinder, waving Ania's panties as a sign of surrender.

***

Renata's response to the moment of her liberation that, against all reason, had finally manifested, was oddly anti-climactic. She simply couldn't absorb it. Was she really free? It no longer seemed possible. Had the possibility of living out her life been restored to her? She was physically debilitated and psychologically drained by spending almost half her earthly span on the run. All Renata could feel, if it even was a feeling, was numb. Whatever thoughts she managed to formulate were thoughts of her brother. If only Alek were alive. Was he?

The G.I.s who stumbled on them shared the contents of their water canteens, distributed bars of chocolate, and then the survivors, for that is who they were now, were left, once more, on their own.

Several days later, shivering and hungry, Renata was scavenging in the ruins of the pulverised streets, foraging for food, when she was caught in last-minute crossfire. Crouching in the rubble of a gutted home, she heard a soldier trying to communicate with a German civilian in a language, she knew, was not German. She waited for the G.I. to finish with the German and, skirting the scraps of metal and loose bricks which littered the devastated streets, she ran after him. [15]*'Jude!'* She shouted. The soldier bristled 'What?'

'Jude!' Renata insisted, pointing at him. The soldier glowered. 'Who the fuck are you?!'

'Jude! Ich bin Jude,' Renata pleaded in desperation, and with a resurfacing sense of hope.

'Oh Jesus!' Finally, light had dawned. 'You…?'

'Ja! Jude! Jude! Ich bin Jude!' Renata beamed, fervently shaking her head.

'Oh Christ!' The Jewish G.I. smacked his own head.

'Kom.' Renata led the overwhelmed soldier to the cylinder along the riverbank where Ania, Camille, and several other homeless slaves cowered inside. Gently, in Polish, Renata coaxed them out. The G.I. passed around his water canteen and handed out bars of chocolate. Then he brought the dazed young people to American Military Government headquarters, to Chaplain Abraham Hasselkorn.

'Sir.' The G.I. explained. I brought these people to you because I didn't know what else to do with them.'

The Jewish chaplain reassured the Jewish G.I. 'You did the right thing.' Chaplain Hasselkorn led the disoriented group to an inner office. On the door of this office a sign greeted them. It read *Lieutenant A. Hutler. Displaced Persons Officer.*

A. Hutler? The group of survivors blanched. It would take them a while to become comfortable with this name. When they did, the name of the Jewish lieutenant from Chicago became the butt of ongoing jokes.

---

[15] Jew

'Al,' Rabbi Hasselkorn informed his fellow officer. 'These people were found hiding in a cylinder on the riverbank. They say they're Jewish.'

Lieutenant Hutler addressed them, collectively, in German, though his eyes were drawn to Renata. The girl had a particularly intelligent look.

'Where did you come from, *mädchen*. Who are you?'

After two years in The Third Reich, Renata's German was passable. 'I come from Warsaw two years ago. I escape Ghetto. I let the Germans catch me so they would bring me here.'

Hutler had yet to grasp the nuances of those hiding in the open.

'My God, why would you want the Germans to bring you into Germany?!'

'To get out of Poland, *naturlich!*' Renata's companions nodded in agreement. Al, the Jewish lieutenant, and Abe, the Jewish chaplain, were dumbfounded. Finding herself designated group spokesman, Renata continued. 'No one except my sister knows I am Jewish, and she is not telling.' Ania announced herself by a curt nod, which seemed almost like a bow. Except for a dangerous slip of the tongue to Camille, her little sister's statement was true.

'My mother's friends outside Ghetto arrange false papers for me. I make everyone believe I am Polish Catholic.'

'And your mother? Where is she?' Hutler asked.

Renata hung her head. Enough said.

'How old are you, *mädchen?*' Gently, Hutler continued to interview.

Renata hesitated. Even if this officer was Jewish and American, she wasn't sure she should tell him.

'Nineteen.' Renata lied. In truth, she was sixteen and a half. But Renata didn't feel like a child, and was afraid of being taken for one.

'And what is your name?'

'My real name?'

Hutler nodded.

Renata looked as if she was about to confess a guilty secret. This was as much of the truth as she felt ready to tell. 'On false papers I am Irena Krystyna. I make everyone call me Krystyna because I like the name. Before war I see film [16]*Krelewa Krystyna* with Greta Garbo, and I want to be like Garbo in movie, so in war, I take the name. My real name,' Renata hung her head, 'is Renata.'

Chaplain Hasselkorn gazed at the girl in wonder. Echoing a Polish girl Renata believed was lost, the chaplain stated, 'In Latin, Renata means 'reborn.' The symbolism and the significance of a survivor bearing such a name made a deep impression on the two American officers.

'It sounds like you've had to create a whole new identity for yourself.' Softly, Hutler offered.

'Oh, I am good liar!' Renata pronounced with pride.

The two officers could do nothing but shake their heads.

'You don't have a place to live, do you.' Hutler stated. It was not a question.

---

[16] Queen Krystyna

'*Nein,* but I know a place where we can live. A German woman who is working in same factory told me about it. She knows a guard from concentration camp who runs away. His wife sewed a P on their jackets, and they run to the mountains. Ha! Now Nazis are pretending to be Polish workers like me!'

'Do you know the location of this house?'

'*Ja.* The German woman tells me. It is nice house in good district. It is not bombed.'

'Follow me. All of you.' Lieutenant Hutler led Hasselkorn and the motley crew out of American military headquarters and onto the street. He motioned to a parked jeep. 'Now Queen Krystyna-Renata, you'll lead us to your castle. Have you any other requests?' Al winked at Abe. 'Your wish is our command.'

'*Ja!*' The teenager retorted. Ania gasped, as her little sister continued to engage the American officer in conversation. 'Can we bring the German woman from factory? Her house is *kaput.* She has nowhere to live, too. She is good woman. She was never mean to us.'

Hutler considered Renata's request. 'We'll employ her as your housekeeper. That way she'll have enough to eat and a place to sleep.' Al signalled. 'Alright Gang! Pile in!'

Approaching the parked jeep, Hutler hopped into the driver's seat. Hasselkorn joined him on the passenger side. Renata and the rest climbed into the back, crowding each other and half-sitting on each other's laps. Hutler hit the gas, Renata indicated the way, and the vehicle rumbled over ruined roads until it reached a residential district unscarred by Allied bombing.

'It's that one.' From the back of the jeep, Renata piped up and pointed out her new residence. Hutler braked, jumped out of the jeep and pushed open the door to the home of a concentration camp guard who had decamped and headed for the hills.

CHAPTER THIRTEEN

'Don't do it!' Renata pleaded with her sister. 'The Americans are here! There's nothing he can do to us, now! You don't have to do it!'

'He says he'll kill me if I don't.'

'He's bluffing!'

Ania didn't tell her sister that Camille had threatened to kill her, too.

'He can't hurt us anymore, [17]*kochana*. No one would listen to him. Even the Germans are running away! Leave him, *kochana*. I'm begging you. Just leave him!' Ania wasn't listening, either. On the verge of VE Day, calculating that he would fare better in the coming post-war world if he attached himself to the clannish Jews, Camille convinced Ania to marry him by aiming the barrel of a loaded revolver at the side of her head.

On the eve of freedom, breathtakingly brave and audacious Ania legally chained herself to the Belgian peasant. Her sister served as a sorrowful witness. Ania and Camille were married in a civil ceremony in Mannheim's [18]*Rathaus* on 3 May 1945.

---

[17] Darling
[18] Town Hall

In the evening, in a private bedroom of the apartment vacated by the fleeing concentration camp guard, luxuriating in a real bed, Renata reached under the mattress and pulled out several cans of Carnation condensed milk. She had punched holes in the cans and inserted straws so that when she woke in the middle of the night, which she did often, she could have instant access to the thick and creamy American milk. Oh, what bliss to lie in a real bed, under a quilted blanket, among soft and clean sheets! Renata hadn't slept in a bed since childhood.

The cans of milk were now within easy reach. Reassuring herself that she wouldn't go hungry, Renata reached to the nightstand, clicked a knob on the [19]*Volksempfänger,* and fiddled with its glass tuning dial. Listening to a foreign broadcast was no longer considered a capital offence. As Renata raised the volume, in faraway Bush House the first four notes of Beethoven's Fifth Symphony were beaten out on a kettledrum. *Da da da DUM!* 'This is London calling.' A rich and plumy voice intoned, in Oxford-accented German. The BBC European Service was speaking to Germany. How wonderful that the concentration camp guard had left behind his wireless. There was little war news because, except for the fighting in the Pacific and the Third Reich's protracted death throes, there was no longer war, but the BBC still aired the recorded music of Major Glenn Miller, who had vanished in the air over the English Channel four months before. Renata came to think of Miller's sweet swing as freedom music. She always would.

Renata's insomnia was now chronic. She resisted sleep in order to avoid nightmares, which were also chronic. If fatigue overwhelmed her and she finally dozed off, it would be with the lights on. Renata had become afraid of the dark.

---

[19] People's radio

For Renata and her sister the war was over, but they had to wait until it was over for everyone.

***

The days were longer and warmer. On a lovely May morning, within a week of Ania's shotgun wedding, G.I.s behind the steering wheels of their jeeps rumbled through the rubble of Mannheim honking their horns and shouting, 'The war is over!' Renata stood in the streets, stunned. It was official. The swastika's hook had been pried off Europe and Renata survived to see it. She would no longer be hunted. She would not be slaughtered. The teenager had spent almost half her earthly span on the run. Now that the gift of life was restored to her, she needed time to get used to the idea. How does one adjust to the idea of being alive?

When the sun set in Mannheim on 8 May 1945, anyone still sheltered in a house with windows intact ripped the blackout shades out of them.

For the next seventy-two hours, freed Russian slaves went on a rampage of looting and vengeance. Their American liberators, some of whom had also liberated the concentration camps, turned a blind eye.

Renata's one attempt at looting ended in farce. In downtown Mannheim, she joined a gang that invaded the cellar of a Woolworth's department store. It was believed to be a wine cellar. Renata expected to grab a few bottles and then barter them for food. Her Russian comrades took axes to the barrels, and smashed them. The contents of the barrels gushed forth and sprayed them all. Renata found herself saturated in ink.

Near the now-defunct Rosol factory there lived a *Luftschutz*, an air raid warden responsible for keeping slave labourers out of shelters during bombing raids. He was a particularly vicious guard who delighted in the terror of slaves forced to brave, in the open, the onslaught of Allied bombs. Because he blocked her entry into a shelter, during one bombardment a young Russian slave, Nina, had her arm blown off. 'We'll fix that bastard,' her male compatriots vowed. 'It won't be long now.' In war's immediate aftermath, during the three-day free-for-all winked at by the Americans, Nina's comrades kept their word. They abducted the *Luftschutz* and dragged him into the street. Urging onlookers to witness and enjoy the show, they stripped the guard naked and hung him, upside down, by his testicles, on the closest lamppost.

As the air raid warden died in agony, Renata's fellow slaves cheered. Renata responded by vomiting. Though she had entertained many fantasies of revenge, when offered the opportunity to realise them, Renata discovered that she wasn't a killer. As she wretched, the freed slave realised that what she most hated was hatred itself.

'What's the matter with you?!' A Polish slave she'd been friendly with in the factory, turned on her. 'Can't you take it?! You're behaving like a fucking Jew!'

The Russian slaves forgot no one, and nothing. They formed a cordon around a neighbourhood bakery in order to protect it from uninformed mobs. The owner of this bakery was a kind-hearted old German who regularly slipped them extra rations of bread.

***

Renata was standing at the counter of the kitchen in their newly requisitioned apartment, spreading jam on bread: the jam and bread, she couldn't help recalling, that the Germans had promised Warsaw's starving ghetto inhabitants in order to entice them to the cattle trains, and their deaths. She had her back to Camille, who was sitting at the table, sipping on a cup of real coffee. The Americans were well equipped, and

Camille knew how to barter with them. Already, he had made inroads into Mannheim's burgeoning black market.

Ania was resting in a bed in a back room, laid low by morning sickness. Within a month of her marriage, she was pregnant.

Camille studied the back of his teenage sister-in-law. She was buxom, shapely, and fattening up quickly on those cans of condensed milk, the ones with the pictures of a silly looking cow.

Cá m'est egal. Camille mused. It's all the same. One sister would do as well as another.

Setting aside his coffee, Camille rose from the table, unbuckled his belt, unzipped the fly of his pants, grabbed Renata, and pressed her against the counter. His intention was clear. Renata, muscular and strong from work in the factory, shoved him away, seized a steak knife from off the counter, and aimed it at the contents of Camille's open pants. 'Take one step closer, you fucking pig, and I'll cut off your balls. I mean it!' Camille knew she meant it. The kid could be as ferocious as her sister. *'Ah, merde.'* Camille backed off.

'What's going on in there?!' Ania yelled from the back room. 'I've got a headache! Can't you let me rest?'

Quickly Camille zipped his fly and buckled his belt. Just as quickly, the wily peasant lied, [20] *'Ta soeur est un putain!'*

'What?!' Renata screamed. 'No!' If Camille couldn't screw her one way, he would nail her another way.

'Why do you think the Americans bring us so much food?!' Camille roared towards the back room, taunting his

---

[20] 'Your sister is a whore'

wife, and setting up her sister. The fact that he was the one supplying the food became irrelevant.

'What do you think she's doing when she goes to military government headquarters? To translate for the people coming back from the camps, for that Jewish lieutenant? Ha! A snot-nosed nothing like that working as a translator for American officers? She tells you such stories, and you believe her?! She's screwing those officers, that's what!'

'It's not true!' Renata wailed. 'It's not true! The Americans are good to us because they're good people! They feel sorry for us. They care! Lieutenant Hutler gave me work so I'll have something to do! The Americans are teaching me! I'm learning English!'

'Oh the Americans are teaching you, alright!' Camille jeered. 'But it isn't English! They're teaching you real good, too!' Camille leered, and spat out, to Ania. 'Your sweet baby sister just tried to fuck me!'

'What?!' Ania bolted out of bed and raced to the kitchen, grabbing hold of her hapless half-sibling. 'You're starting up with my husband? You're trying to take my place?!'

'No, no! He's lying, Ania! Can't you see he's lying! It was the other way around! It was the other way around! He's lying about me in order to defend himself! You know me, Ania, you know me!'

Renata knew Ania, too. There was no reasoning with her. Ignoring every warning, Ania married the creature Renata recognised as a vicious animal. Now he was the father of her unborn child.

Ania couldn't afford to hear what she knew to be true. As Camille lolled against a wall, grinning with satisfaction, Ania struck her younger sister across the face and screamed, 'You tramp! You whore! Get out of my sight! Go to your

Americans! Let them take care of you!' Desperately attempting to justify her acceptance of Camille's behaviour, Ania cried, 'I'm standing up for my husband! You are not welcome in our home!'

CHAPTER FOURTEEN

'The bearer of this document is to receive all aid and assistance from American army personnel.' The officer signed the pink-coloured note, *Lieutenant Albert Hutler, Seventh Army*. 'Here, kid. Good luck.'

Pocketing the precious pink document, Renata joined an army of searchers propelled to the cities and towns from which they were deported, in the hope of finding a loved one alive. Renata refused to believe that Alek was dead. Nightly, he called to her in dreams. Armed with the official pass signed by Lieutenant Hutler, Renata freely crossed borders and military zones. She caught rides on American army trucks and jeeps, and rode on the roofs of German coal and cattle trains, growing filthy from soot and rendered half blind by smoke. The roads were choked with refugees from the east, survivors of the death camps, and escaping Nazis. Among them marched the teenage returnee.

Renata reached the remnants of what had been Warsaw. The elegant city of her birth and childhood was transformed into a surrealist landscape of physical and moral devastation. Amid the rubble, jagged edges of walls rose in fields of ruins. Stumbling through Warsaw's remains, Renata came to a large clearing. No half-destroyed building, no piece of wall loomed in mute witness to the disease, the misery, the starvation; to the round-ups, the resistance, the raging fires and outright murder committed on a plot of land that once held city streets. The only surviving physical structure was a church, which the Germans left unharmed. Here was the site of the infamous Warsaw Ghetto and, except for the empty symbol of faith, there was only flat, bare ground.

Renata turned back and retraced her steps. Instinct led her to the river. Since the Germans had destroyed the bridges, Renata crossed over on a makeshift pontoon. A lift in a peasant's cart led her to what, at first, seemed a mirage. One solitary house that she remembered still stood on the road. It was the house in which she received sanctuary after her escape through the sewers. Anxiety rose as high as hope.

Renata knocked on the door. A withered, seemingly old man unlocked the door, opened it a crack, and peered at her.

'What do you want?' Renata recognised Count Czerniakowski by the sound of his voice. The count was Leszka's father. Leszka was the Underground contact who served as rescuer and go-between while Renata was still in Warsaw, and after she was deported to Mannheim. The count was a high-ranking officer in the Polish military. Now he quaked in terror. At any moment he expected a summons from the Soviet authorities. The Russians were their masters, now.

'*Pan* Czerniakowski.' Sadly, Renata smiled. 'Don't you know me?'

'Oh Lord!' The count crossed himself. 'Natalia's child!'

From the count, Renata learned that Leszka and her mother were working in a military hospital near the German border. She accompanied him to the Central Committee of Polish Jews and signed a sworn statement testifying to his family's help, commitment and loyalty during her time of direst need. Before leaving, Leszka was able to get a message to her father, informing him what had happened to Renata's brother, Alek.

The count invited Renata to rest in his home, but when she heard that Alek was alive, she could neither rest nor tarry. She set off again – on foot, on the running boards of old trucks, in farmers' wagons, and finally, by train. Lifted into a freight car by Polish soldiers, Renata rode the rails. Her foot slipped, and a heel on her sturdy new Oxford shoes, a gift from the Americans, came unglued. Renata pocketed the dislodged heel next to the pink document.

Before the war, the trip to Gdansk would have taken eight hours. Now it took two days, as the train took long rests in the countryside while more imperative transports rode by.

Jumping off the roof of the train in Gdansk, Renata limped to the newspaper office where her brother worked as a journalist. She reached the office shortly after five p.m. It had just closed. Its employees were gone for the day.

As she hobbled along the hot pavements, passers-by took pity on her. It was early summer; late June. A cobbler in a shoe shop offered to glue Renata's heel back onto her shoe. Regretfully, Renata informed him, 'I have no money.' No matter. The sympathetic cobbler understood that she was on a mission, and offered to fix her shoe for free. Gratefully, Renata stopped at the cobbler's shop just long enough to repair her shoe before continuing on her search for her brother.

A group of young boys were kicking a ball around the courtyard of the apartment block where, Renata had been told, Alek now lived.

She approached the building. The boys, curious about the stranger in their midst, approached her. Renata entered the corridor leading to Alek's apartment. The boys dropped their ball, and trailed her. The apartment was empty, and its front door locked. To the watchful children, Renata explained her mission. They pointed to the back of the building, indicating an open window. Renata hurried to the back, followed by the boys. The sixteen-year-old girl climbed a spreading maple tree, which impressed them, and scurried along its branches like a hungry squirrel. She let herself into Alek's apartment through its open window. On the ground, the group of boys applauded and cheered in a vociferous demonstration of admiration and respect.

Inside the apartment, Renata began to explore. There was a kettle on the gas stove, still warm to the touch. The apartment could not have been empty for long. There was a crib in a corner. Renata did not yet realise that she had become an aunt. As if waiting for her, there was a cosy sofa tucked under the open window, allowing in a breeze. Having found her heart and home at last, the focused young girl dropped onto the sofa, and promptly fell asleep.

Once more, in her dreams, Renata heard Alek calling to her. He was cradling her in his arms. His eyes were moist with tears. Renata woke to discover that, this time, she wasn't dreaming! Upon opening her eyes she found herself cocooned in the warm, strong arms of her big, beautiful, life-size brother! Alek's large head cradled in the crook of her neck. He was weeping on Renata's shoulder.

'He said you were dead! He said you were dead!' Alek almost chanted as he rocked and swayed, clutching the warm, living body of his lost-and-found little sister.

'What? What are you talking about? Who said I was dead?'

Alek stopped rocking. Coming to stillness, he explained, 'Broniek. From Sochaczew. He came back from the camps. He said he saw you shot, so he could claim your father's house.' The ultimate betrayal had come, not from their Catholic neighbours, but from one of their own.

'It doesn't matter about my father's house.' Renata tried to comfort the large, sorrowful man. 'As long as I have you.' Renata's half-brother was almost twice her age.

'Don't try to go back to your father's town.' Alek had few illusions of the new Poland. 'They let Broniek have your father's house, maybe because he came early, but they're killing Jews who try to come back.'

'But you're here.' Renata was slow in absorbing the depth and intensity of hatred from those she had considered countrymen.

'No one except Irena knows who I am,' Alek confessed, almost ashamed. Then he confessed more. 'I, too, have stolen something from your father.'

'What do you mean?' Renata's slanted blue eyes bore into her brother's slanted brown eyes. Looking away, Alek announced. 'I took your father's name.' Aleksander Młynek was now Aleksander Skotnicki. His son, and the sons not yet born, would be Skotnicki, and their children would be Skotnicki. Łucjan's name would live on through Alek's line.

'But that's wonderful!' Renata erupted.

'You don't mind?' Alek gazed mournfully into her radiant face.

'Do I mind?' She hugged her big, sad brother. 'I think it's great!'

Brother and sister sat up all through the night, trying to make up for lost time. Who was lost? Who had been found?

'Mandelstam came back from Russia. He's been asking for Ania. I didn't know what to tell him.'

Ania's pre-war fiancé had returned from the Soviet Union. He had carried Ania in his heart throughout the war, and still wanted to marry her. To Renata, this was glorious news. She recognised it as a form of rescue. Alek disagreed.

'Since she's married and pregnant now, we mustn't disturb her peace.'

Renata felt uneasy about withholding such information, but assumed her older brother was naturally wiser. Ania's pre-war fiancé would be told she married and was with child, but Ania would never know he survived and that she was still loved, wanted and remembered. How different the rest of her life might've been, if she had. Her life was spared, but she would never know joy, nor find peace.

In time, Alek gave Renata a photograph of his pre-war fiancé Marysia, for safekeeping. 'If Irena finds it,' he stated sadly, 'She'll destroy it.'

On the enchanted evening of their reunion Renata told Alek about Irena Podbielska, the schoolmate in Białystok whose identity she had usurped in the latter part of the war. 'I assume she was killed when our school was bombed, but I didn't see it happen.' Alek would place an ad in the newspaper he worked for, asking for news of Irena Podbielska. The ad was never answered.

'What about the Golombeks and Janek Bartczak? They were so good to me, especially Janek. Are they alive? Are they safe?'

'The Golombeks are alive, but not really safe. As a policeman, he is considered suspect by the Soviets. The last time I saw Janek was on the barricades, during last year's uprising.' Alek was referring to Warsaw's second and doomed uprising in which Polish Catholics, and a few Jewish survivors of the Ghetto once more took up arms against the Germans.

'I saw him from a distance. There was a lot of shooting. It was chaotic. I haven't heard from nor seen him since.' Both Alek and Renata drew the logical conclusion that Janek Bartczak hadn't survived.

As brother and sister talked and laughed and cried and hugged, oblivious to everyone and everything around them, a woman crept in and placed a year-old toddler in the crib. She lingered at the doorway, in the shadows, watching and listening, witness to the fierce and loving bond between brother and sister. Then, like a snake in the grass, she slithered away.

CHAPTER FIFTEEN

The toddler gazed curiously at the teenage girl sleeping on his parents' sofa. His mother shook her awake. With the emerald green eyes inherited from his mother, he gaped at the waking stranger. Coming to consciousness, Renata gaped back. 'Who are you, little boy?' Renata coaxed.

Dryly, the woman answered for her child. 'He's your nephew.'

Alek had gone to his office at *The Baltic Journal*. It was a so-called free press. Though the Soviets were entrenched, the Iron Curtain had yet to clamp down.

Irena Bobinska went to a drawer, removed a medallion, and instructed Renata to hang it around her neck. 'You'd be better off keeping your Jewishness to yourself. If you're staying, you'll have to earn your keep. You can start by keeping house. I won't have a freeloader in my home.'

By coming to her brother, Renata believed she was coming home. Instead, she found herself once more enslaved.

In Poland in the summer of 1945, Renata suffered nightmares every night. The new communist satellite seemed one vast, invisible Jewish cemetery.

'I came here to get you out.' Renata pleaded with her brother. 'Why won't you leave?'

'This is Irena's home.' Alek avoided giving a direct answer.

'But it isn't our home anymore.'

'I can't leave a child.'

'Do you love Irena?' Renata broached the subject another way.

'I don't know.' Alek sighed. 'I never got a chance to find out.'

Ania had paid Irena Bobinska to hide her brother Alek. He wasn't scheduled to stay for long but the scenario changed when, after a few days under her roof, Irena refused to allow partisans to bring him with them into the forest. Irena's fiancé was fighting at the front. She liked the look of the large and handsome Jew. She also held the power. Alek was compelled to fuck for his life.

When Irena Bobinska became pregnant, Alek was obliged to emerge from the oven he hid in during the day. Irena had staked her claim, and then she secured her territory. A new Christian identity was created for Alek, and the couple went through a Catholic marriage ceremony led by a priest ignorant of the groom's true identity.

As Renata pleaded with Alek to leave, Alek pleaded with Renata to stay.

'I'll send you to school. You're still young enough to go back and get an education. What will become of you if you leave? You will have no money, no profession, and no home. You'll grow wild. You'll be nothing more than a stateless refugee.'

Renata couldn't refute Alek's argument, but he appeared oblivious to Irena's hostility towards her. Now that Alek was a father, Renata knew she couldn't come between them.

A distant relation put Renata in touch with the [21]*Bri'ha,* and she announced her impending departure.

'Ha!' Irena snorted. She was glad to see the back of her sister-in-law, who was not only inconveniently Jewish, but also competition for Alek's ambivalent affection. Still, she couldn't resist a parting shot. 'Don't believe all that high-minded talk about wanting to live in freedom in a free new world. The kind of freedom your sister wants is the freedom to whore around!' Perhaps, given her own pattern, Irena really believed it.

Like Ania in Mannheim, Alek sacrificed his vulnerable sister to a malevolent spouse. 'You're leaving because you want freedom to whore around!' Alek parroted.

Renata had learned her lesson in Mannheim. She knew it was useless trying to defend herself. She left the premises under a cloud of recrimination and became, as Alek predicted and Irena made sure, a homeless and stateless refugee.

It was harder getting into the American zone than it had been getting out. At a border patrol, Renata offered her services to the Soviets. She was put to work processing returnees. For two days Renata sat at a wooden table which served as a desk, stamping documents. At the end of the second day, when the patrol guards retired for the evening, Renata stamped a stack of documents, stole them, and bolted. Handing out the documents, one at a time, at

---

[21] The Hebrew word for 'escape' or 'flight', the Bri'ha (sometimes written 'Bricha') was an underground organization, mainly comprising Palestinian Jews, whose task was to guide Holocaust survivors out of Europe and into Palestine pre-1948

intermittent checkpoints, eased Renata's way into the American zone.

CHAPTER SIXTEEN

'The displaced persons' camps were crude installations. They were carefully isolated from the surrounding communities. Though 'liberated,' the DPs were treated worse than vanquished Germans. In some camps DPs were penned behind barbed wire and needed passes to leave the grounds. There was no psychological counselling, no group therapy sessions. No educational programs. We were treated as if the Holocaust had never happened. In my case, as if nearly six years of terror and starvation which left me sweating and screaming in the night, as if the termination of my formal education, the murder of my people, were but everyday occurrences in a young girl's development. There was no insight or empathy for youngsters like me... Our desperation was further deepened by the conviction that we had been abandoned... We became an international nuisance, cast-offs, unwanted. As far as I know, no one in any position of authority paid the slightest attention to the high incidence of suicide among the Jewish survivors... We reached out to the world that had betrayed us and discovered that if we were to continue we would have to do so on our own. And by and large, we did.'

From the private memoir of Renata Skotnicka-Zajdman

Back in Mannheim, Renata registered at Camp Bensheim, a newly created displaced persons' camp. She reported to American military government headquarters, and Lieutenant Hutler, who put her to work translating oral testimonies of Polish-speaking concentration camp survivors. Renata worked alongside another orphan, a native of Mannheim, who survived Auschwitz, made his way back to his home town because he had nowhere else to go, and was acting as a translator for German-speaking returnees. Ernst Michel, later known in the United States as the high-powered fundraiser Ernest Michel, and even Ernie, returned to Mannheim while Renata was in Poland. They worked side by side under the supervision of Lieutenant Hutler, who became Michel's mentor. Before the end of 1945, Hutler, now a captain, returned to civilian life in America, and in 1946 Michel followed. Before he left, Hutler dictated and signed a document restoring the fictional Irena Krystyna Podbielska's true identity. The date of birth on the surviving document is correct, but the year of birth is wrong. Renata continued to lie about her age, claiming to be three years older. In reality, Renata was an exact contemporary of Anne Frank and Elie Wiesel. She was young enough to be eligible for Canada's War Orphans' Project and, like Wiesel, she might have been transported to western Europe and given the formal education she was owed and deserved. Instead, Renata chose to go it alone. She would pay an exorbitant price for her self-imposed isolation.

In hindsight, her decision seems a mistake, but having come through the greatest cataclysm of the twentieth century only to be further abused and betrayed by the only family she had left, Renata trusted no one. External authority became anathema. She couldn't allow any organisation, no matter how benevolent it might seem, to control her destiny and determine her fate.

In the displaced persons' camp Renata made friends, fell into First Love, got hurt and got over it. She also relinquished her childhood dream of becoming a lawyer, like her father, and set out to earn a nursing diploma. She reasoned that having a portable profession would enable her to earn her keep anywhere in the world. After initially training as a nurse's aide in the camp, Renata was sent for further training to Hanau, in Frankfurt-am-Main.

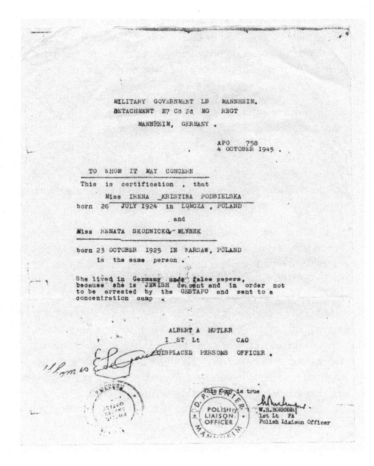

Figure 4: The 'Hutler letter', the official US Army document restoring Renata's identity

Over the course of the next three years, Renata studied and worked in the Jewish ward of a *Krankenhaus*, and in the outpatient clinic inside Camp Bensheim, which cared for patients who refused, sometimes hysterically, to be treated by German nurses and doctors. She saved her earnings, accumulating 300 U.S. dollars. Concurrently she applied for immigration to most countries that might accept her. The further away, the better, as far as she was concerned.

At the American consulate, Renata applied for immigration to the United States. The U.S. quota for Polish nationals, which is, ironically, how Renata was categorised, extended into 1951. England was accepting charwomen, but Renata didn't want to go to England. In the later 1940s, during the period leading up to Israel's War of Independence, the British were even less popular with the Jews than the Jews were with the British.

For a time within the camp, rumours circulated that Australia was offering a one-year contract to nurses to work on an Australian ship. Renata toyed with the idea that, before the contract was up, she might jump ship and marry an Australian in order to acquire Australian citizenship. It was a fanciful idea, and the chance of successfully executing it was almost nil, but Renata was getting older and becoming fearful of the future that it seemed, for so much of her life, she would not have. Would she never escape this horror-haunted and blood-soaked continent? Before the decade was out, Renata would turn a preternaturally mature twenty. She felt ancient. In some ways, she was.

In 1948, when Canada changed its government, the gates to a country that conducted itself like an exclusive country club began to creak open.

Determined to get through the gates, Renata bought a nursing contract in Canada from a Polish-Jewish racketeer. The gentleman was originally from Sochaczew and his family name was Wlodawsky. His first name was Joseph. Joseph Wlodawsky was an older and sophisticated man.

The details of his survival were shady, like the man himself. At war's end Wlodawsky landed, on his feet, in Germany. Renata hadn't known Wlodawsky before the war, but Wlodawsky claimed to have known Łucjan. It was possible. Wlodawsky's younger brother Arthur was the lawyer who fronted for Łucjan after he was disbarred. Arthur Wlodawsky met his end in the Warsaw Ghetto.

Imagine finding someone from Sochaczew, someone who had known Łucjan, in post-war Mannheim! By exploiting her father's memory, Wlodawsky gained the young girl's trust. When Wlodawsky emigrated to Canada with his wife and small son – he was one of the first refugees to get in, or buy his way in – Renata handed over to him the entire 300 U.S. dollars she earned in three years so that he would purchase for her, as he promised to, a nursing contract.

Anxiously Renata awaited a summons to Butzbach, for the physical examination required by Canadian Immigration authorities. She had already passed their IQ test stating, truthfully, that she was not, nor ever had been a member of the Communist Party. The physical examination was the last test she would have to pass. When the time came, Renata sent in a look-a-like with clean lungs to undergo the physical. Exposed on X-rays, the pattern of scars on Renata's lungs would baffle Canadian doctors who read them, for decades to come.

***

On 1 December 1948, at Bremerhaven, Renata, among a group of twenty young and unattached displaced persons, boarded a ship taking them to England. Renata carried a small red suitcase. It was her only piece of luggage. Before embarkation, the refugees were obliged to sign a statement swearing that should they be maimed or killed during the projected two-week journey by sea and air, no kin would claim compensation.

After a turbulent crossing through Hoek van Holland and the churning English Channel, the seasick band of refugees arrived at Harwich, where they were greeted by a welcoming committee dispensing biscuits and tea. On 3 December they were sent on to London by train.

Even in their diminished state the refugees were young, free, fed well enough, and even in its diminished state, London was one of the greatest cities in the world. Bunked in an underground shelter which served as a dormitory during the war, the band of young refugees quickly recovered their balance and bearings, and each morning, for a week, after breakfasting on meat pies in a nearby cafeteria, they embarked on an improvised version of a London package tour. Though Renata would later characterise her first London sojourn as a blur of 'meat pies, ruins and rain,' being a refugee in post-war London had its perks. Provided with slips of paper on which they carefully penned and misspelled the names of historic landmarks and tourist sites, these inadvertently revealing notes transformed into free passes as friendly bobbies and conductors on double decker buses helped them up to the top deck for a better view of the beloved capital, and then helped them on their way. By the end of 1948, stateless refugees in transit were a common sight in London Town, and its citizenry, in one more display of London Pride, acted as amateur guides. London could not only Take It, but it could also give of itself, and did. Londoners' hearts were as warm as their rain was cold. Within the week allotted to them, the increasingly merry band of refugees availed themselves of almost every pleasure London offered.

During the second week of December, the displaced persons boarded a *North Star* at Gatwick, bound for Gander,

Newfoundland. In Gander, Renata's journey was delayed by a classic Canadian blizzard. While waiting for the storm to pass and the plane to refuel, Renata noticed a bucktoothed, weak-chinned woman sitting on the opposite side of the intimate lounge. She recognised the woman from movie newsreels. The woman was travelling with her son James. She was returning from Paris where, at a United Nations General Assembly, she chaired the session which ratified the document she had drafted, a document which would become her greatest legacy; The Universal Declaration of Human Rights.

Extracting from her little red suitcase an American dollar bill, Renata approached. Waving the bill at the woman, she mimed the motion of writing.

'Pani Roosevelt. *Prosze.'* Renata was offering the bill to Eleanor Roosevelt so she could sign her name on it. A lesser being might have been startled by the apparition of a homeless refugee waving money at her, but FDR's widow took it in her stride. Obliging, she fished for a pen in her purse, and good-naturedly signed her autograph on Renata's bill.

It was the least she could do, and one imagines she knew it. Though considered a bleeding-hearted pest during her time in the White House, even FDR's widow underestimated the danger to Europe's Jews. One of the first to sound the alarm, she faltered in following through, failing to spur Franklin into enacting legislation which might have saved many. As much as the former First Lady had achieved, and would continue to achieve, her failure to rescue Europe's Jews, through her influence on the late president, plagued her conscience for the rest of her life.

In early winter, the *North Star* flew from Gander to Toronto. All the other refugees on this flight would settle in Toronto. Renata was going to Montreal. A representative of

The Canadian Red Cross handed her a five-dollar bill with which to begin her new life in a new land. Protectively, Renata tucked the bill into the cleavage of her brassiere.

On their immigration application forms, the displaced persons were given a choice of settlement in either Toronto or Montreal. Renata chose Montreal because of the tales of this city told to her by the Parisian prisoner-of war, Roger Briand.

***

Renata sat ramrod straight on the hard back seats in the coach compartment while passengers filed past on their way to the club car. The scent of roast beef and mashed potatoes wafted through the compartment. Renata breathed it in, as if the smell alone could nourish her. She was faint with hunger.

A black porter in a black uniform and black cap approached Renata, pen and note pad in hand. 'What would you like for dinner, Miss?'

Renata flinched. The sight of a man in a uniform, in any uniform, frightened her. She stiffened.

'Can I get you something to eat, Miss?' The porter put it another way. Because she didn't understand the question, Renata didn't answer.

The patient porter handed his pen and notepad to Renata. 'You write down what you would like to have, Miss.'

Renata was terrified. She wrote her name, social status (D.P.) and place of destination. She handed the notepad and pen back to the man in the uniform. The porter's warm dark eyes widened. Chuckling, he shook his head and returned to the dining car. He seemed to have given up, but no, a few moments later the kindly porter was back, balancing a cup of hot black coffee and a warm white roll. As famished as she was, Renata didn't dare break her five-dollar Canadian bill, nor even her one-dollar American bill – certainly not now that it had Eleanor Roosevelt's autograph on it! To the porter she pointed out her empty pockets. The sympathetic porter indicated that the coffee and roll were on the house.

Gratefully Renata almost grabbed the offering out of his hands, gulped the coffee, and devoured the roll. The black man's warm dark eyes lingered on the poor young thing, and then he returned to the club car.

At Montreal's Windsor Station, on the evening of 13 December, a stranger awaited Renata's arrival. Wlodawsky had sent an emissary. He was a business associate. His name was Albert Weiner. Weiner welcomed Renata to her new life in Canada with a bouquet of flowers, and a bouquet of food. This gentleman almost became my father.

PART II

A NEW LIFE IN A NEW LAND

CHAPTER SEVENTEEN

What I have been able to piece together about Albert Wiener is that his name was not Albert but Abram. He was a Polish Jew from a wealthy family who had managed, as late as 1941, to bribe his way into Tangier, and then escape to Portugal and Spain, before reaching Canada. He travelled light and alone. I do not know how he became involved with a man like Joseph Wlodawsky but I do know, due to the circumstances surrounding Renata's arrival in Canada, that their relationship would abruptly end.

At some point during his flight across the continent, Weiner decided that being an Albert was healthier than being an Abram, and that is who he became. Certainly, being an Al Bare was convenient once he settled in Québec.

At Windsor Station on the evening of 13 December 1948, what Renata saw was a short, dark-eyed, bespectacled gentleman of indeterminate age (Albert would claim to be fifteen years older than Renata, but the true age difference was closer to twenty). He stood waiting for her with a bouquet of flowers in one hand and a bouquet of food in the other.

The yeasty aroma emanating from the Five Roses flour mill mingled with the frigid air, as the day's last scheduled train from Toronto pulled into Windsor Station. Clutching her little red suitcase, Renata descended the steps from a train car to the platform. Snow began to fall. Tiny white pellets struck her bare head and the peaked collars of her coat, heralding the onslaught of a classic Canadian blizzard. Renata was wearing sturdy shoes. She had no boots.

It was not difficult for Albert to identify the exhausted young woman coming off the train. Her luxuriant, dark hair was uncovered. She wore leather gloves and a warm, elegant coat. It was a treasured article of clothing she acquired in Germany, on the black market. She had even clipped a broach onto the collar of her coat, which was a gift from *Frau* Duplessis's mother. Renata had standards and despite her circumstances, she was determined to maintain them.

'You must be Renata. Welcome to Canada.' Albert introduced himself and brought Renata to a nearby boarding house, where temporary shelter had been pre-arranged. He found a glass and filled it at the washbasin embedded in a wall of the room rented for her. Then he inserted the floral bouquet, which had been hard to come by, in December. He placed the food on a windowsill. Its pane was laced with snow. Certainly, the bottle of whole milk, the loaf of rye bread from Ben's Delicatessen, and the cluster of Macintosh apples would be well refrigerated there.

'Have a good night.' Albert took his leave. 'Rest well. Sleep as long as you like. I'll come by tomorrow afternoon.'

What was Renata thinking as she lay sleepless in a strange room, in a new land, a country that caught her imagination when, as a child in Sochaczew she read, in translation, Anne of Green Gables? A land she imagined as a peaceful sanctuary filled with nothing more threatening than snow? It was her first night in the country that would become her adopted home. The brightness of the blizzard raging outside the window silhouetted a stranger's thoughtful edible offering. Hopes, fears, and nightmarish memories must've overwhelmed her as she lay alone in the semi-dark, slicing pieces of apple with a penknife, and chewing on chunks of bread.

Though she could ill afford to, Renata would soon discard her little red suitcase. I will live here and I will die here, she told herself, as she tossed what represented, to her, a symbol of wandering. My life on the run is over, she told herself. No one will ever hunt me again.

The next day, despite the weather, Wlodawsky appeared before Wiener did. Renata greeted him cheerfully. She was eager to begin her new life.

'When do I start work in a hospital?'

'You don't.' Wlodawsky's words felt like a slap across the face.

'What do you mean? I sent you 300 U.S. dollars to pay for a nursing contract.'

'Your German diploma is no good here. The nurses' union won't accept it.'

'Then what am I going to do?' Renata looked like a startled deer. Wlodawsky avoided her fearful look. 'I'll take care of you. You don't have to rot in this shabby room. I'll arrange a pleasant place for you to live. I'll arrange an entire apartment.'

'You don't have to do that.' Renata hadn't yet caught on. 'Since you weren't able to buy a nursing contract, I still have the 300 U.S. dollars.'

'No. You don't.' Wlodawsky eyed her evenly.

'I don't understand.' Renata was nervous. 'What happened to it?'

'The money is safe.' Wlodawsky assured his prey. 'I've got it.' He added emphatically, 'I mean to keep it.'

Renata stiffened, in alarm. Had she once more been robbed and betrayed?

'I worked three years for that money. It was everything I had.'

'You'll be well taken care of.' Wlodawsky reiterated. 'If you'll be good to me.'

Renata was absorbing the full import of Wlodawsky's proposition. 'You're a married man.' She reminded him. 'You have a child. I was someone's child too. You knew my father. You said you were his friend.' Renata appealed to Wlodawsky's humanity. 'You're one of us. You went through what we all went through. How can you do this to me?'

'Oh don't be melodramatic.' Wlodawsky scoffed. 'I haven't done anything to you. On the contrary, I'm offering you a good deal. You're a pretty girl. Your looks haven't been ruined, like those scarecrows who crawled out of the camps. Be smart and take advantage of what you've got. Your youth won't last forever.' The devastated expression on Renata's pretty face was almost unbearable, even for a creature like Wlodawsky.

'Who do you think you are?' He roared suddenly, unable to handle his victim's anguish. 'You crawled out of a sewer! You're just another Ghetto rat who managed to avoid the gas chamber!' If Wlodawsky had moral brakes, he didn't feel the need to use them. 'Be reasonable.' He argued. 'Think logically. You're alone in the world. You have no family, no friends, no money, no education, and no home. You can't even speak the language. What can you do if you refuse me. You can work as a cleaning lady. That's all your good for.'

Renata's eyes widened. Evenly, with eerie calm, she stated, 'Thank you for the suggestion. That is what I will do.'

133

'Ouf! You're impossible!' Wlodawsky extricated himself from the web he had woven. 'I'm finished with you! You're on your own!' He turned on his heel, walked out, and slammed the door.

Renata doubled over. Outside the window, snow drifted and whirled. Where could she go? What could she do?

There was a knock on the door and, like a *deus ex machina,* Albert appeared. The look of hurt and horror on Renata's face sent him into alert.

'My God. What happened?'

'I need a job. I need to make money. Can you get me a job? I'll do anything!'

'*Shaa.* Slow down. Tell me what happened.' She did. 'Oh I'm sorry. I'm so sorry! I thought he was helping refugees!' Albert clapped his hands on his head. 'That son of a bitch is helping himself!'

'Please find me a job. I'll start today if anyone will take me.'

Albert wanted to offer money but realised that, in her present state, Renata might misunderstand and become offended. He felt like a pimp for the role he had unwittingly played in Wlodawsky's charade. He felt tainted by association.

'It's not as bad as it seems,' Albert tried to reassure Renata, and himself. 'I'll find you a job.' But when, he could not say. Albert was well connected, but who would hire a young woman just off the boat ten days before Christmas? Renata had used two of her five dollars to pay the advance on the room for a week, and Albert had every intention of discreetly paying the landlady further advances.

'You'll go crazy if you sit here alone. Come. I'll take you to dinner.' Albert took Renata to dinner, on and off, for the next four years. He would find her furnished rooms and homes to live and work in. As her English improved and her intelligence was recognised, he would find her increasingly lucrative jobs. Albert steered Renata to the English-language classes held at the Jewish Public Library. These classes were conducted by the struggling poet Irving Layton, who donated teaching time to the influx of disoriented refugees. Layton, in a rumpled brown suit, dashed into the library on dark winter afternoons, clutching a battered brown briefcase. He was patient and tender with the traumatised refugees. All the female students had a crush on him.

Renata earned a reputation as a dedicated student because she was the first to arrive in class and the last to leave. The reason Renata appeared so eager was that she could tuck her feet under a desk before her classmates and Professor Layton might see them. Her sturdy Oxford shoes had become so worn that they developed holes. In the dead of a Canadian winter, Renata was tramping around with holes in her shoes.

Despite the condition of her footwear, Renata was quick at her studies. Within months, she was reading the foreign correspondent John Hersey's hot new novel about the Warsaw Ghetto, the best-selling *The Wall*. It would take longer to afford a pair of new shoes. In time, Renata would own a closet full of shoes. She would also develop a large, multi-lingual private library.

Irving Layton's warm-hearted response to the Jewish refugees who streamed into Canada in the late 1940s and early 1950s was an exception that proved a rule. Montreal's mainstream Jewish community ostracised the newcomers. Their established brethren were embarrassed by them, fearful of them, and even hostile to them. Montreal's mainstream Jewish community didn't seem to understand that the devastated remnants of European Jewry were steeped in deep collective mourning, and clearly, they didn't care. They wanted neither to deal with their anxiety, nor hear their stories of horror.

Marginalised once more, the refugees turned inward, and toward each other. [22]A survivor of Buchenwald, who endured his sojourn in hell by fantasizing about bread, set up a bagel bakery on St. Viateur Street, rising at five each morning to hand-knead fresh batches of yeast and dough. [23]A Russian housewife who dreamed of becoming an actress reinvented herself as a director of plays performed in Yiddish.

The refugees found ways of making their own fun. Albert introduced Renata to the winter wonderland on Mont Royal Park and the summer oasis at Crystal Beach (now Cap St. Jacques). He took her to classical music concerts, and accompanied her to French-language plays at the *Monument Nationale*. With Albert, Renata saw Gratien Gelinas in the original stage production of Tit-Coq. She saw Edith Piaf perform during a North American tour. Albert also took Renata to Bar-B-Q. Chalet. Once.

'What are you doing?' Renata queried her date. They had settled into their seats in the chalet that wasn't a chalet. At their table the waitress had just deposited two plates of sizzling chicken pieces, along with a heaping side order of French fries. The chicken skins were so dark and highly spiced that they glowed like amber.

---

[22] The St. Viateur Bagel Shop became a Montreal institution. It was immortalised in the 1973 short story collection Saturday Night at the Bagel Factory. The book won The Stephen Leacock Award for Humour

[23] Dora Wasserman, founder and first director of The Montreal Yiddish Theatre, who would ultimately tour the world with her troupe, including Wasserman's native Russia.

Figure 5: Mont Royal A quiet land of snow and peace (1949)

'I'm eating,' Albert responded, logically. He had just lifted a drumstick, and was biting into it. 'Why don't you eat too?' He waved the drumstick as if it were a baton, indicating Renata's plate. 'Dig in.'

'Don't be silly!' Renata huffed. 'We're in a restaurant! I'm not going to eat with my hands! How can you? The war is over, we don't have to behave like peasants anymore.'

Albert chuckled. 'Suit yourself. But look around you.' All the diners at neighbouring tables were eating with

their hands. Renata was nothing if not adaptable. Well, if this is how it's done in Canada… Reluctantly, Renata lifted a seasoned breast. She liked the white meat of chicken.

The rest of the meal proceeded without incident. When their plates were cleared off the table, the waitress brought two bowls holding warm water, with a slice of lemon floating on top of each.

'What am I supposed to do with this?' Renata appealed to the mentor who was initiating her into the curious ways of the New World.

Albert paused. He had a warm, open and friendly face. Innocently, he instructed his protégée. 'You drink it.'

Trustingly, Renata raised the bowl to her lips and sipped. All eyes in the restaurant were on Renata. 'Like this?'

Albert smiled sweetly. 'Look around you.' Their fellow diners were dipping their hands into the bowls and rubbing them with lemon slices, in order to wash off chicken grease.

'Oh you!' Renata hurled a napkin at her date. 'Yes, I know.' Ruefully Renata shook her head and announced, in English, 'Me, dumb immigrant!' Albert guffawed. So did the neighbouring diners.

Renata was a good sport, and accepted Albert's affectionate practical joke in the spirit in which it was played. Albert was her anchor, confidante, and best friend. In time, they became more than friends. Renata suggested to Albert that he marry her.

Albert was amenable to the suggestion, yet hesitated. He said he wanted to wait until he was more financially secure, but Renata sensed the real reason was that he was embarrassed by the prospect of having Ania and Camille as in-laws. Renata hadn't been able to leave them permanently behind. After enduring six months on Camille's family farm in Belgium, Ania escaped back to Germany. Camille followed. She wrote to the younger sister she had unceremoniously dismissed, demanding that she and her husband and child be brought to Canada. Jewish charity organisations would have nothing to do with her because Camille was Catholic. 'You owe it to me. I saved your life.' Emotional blackmail was an effective weapon. It fell to Renata to sponsor her sister and the dependents, and to pay for their passage to Canada. With money borrowed from Montreal's Hebrew Free Loan and paid to the Canadian Christian Council, Renata was able to bring Ania and her family to Canada.

Ania, Camille, and their young boy arrived by ship, docking at Québec City's port in June of 1951. Renata travelled from Montreal by bus, to greet and bring them to Montreal. The boy, born in 1946 in Mannheim, was named Leopold after Ania's father, and oddly, for a woman who detested her step-father, she had added a middle name: Łucjan. Little Leopold Łucjan, when he grew up, would insist on being called Leo, but in the meantime, the family called him Poldi.

In 1952 Ania had another child, a daughter she named Eva Natalia. Eva inherited her father's dark nature. Early on, I learned to steer clear of my cousin Eva.

Albert loved Renata sincerely and always would, but he had difficulty coping with the prospect of these relatives as family. He kept stalling, using money as an excuse, even though he was rapidly on his way to becoming a millionaire.

Without Albert, on lonely evenings when she had no piece work with which she earned extra cash, Renata went to the movies. She loved cinema. Once

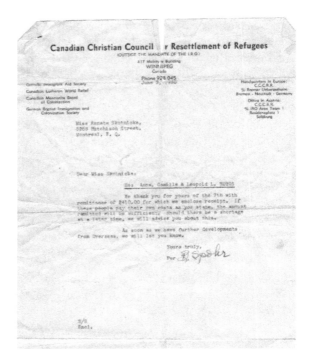

Figure 6: Letter from Canadian Christian Council (1950) regarding the immigration of the Hoyos family. The letter reads:

Dear Miss Scotnicka,

Re: Anna, Camille & Leopold L. HOYOS

We thank you for yours of the 7th with remittance of $410.00 for which we enclose receipt. If these people pay their own costs as you state, the amount remitted will be sufficient. Should there be a shortage at a later time, we will advise you about this.

As soon as we have further developments from Overseas, we will let you know.

she had access to the cinemas of post-war Germany, Renata discovered Italian neo-realism. Rossellini's *Roma: Open City* spoke to her in a way that no Hollywood concoction could. On the verge of emigration to Canada, Renata stood in the streets of Mannheim watching Howard Hawks direct one of the first on-location American films, his minor classic *I Was A Male War Bride*. In an early example of her instinct to document life, Renata requested and received Ann Sheridan's autograph. She didn't dare approach Cary Grant. The male star and the story's war bride appeared an aloof and forbidding demi-god. Even if she had, it was unlikely that Grant would have granted an autograph because he charged twenty-five cents for them and Renata didn't have twenty-five cents.

In her first years in Canada, semi-isolated and intensely lonely, Renata sought solace in Montreal's movie palaces. A cinema is a place one can enter without an invitation or an escort. Matching dialogue to images speeded and increased Renata's comprehension of the English language. The first film she saw in Montreal was the 1948 *Portrait of Jennie*. In Jennifer Jones's sweet visage, the young refugee saw the face of her mother. (When I was twenty-five, I saw *Portrait of Jennie* at a screening at the then-Sir George Williams University's Conservatory of Cinematographic Art. On the way out, I was stopped on the stairs. 'Has anyone ever told you that you look like Jennifer Jones?' I smiled. Truthfully, I answered. 'Yes.'

In Elia Kazan's film adaptation of *A Streetcar Named Desire*, Renata saw the triangle between herself, her sister and her brother-in-law. Like other healthy young women, Renata developed safe crushes on the tough-tender personas of William Holden and Jeff Chandler. Years later, married and a mother, Renata helped me to access her past through film.

CHAPTER EIGHTEEN

'In 1953 I met Abram Zajdman and stopped noticing the loneliness. It was real love – a friendship that caught fire. It took root and grew, one day at a time. It was a quiet understanding and mature acceptance of imperfection. He was a sweet and decent man, a man with whom I could walk side by side. His humour, his intelligence, his tenderness; those were balms for my wounds. I couldn't have made it without his trust and support. It took will, luck, work, maybe a bit of magic – and his wisdom to teach me how to laugh again.

From the private memoir of Renata Skotnicka-Zajdman.

The 18th of January 1953 dawned as a dull, grey, dead-of-winter day. Renata left her office early in order to keep a dental appointment. She was now working for an import and export company. She had begun by sweeping its floors. Her intelligence was recognised, and she progressed to the point where she was now a buyer. Since Renata's written English still wasn't up to snuff, the company's owner provided her with a secretary to write letters on her behalf. Renata Skotnicka, the buyer for the company Elias Brothers, signed her business correspondence, 'Miss Scot'.

Trudging home from the dentist's office, Renata encountered a co-worker walking with a companion. The co-worker nodded. It was all Renata could manage to nod back. She had a swollen jaw.

The co-worker, a fellow refugee, resented Renata because she had advanced so quickly in the company, while he remained behind in the shipping room. He didn't say much. His companion, who had better manners, asked to be introduced.

'This is Abram Zajdman, from Radom.'

As the tall stranger's penetrating dark eyes sized her up, Renata quivered. What a handsome man, she thought. He looks like a movie star, not like a Polish Jew. How ugly I must seem to him, with my swollen jaw.

'Pleased to meet you.' Abram removed the glove on his left hand, and extended it to her. The touch of the stranger's hand sparked a current between them. Renata averted her eyes, but she did not withdraw her hand.

The trio standing in the snow-covered street uttered the customary banalities, and then Renata moved on. Abram turned to take another look at her.

'She's a sweet girl,' he summed up, correctly. 'Attractive, too.' The swollen jaw was a temporary aberration. Abram was undeterred by surface appearances.

'Oh, she's not so sweet.' Renata's co-worker saw an opportunity to wound his colleague, and seized it. 'She's easy, if you know what I mean. You could have a good time with her.' How easy it was to defame a defenceless young woman struggling to survive on her own. The false accusation was so unoriginal that it became a cliché. Yet it had worked with Ania, it had worked with Alek, and it would work with Abram, too.

'Oh really? Well then, give me her phone number.' Abram was game.

At thirty-five, tall, dark, handsome and virile Abram Zajdman had a reputation as what was then called a lady killer. He had earned it. In the early days of the war he was engaged to a girl named Sabena. Abram's first love and first woman were the same. Abram pleaded with Sabena to escape with him into the Soviet Union. Sabena refused to leave her parents. Ultimately, she would share their gruesome fate.

The youngest son in a tribe of what, originally, had been ten children, Abram fled first, and alone. Most of his siblings joined him, and those who did, survived. In Central Asia Abram worked as a field hand and manual labourer in order to support his siblings and their appendages, the same siblings who cut off his education and put him to work in the family distillery when their father died, a year short of Abram's high school graduation.

Abram Zajdman spent his formative years in [24]*cheder*. His ultra-Orthodox mother, who kept *kosher* and wore a [25]*sheitel*, hoped to see her youngest son become a rabbi. It wasn't going to happen. Abram rebelled. He questioned his teachers and was told to question less and obey more, so Abram questioned more. In adolescence he turned to socialist rebellion, becoming indoctrinated into the far-left wing of the Zionist movement. His appetite, always hearty, became heartier on *Yom Kippur*. His father Michal, selling wines to Jew and Gentile alike, enrolled Abram in a secular Polish high school. It took brains for a Jew to be accepted into a Polish high school, and it took fists to stay in. Abram proved he had both.

---

[24] An elementary school teaching the basics of Judaism and Hebrew

[25] A wig worn by Orthodox Jewish women

After his father died suddenly of a heart attack, Abram deferred his plans to make [26]*aliyah* in order to care for and support his widowed mother. On the verge of graduation, Abram dropped out of school and took over the daily management of the family business.

After the war, having trekked to France to find an uncle, Abram was on the verge of emigration to Palestine when he was summoned to assist siblings already in Canada. The youngest son chronically ignored his needs and deferred his hopes and dreams in order to comply with demands made by those who passed for family. In this, Abram and Renata, so different in so many ways, were mirror images of each other.

Shortly after Abram's arrival in Montreal in June of 1948, a fellow refugee invited him to dinner. The two men were close in age. They shared a birthday. Abram's host had a much younger wife, the daughter of a dead friend. The woman and her mother survived Auschwitz. The father did not.

Abram and his young hostess were intensely attracted to each other. Guilt at the prospect of betraying his friend made Abram hesitate, but ultimately it didn't stop him. Abram and his friend's wife became lovers.

In the refugee community, their affair became an open secret. Abram pleaded with his lover to leave her husband and marry him. She refused. Her husband was making a good living as a printer, providing well for her and her mother. She had married him for security, and he was keeping his end of their deal.

---

[26] In this context, emigration to what was then Palestine, and is now Israel

On the other hand, as a travelling salesman, Abram was barely surviving. He had no training, except in the distillery business, and he knew better than to compete with the former bootlegger Bronfman. As a *halutz* he had received agricultural training, but that didn't serve him in a city. Having spent eighteen months in France after the war, Abram's French was fluent, but his English was fractured. He had no profession, and scant education. His older siblings had seen to that.

The torturous affair with Tosha dragged on for four years. Abram was always leaving, and Abram's siblings, entertained by the affair's soap operatic elements, found ways of tossing the lovers at each other in social situations, to see how long Abram could hold out in his determination to break free.

At the start of 1953, Abram decided he'd had enough. He made a New Year's resolution to marry, though he had no idea who his bride was going to be. He wanted children of his own. He wanted to seed a new breed, tough and resilient, able to withstand whatever the world might throw at them. He wanted a woman of his own, who would see and accept him for who he was. Abram considered himself a simple man, but he was not. Abram was, along with his pronounced streak of irony, what he would come to accuse me of being: 'Too sensitive, too intelligent, and too honest!' Abram was all three, though there was no evidence of it in his first phone call to the woman he would make my mother.

'*Pani* Renata, I have news of relatives of yours, in Poland.'

'You do?!' Renata's reticence dropped away. '*Prosze, Pan* Abram, come over and tell me about it!' It was an original pick-up line, guaranteed to work on a refugee hungry for remnants of family.

146

Once inside Renata's room, Abram grew embarrassed. Abram wasn't Wlodawsky. Still in his overcoat, with his gloves on, he demurred.

'I'm sorry. This was a rotten thing to do. I'm ashamed of myself. I'll leave. I won't disturb you again.' Abjectly, Abram turned toward the door.

Renata was impressed with the man's sincerity. She also felt sorry for him.

'*Pan* Abram,' she suggested, 'Why don't you take off your coat, and we can start over.' She extended her hand. 'I'm Renata Skotnicka. Pleased to meet you.'

Abram perked up like a puppy. He removed his gloves and offered both hands.

'I'm very, very happy to know you!' On Abram's right hand, where there should have been a ring and pinky finger, there were only stumps. Renata was startled to discover that the tall dark stranger with the movie star looks had a crippled hand. Now she understood why, the first time they met, he had extended his left hand to her.

The following day, Renata came down with the flu. For the next ten days Abram presented himself at her door, bearing Bayer's Aspirin and copies of Life magazine, along with freshly squeezed orange juice. He sat in a far corner of the room, on a hard-backed chair, his hands folded on his lap, talking to Renata and tending to Renata. Most significantly, he made the patient laugh. As I remember, Abram made it his mission to replace sadness with laughter, whether it was on the face of a child or a fellow Holocaust survivor. When Renata recovered from the flu, *Pan* Abram, true to his New Year's resolution, asked her to marry him.

'But I don't know you!' Renata protested, shocked at the speed of the courtship and the suddenness of the proposal.

'I know all I need to know.' Abram was sure, and resolute. 'Look, I have to go to Toronto on business for a week. Take the week to think about it and when I come back, I'm going to ask you again.'

While Abram was in Toronto, Renata reflected on her parents' marriage, and the marriages of her siblings. Their examples did not inspire confidence. When Abram returned, Renata suggested, 'Instead of getting married right away, why don't we live together first?'

Abram was not only shocked; he was affronted. In his mind, he vetoed the idea. No way. No one is going to test me!

'You need another week to think about it. I'll be back.' Two decades later, with hindsight on his side, Abram would say to me, 'I knew your mother really wanted me; she was just saving her face!' Was he that confident in his courtship? I'll never know, but I doubt it.

In the meantime, Tosha and Albert got wind of the new development. Those two had been confident, even overly confident, of their hold on their paramours. Both now recognised that the relationships they took for granted were under serious threat.

Tosha contacted Abram. 'I've decided to leave Srulek so I can marry you.'

Abram's response stunned her. 'Too little, too late.'

Albert contacted Renata. 'You win.'

'What do you mean, 'I win.'

'I mean you win. We'll get married. Isn't that what you want?'

'Albert,' Renata grew irritated. 'I wasn't playing a game.' At that moment, Albert's presumption cemented her decision. 'I can't marry you now.'

'What do you mean, you can't marry me now?'

'I can't marry you,' Renata was relishing her punch line, 'Because I'm going to marry Abram.'

On Saturday morning, Abram and Renata met in the Miss Montreal coffee shop. Abram sat silent and attentive.

'Albert asked me to marry him,' Renata began.

'Oh, well of course I understand! You've known him a long time, and you've just met me.' Abram was gracious in defeat. 'I hope the two of you will be very happy.' His congratulations were misplaced.

'Hang on! I haven't finished what I was going to say!' My father's forte was comedy, both intended and unintended, but my mother was a master of the dramatic.

'I'm not going to marry Albert. I told him so.'

'You're not? Why not?' Abram was truly mystified.

'Because.' Back in control of the scenario, Renata savoured the climax, as well as the anticipated effect it would have on her audience. 'I'm going to marry YOU.'

As the import of Renata's words sunk in, Abram's warm dark eyes widened. 'Oh. Ohhhhhh!' He clapped his hands over his heart, as if to warm and secure it. Then he became practical. 'Renia!' It was the diminutive he would use when addressing my mother, for the rest of his life.

'Can you give me a dime?'

'What?' Now it was Renata who was mystified. 'Of course I can give you a dime.' She fished in her purse, and pulled out her wallet. 'May I ask why?'

'Because!' To Abram, the reason was so obvious it didn't seem to need explanation. 'I want to call my sister! I have to tell her the wonderful news! Oh!' He raced to the nearest phone booth, clutching Renata's dime. 'I'm so happy! I'm so happy!' I imagine tears welled in Abram's warm and wonderful eyes. I also imagine he must've thought, as he would often say, when something happy happened, 'If only *mein* mother could see.' (Years later Abram would instruct me, 'Always have a dime on you for a phone call. Just in case.')

***

Not everyone was so happy about Abram and Renata's impending nuptials. On both ends, all hell broke loose.

'Are you insane?' Ania flew at her sister. 'You're throwing aside Albert for this?! Albert is willing and able to give you everything! This man is a pauper! Marry him and you'll never stop struggling! You'll be poor for the rest of your life!'

Renata conceded the logic of her sister's argument, but euphoria rendered her beyond the reach of logic. To Ania, the only explanation Renata could offer was, 'I can't help it. I have to marry him. He makes me laugh!'

While Ania was ranting at the prospect of Renata marrying Abram, Abram was pressing Renata to introduce him to Ania.

'I want to meet your family. Why won't you introduce me to your family? Are you ashamed of me?' Renata had met her match. Abram was as proud and sensitive as she.

'No! Of course not!' Renata could not bring herself to tell her intended that it was her family who embarrassed her. She sensed Albert's ambivalence had stemmed from his distaste for her sister, and particularly, his revulsion for the ape-like Camille. Who wouldn't feel repelled by such a beastly brother-in-law? Renata was afraid that, once Abram met her family, she would lose him. Finally, she could put off the meeting no longer. With a heavy heart, she brought Abram to meet Ania and Camille.

To Renata's wonderment, within moments Abram charmed Ania and had Camille eating out of his hand. With his prospective brother-in-law he found common ground in the French language, and in their mutual appreciation of *salade endive* and cognac. On the afternoon of that first encounter, Abram worked magic. Winning Ania's admiration and Renata's everlasting gratitude, Abram tamed the beast.

The Zajdman tribe's objections to Renata were vague, but equally virulent. They could not dismiss her on financial grounds, since she was earning more money than their brother. They could not fault her family background, because she came from a higher social class than they did. They picked on the fact that Gentiles had married into her family. Renata didn't speak Yiddish. She wasn't religious enough; she wasn't Jewish enough. They were too primitive to be aware of their real objections: Renata represented a threat. Their family servant was about to become a family man. He was going to have children of his own. He would no longer be on call to baby-sit and tutor the children they neglected. He might have less time to drive his sisters and sisters-in-law to their appointments with hairdressers. They might have to rely on him less, and share him more. The Zajdman tribe was not about to share with anyone.

For her part, Renata idealised large families, having lost so many relations during the war. She was impressed by Abram's devotion to his siblings and their children. He was a loyal brother and a playful and engaged uncle. Watching Abram cavort with his nieces and nephews Renata recognised, rightly, what a wonderful father he would be. She also believed that in marrying Abram she would be giving her unborn children a sheltering tribe of loving aunts and uncles and cousins. In this, she miscalculated. Badly. Renata had been too young to understand the overwhelming pressures relatives placed on her beleaguered mother Natalia, and Natalia hadn't survived to guide her daughter, and warn her. Renata was about to enter a hornet's nest. Its sting would reverberate into the next generation.

Dangling like a loose thread was Abram's married ex-lover Tosha. Abram felt obliged to speak with her directly. Tosha refused to accept Abram's decision. 'But I said I would leave Srulek and marry you!'

Sadly, Abram shook his head. 'Would you have said it if I hadn't met Renata? For four years I've been begging you to leave your marriage and live with me openly and honourably. I would've done anything, taken any kind of job, worked at two jobs, if need be, to keep you and your mother comfortable and safe. But you strung me along while having it both ways. Now I've found a woman who accepts me as I am. She isn't afraid to work and struggle with me.' The silver lining behind the cloud was becoming clear. 'Perhaps you did me a favour.' Abram mused. Sincerely, he told her, 'Tosha, I wish you well. Now let me go.'

Tosha wouldn't let go. In hysterics, she called her mother. Tosha's mother called Abram's eldest sister. 'Give me that woman's phone number.' The sister Abram revered was delighted to oblige.

'Miss Skotnicka,' The tongue of Tosha's mother dripped acid. 'Would you like to know where your boyfriend is? He's with my daughter, that's where!' The woman grew as hysterical as her daughter. 'Who do you think you are, trying to come between them? Abram will never give her up! Tosha will never let him go!'

After parting from Tosha, Abram headed directly to Renata's room. She opened the door and tossed Abram's ring at him. Though he could ill afford it, Abram insisted on buying an engagement ring. It was an inexpensive item, which he would replace with a small diamond fifteen years into the future.

'Get out!' Renata greeted him. 'Get out, get out, get out!'

Abram barely recognised this virago. 'What's got into you? What's going on?!'

Renata burst into tears. Sobbing, she attacked Abram. 'How could you?! How could you?!' She wailed.

'How could I what? What are you talking about?!' Swallowing her tears and gulping for air, Renata told him about the phone call.

'What a bitch. What a vicious bitch.' Abram muttered to himself.

'But it's true! Can you deny it? You were with Tosha, weren't you?!'

'Yes. I was with Tosha.' Abram admitted.

'Well then what do you expect me to say? What do you expect me to do?'

Once more, Abram conceded defeat. He couldn't cope with cunning and deceit.

'I'll leave.' Abram was near tears. 'You'll never see me again.' Abram, too, could be a dramatic Slav. 'But before I go,' he made a last-ditch plea for understanding, 'would you at least allow me to explain? Would you give me that chance?'

Abram looked so forlorn that it gave Renata pause. My paternity hung in the balance. At that moment, if Renata hadn't listened, Albert might have become my father.

Abram explained himself. Intensely quiet, Renata listened. When Abram was done, she buckled at the knees. Who knew better than she what it felt like to be victimised by distortion and slander? Instead of taking the coward's way out, through silence or a phone call or a letter, Abram faced his long-time lover and ended the relationship cleanly. As a result he was on the verge of losing his new love because she was on the verge of driving him away.

'I'm sorry I didn't trust you.' Renata told this gorgeous hunk, who had proven to be a sweet and decent man. 'It won't happen again.' Abram heaved a massive sigh of relief, and offered his bride his five-fingered hand. She did not accept it. Instead she lifted her groom's crippled hand, and held it. Renata would fall asleep clinging to the stumps of Abram's crippled hand for the next thirty years.

CHAPTER NINETEEN

Abram and Renata had no honeymoon. They couldn't afford it. On the evening of their marriage they moved into a large apartment on Ducharme, where Abram was living with a sister, a brother, their spouses and children. The newlyweds were allotted a third of the space, and obliged to pay half the rent.

The first dispute in their married life was triggered by the Rosenberg case. Julius and Ethel Rosenberg, an American-Jewish couple and the parents of two young boys, were tried and convicted of spying for the Soviets. The Rosenbergs were executed in June of 1953. Renata was aghast.

'How can the Americans murder a mother?' She implored her groom. Abram, whose sojourn in the Soviet Union turned him into a ferocious anti-Communist, sided with the prosecution.

'You have no idea what the Soviets are capable of.' For the next ten years, their disputes revolved around Abram's siblings. Abram refused to believe what his siblings were capable of.

'You must have done something to offend them,' he reasoned. 'Why would they want to hurt you?' Abram had yet to learn that hate doesn't need a reason. Hate is its own reason.

Three months into their marriage, Renata underwent emergency surgery to remove an ovary. Like many severely malnourished women in wartime, she had lost her menses, and after the war underwent radiation treatment in a German hospital in order to restore them. Many female Holocaust survivors were plagued with gynaecological disturbances. Her in-laws demonstrated a bit of sympathy, then. In her hospital room, as Renata faded in and out of consciousness, she heard one of them remark, 'Poor Abram. He'll never have children now. He should've married Tosha. The [27]*potz* went and saddled himself with damaged goods.' What the smug Zajdman tribe did not know was that, in Auschwitz, Tosha was one of Mengele's experiments. The infamous doctor stopped short of murdering her, but he rendered her infertile.

When Renata recovered from the operation, she and Abram set out to create their own fun. During the week they worked long and hard, but on weekends they went out and partied. In the 1950s, Montreal enjoyed a vibrant nightlife. For a dollar one could go dancing in the neon-marqueed nightclubs lighting up St. Catherine Street. All the clubs had glitzy floor shows, and housed lounges which featured more intimate entertainment. For more than a dollar, one could go clubbing at the El Morocco. Montreal's top club featured the prettiest showgirls and the hottest bands. It served the best liquor and the juiciest steaks. By nature a *bon vivant,* Abram's *joie de vivre* often found expression at the El Morocco. On Saturday nights Renata put on a pair of high heels and her one party dress, a shiny black item whose halter top accentuated her well-spaced, sturdy shoulders, and pleats that accentuated her strong, shapely legs.

On Sunday mornings, after soaking her sore feet, Renata headed back out with Abram to St. Catherine Street. On Saturday nights the street sizzled, but on Sundays, it was silent. On Sundays, nothing was open in this Catholic city,

---

[27] Loosely translated: idiot

except for the churches. Renata and Abram would take a trolley car to the downtown shopping district and Abram, with his penchant for whimsy, treated Renata to a window-shopping spree. The newlyweds strolled hand in hand along the empty boulevard, commiserating in front of department store display windows.

'Go ahead, *kochana.* Take your pick. Take it all. Today you can have anything you want.' On Sundays in Montreal in the 1950s, no fur coat was too expensive; no ball gown was out of reach. On Sundays, prompted by displays in the windows of Simpson's and Eaton's and Morgan's, in her imagination Renata could furnish her dream home. On Sundays, if she chose, Renata could buy out the posh and elegant Ogilvy's. On Sundays, Abram urged Renata to choose diamonds from the display window at Birks. On Sundays, Abram and Renata were the wealthiest couple in the world. Always, and only, on Sundays.

What Renata wanted, more than any material possession, was a child. So did Abram, but he didn't want to make his bride feel worse by admitting it. Instead, he told her, 'When I was in Siberia during the war, an old gypsy woman took my hand and read the lines in it. She told me I would survive the present terrible time, and travel over the seas and settle in a land far away. She told me I would become prosperous, and I would have two children. Don't worry, *kochana,* not only will we have one child, but we are going to have two!'

***

Every month, when Renata bled, she cried. Every month Abram reminded her of the gypsy's prophecy. Renata was fed up with Abram's gypsy, and Abram was fed up with Renata's thermometers. It must've been early in 1955 when Abram diagnosed the problem, and proposed a solution.

'The reason you aren't getting pregnant is because you're too tense! You need to relax. Quit your job!'

'What? We can't afford to lose my pay check!' Renata protested.

'We'll manage.' Abram was sure, and serene.

But how can I quit my job?'

'Simple.' Abram advocated simplicity. 'You go to your boss and say, 'I quit!''

'Oh, come on!'

'Try it, and you'll see!'

Renata was unconvinced. 'What if I quit my job and I don't get pregnant, and my boss doesn't take me back?'

'There's only one way to find out.'

Renata quit her job. The next month, she was pregnant. She hoped she was carrying twins – the gypsy said she would have two children, after all. Alas, there was only one of me.

The summer of 1955 was a scorcher. Air conditioning was in its infancy. Even Marilyn Monroe was reduced to standing over a subway grating, in order to get a bit of relief from the heat. Abram was intent on getting Renata out of the city, and into the hills.

In their early days in Canada, the struggling [28]greeners, a creative lot, found ways of arranging vacations in summer. They couldn't afford to stay at resorts in the Laurentian Hills, even those that accepted dogs and Jews, so they pooled their resources and rented farm houses. Each family was allotted a room, while sharing the bathroom and kitchen. It was a

---

[28] Greenhorns. A pejorative term for newcomers

form of communal living, and Abram, a ferocious anti-communist, dubbed their summer premises 'the [29] *kolhhoz*'. At the *'kolhhoz'* Dr Abram, who had taken charge of Renata's pregnancy, sponged her down while she soaked her feet in a pan of cold water. Counter-intuitively, he had her drinking hot tea, rather than iced tea, so she would perspire and her body temperature would lower naturally. He had her resting in the shade of trees during the days, and took her for walks in the evening shade. What Abram refused to do was prepare the accoutrements needed for me. There was to be no crib, no clothes, no blankets nor any bottles visible, until the moment I manifested. Abram's early religious training surfaced, then. Medieval rabbis, in their wisdom, and in this, they were wise, decreed that no material sign of an impending new life be visible to taunt an expectant mother, in case she was unable to carry her baby to term.

'Don't worry, *kochana*. When the child arrives, I will arrange everything. But not now. Not yet.' One didn't risk tempting The Evil Eye.

An idyllic summer ended, and Renata was back in the *kolhhoz* on Ducharme. She was nearing the end of her seventh month of pregnancy, resting on the sofa in the corner of the living room allotted to her and Abram, when Abram's seven-year-old niece Roma decided she wanted the space.

'Get up Renia. I want to sit there.'

'But Roma, I'm resting. You can see that I'm carrying a baby.' Renata patted her swollen belly.

'I said I want to sit there! Get up!' To drive home her point, Roma punched Renata in the stomach. In effect, she punched me, setting the template for how relatives on both

---

[29] The term for a collective farm in the Soviet Union

sides and into the next generation, believed they could treat me.

Renata gasped and doubled over. She stared at the holy terror in terror.

'If you tell,' Roma threatened, 'I'll do it again, and I'll say you punched me!'

Protectively Renata wrapped her arms around what, despite my cousin's assault, was soon going to be me.

Abram walked into the room. Roma glared. Renata told.

'Get out of *mein* sight before I kill you.' Quietly, he warned his niece. Bullies are also cowards. Bullies are always cowards. Roma bolted. Abram then raised a stink with Roma's parents.

'Why are you making such a fuss? She's just a child!'

The next morning Renata called her obstetrician. The doctor called in Abram.

'If you don't get your wife out of there,' he warned the expectant father, 'She's going to lose the baby.'

It was the cusp of winter. The traditional moving time was May. Nevertheless, Abram ensured my survival by locating an available and affordable apartment almost immediately.

CHAPTER TWENTY

I was expected to be a Christmas baby. However, during a check-up on the afternoon of 5 December, the obstetrician informed my mother I was so eager to meet her that it would take but a nudge to coax me into the world. My mother was equally keen to greet me, so I made my entrance at Montreal's Jewish General Hospital during the wee hours of Tuesday morning on St. Nicholas Day. It would have been Łucjan's sixty-sixth birthday. It would have been Rafał's birthday, too.

In childhood I imagined myself as Santa's gift to my parents, though often I suspected I'd been dropped down the wrong chimney. I don't believe that, now. I believe I was born to the people who needed me.

My parents brought me to their new, private and safe space in apartment 15 on 7 Plamondon Road. I was born into freedom, though there was the unresolved issue of my name. My father wanted to name me Sarah Leah, after his mother. In the Jewish tradition, it is the mother who has first rights in the naming of a first-born. In order to please my father, my mother was prepared to waive her rights, but she cringed at the thought of naming a daughter Sarah. Sarah was the name the Nazis stamped on Jewish women's documents. For Mum, to name me Sarah was to stigmatise me.

A compromise was reached when my parents heard that a friend, another *greener,* had married a [30]*gheler* named Sharon. This Sharon was named after her grandmother Sarah. My mother liked the soft sound of Sharon. It was pure. It carried no echoes, raised no associations. It felt fitting to bestow upon a new life in a new land a name as fresh as December snow.

Still, my mother wanted to remember her mother through me. (Her wish would be granted beyond all expectations as I developed and my face formed into Natalia's face.) It was decided that I would be given the names Sharon Natalie.

With the intention of registering my birth, in late February of 1956, with one of his brothers-in-law in tow, my father headed to *Vieux-Montreal,* to the *Palais de justice.* I imagine they took a streetcar to St. Catherine Street, and then walked down to the Old City. My mother was at home with me.

'But Mama wasn't just Sarah. She was Sarah Leah. We can't leave out the Leah!' protested Uncle Leon. Uncle Leon had been devoted to his mother-in-law Sarah Leah. At the outbreak of war, persuaded by his mother, Abram escaped into the Soviet Union. Leon remained in Radom with his bride Cesia and her mother Sarah Leah. In August of 1942, when the Germans came, Leon brought his healthy, sixty-two-year-old mother-in-law to the local hospital, believing she'd be safe there. Instead, Sarah Leah was shot in a hospital bed. Abram never knew how his mother died and warned those who did, not to tell him. Still, he knew that Leon had done his best to protect Sarah Leah. Because they stayed behind, both Cesia and Leon were deported to Auschwitz.

---

[30] Yellow. Since the established Jews called the newcomers 'greeners,' the newcomers retaliated by calling the established Jews 'yellow.'

Abram not only respected his brother-in-law; he also felt indebted.

'Kaminer!' Abram called Leon 'Kaminer,' because Kaminer was Leon's last name. 'This wouldn't be fair to Renia. She let me have the first name; I shouldn't take away from her the second name!'

'But what kind of a name is Sharon?'

'It's a good name. A Hebrew name. It's in Israel. It's in the Bible.'

'But what kind of a name is it for a girl?'

'Kaminer!' Perhaps Abram pulled on the earflaps of his lumberjack hat. Did Abram already have his lumberjack hat? It was such an ugly hat, but it kept his head cosy and warm. Though it was late in February, it was still starkly cold. I recall Abram wearing that hat every winter for decades, until Mum finally wrenched it away from him.

'I'm warning you, Kaminer! Don't give me a hard time!' Crusts of ice crunched under the impact of Abram's boots. For a man of his time and place Abram was tall, and Uncle Leon was pint-sized. As Abram strode purposefully through the frosty, cobblestoned streets of Old Montreal, Uncle Leon would've had to scurry to keep up with him.

'But the Sharon part is only for Sarah!' Uncle Leon yapped at Abram's heels. He may have been diminutive, but he was persistent. 'What about the Leah part? How can you do this to a child?! You can't leave your daughter with half a name!'

'*Oysh!*' Abram drew a sharp, visible breath in the crystalline air. 'So what would you suggest?'

'How about 'Lynn'?'

163

Abram halted in his frozen tracks. '*Vot?*'

'Lynn.' It's a Yinglish name, but it starts the same way 'Leah' does.'

Abram was intrigued. 'Kaminer! How did you find up such a name?'

Leon sensed his brother-in-law was on the hook. He was still wriggling, but he was on the hook.

'I heard it.'

'Where did you hear such a name?'

'I don't know. On the radio, maybe. In the movies, maybe. But I heard it. It's a *goot* Yinglish name for a born Canadian. Your daughter is the first-born Canadian in our family. Why shouldn't she have a Yinglish name?'

Abram conceded. Kaminer had a point. Renia wanted to cut ties with the Old World. Maybe Kaminer was right. A born Canadian should have an English name. Renia already had Natalies in her family. Her brother's daughter was Hania Natalia and her sister's daughter was Eva Natalie. Why should his daughter be the same? No! Abram's daughter should be different. Abram's daughter WAS different. And different in a special way. His daughter was special! The first-born Canadian in their family!

Abram marched along Rue Notre Dame, to the columned front entrance of the *Palais de justice*. As he passed through its heavy doors and stood under its high ceiling he would've doffed his hat, whichever hat it was, in a demonstration of respect. Little Uncle Leon tagged after him.

The two *greeners* found their way to the offices of the Superior Court. In the Department of Health, in *le division de la demographie*, in *le bureau du greffier*, Abram approached the clerk on duty, and stated his business. 'I have a new daughter.'

'*Felicitations.*' Monsieur Ouellette offered his congratulations.

'*Merci.* I want you should put her down as a real person and a real citizen.'

Abram couldn't hide the pride he felt, and didn't try.

'When was your daughter born?' The clerk Ouellette prepared to take dictation.

'Ach! It is more than two months! On 6 December.'

The date of my birth was duly noted.

'And what is your daughter's name?' Blandly, Monsieur Ouellette awaited Abram's answer. From Uncle Leon, there was an audible intake of breath.

'*Mein* daughter's name is…' Abram hesitated, decided, and forcefully stated, 'Sharon LYNN!'

Abram was handed my birth certificate. It was official. *'On this twenty-third day of February one thousand nine hundred and fifty six I, the undersigned, registered the birth of SHARON LYNN born in this City, on the sixth day of December one thousand nine hundred and fifty-five, daughter of Abram ZAJDMAN, Salesman, of this City who has signed and of Renata SCOT (sic) NICKA his wife who has not signed.'*

The act was read; the deed was done. Their mission accomplished, Abram and his sidekick departed the *Palais de justice*. On the snow-covered cobblestoned streets of Montreal's historic Old City, the first-time father looked beyond the horizon to the returning light. For the rest of his life, Abram vowed he would do what he *had* to do to ensure that for the rest of her life, his daughter could do what she *wanted* to do.

Uncle Leon checked his watch. 'We made good timing. Maybe we can still have supper at sex o'clock.'

Invariably, Auntie Cesia called supper for 'sex o'clock.' For years Cesia called it and Leon announced it. Despite the attendant titters and stifled guffaws, neither of them heard what they were saying.

When I was eighteen and accepted into theatre school, I decided to correct Daddy's well-meaning mistake. Since I intended on becoming an actress, I felt entitled to change my name. I wouldn't relinquish Sharon, but Lynn had to go. I didn't feel comfortable being a Natalie; that name belonged to Natalie Wood. Natalia felt too foreign, and Natasha felt pretentious. Mum and I reviewed the derivatives of Natalia. There was Nadja, which was Russian, but Mum assured me that it could pass for a variation of Natalia. Also, in translation, the name means Hope. I felt this version worked well with my surname and would look good on a theatre program. When I was twenty-one I had the change legalised. Daddy took to calling me Comrade Krupskaya, after Lenin's wife Nadja.

***

The first year of my life proved an eventful one. I didn't cramp my parents' style so much as alter it. Daddy no longer danced at the El Morocco. Instead, he danced around the living room, his arms filled with me. If my mother wanted to kiss me, she had to wipe off her lipstick. Daddy would admonish, 'You're not touching my child's skin with those chemicals on your mouth!' Daddy was an environmentalist ahead of his time.

In the days before Canadian Medicare, the price of my delivery decimated my parents' savings, so they began saving money again, and soon were able to lay a carpet on the living room floor. Only then was I lifted out of my crib and placed on the padded surface 'so the child should crawl freely, without hurting her knees.'

When the worst of winter was over, before leaves appeared on the trees, I was bundled up and taken to the Botanical Gardens 'so the child should see and learn to love flowers,' though flowers were not yet in bloom. According to my father, it was never too early to learn.

In the summer of 1956 my mum announced to Daddy, 'Sharon wants to go to New York.' I don't know how she knew, but since my wish was my daddy's command, we set off for New York. We stayed with my mother's friends, who lived in Brooklyn. They had been together in Germany, after the war. Immediately after the war, Mum's friends were married by the American army chaplain Hasselkorn in Heidelberg's synagogue. It was the first Jewish wedding held in post-war Germany. Jewish G.I.s arranged the wedding, and concentration camp survivors strong enough to participate were trucked in to attend the event. Mum served as bridesmaid. Mum's friends were able to emigrate to the United States early because the bride – really – did have an uncle in Brooklyn.

In New York, I was taken to Rockaway Beach, where my Daddy removed my diapers.

'Abram. Don't do it,' Mum warned.

Daddy didn't heed the warning. 'I want she should get an all-over tan. The child's skin should breathe!' Parked in a deck chair under a sheltering umbrella, Mum peered from behind her sunglasses.

'Abram. You're asking for trouble. Don't do it. Just don't do it!'

I imagine I smiled blissfully. Anything my Daddy did was fine with me.

'Freedom!' My father exhorted. At that moment, freedom superseded hygiene. 'The child needs to be free!' So saying, I was liberated from my diapers and paraded along the beach. When the inevitable happened, Daddy came running back to Mum.

'Renia! Look! What should I do?!'

Mum roared with laughter. 'Don't come running to me! Take her into the water and clean her off!' Even freedom has its limits.

The limits of freedom in America were tested when my Daddy took me to the Visitors' Gallery of the United Nations Security Council in August of 1956. I was already seven months old, and it was high time to introduce me to international affairs.

In August of 1956, the Suez Crisis was escalating. The Russian delegate was speaking, and he was making his point vociferously. When he finished, there was a squeal from the Visitors' Gallery. Apparently, I was protesting. 'Knee yeah! Knee yeah!' My Daddy translated my outburst. We always understood each other.

'Vetoed!' My Daddy exclaimed, to the members of the Security Council and to the members of the Visitors' Gallery. 'Right here!' Proudly he pointed to the budding anti-communist in his arms. 'Your motion has been vetoed! *Mein* daughter says '*Nyet!*'

***

I can't recall if the words I uttered in the United Nations Security Council were my first, but when verbal communication began, it flowed freely. I recall my earliest monosyllabic sentences being 'Cookie!' and 'Up, up!' The latter was illustrated with raised arms. The meaning of 'cookie' needed no illustration. Sucking on a biscuit while enveloped in my Daddy's embrace was all I needed to be content.

When I graduated from a crib to a bed, my Daddy would lie beside me in the evenings and invent what were referred to as bedtime stories. The intention was to put me to sleep, but how could a story put me to sleep? I loved listening to stories, and I loved listening to my Daddy tell them. These stories remained forever unfinished because Daddy always fell asleep before he could invent an ending. Each evening his narrative began, 'Vunce upon the time there vas a little girl with biiiig brown eyes and loooong brown braids – who talked too much!' Daddy's big brown eyes widened, and his forehead would touch mine. Playfully, he inquired, 'Now who could this be?' Mirroring my Daddy, I widened my big brown eyes, while my fingers combed through the wavy mane of my unravelled braids.

'I don't know.' I knew full well. 'Why don't you tell me?' I prompted. And so the evening's story began. When Daddy's bedtime stories put him to sleep, I would carefully and quietly crawl around him and out of the bed, shushing my astonished mother and warning her not to make noise so Daddy could sleep.

It was Mum who couldn't sleep. She put on a brave front during the day, but at night her untold story overwhelmed her. She dreamt of infants smashed against Ghetto walls and babies tossed and shot in the air, like pigeons. Once more she witnessed a toddler kicked to death because the murdering German soldier couldn't bother to waste a bullet on the child. In reality, she was forced to remain silent. In delayed response, in her dreams, she screamed.

When Mum could no longer fend off sleep, again she saw the children of Warsaw's Ghetto dislodging bricks in the walls and crawling through the holes to the forbidden Aryan side, begging for bread with which to keep their parents alive one more day. In all of Mum's nightmares, all the phantom children were me.

When Mum woke, weeping and screaming, Daddy would wrap his arms around her and lead her to my bed, where I was (finally) asleep.

'Look, *kochana*. The child is here. The child is safe. Don't cry anymore, *kochana*.' Weary with exhaustion, Daddy pleaded, 'Please.'

Mum never felt safe enough which meant, in her mind, that I could never be safe enough until I had a sibling of my own.

'One day we'll be dead and she'll be alone in the world. What will happen to her then?'

After my birth, Mum sustained a blood clot and was warned that it would be dangerous to have another child. She made the round of obstetricians until she found one willing to take the risk, and then she lied to my father in order to get pregnant. The ensuing pregnancy was grotesque and Mum was offered a therapeutic abortion which, in 1958, was almost unheard of. She turned down the offer.

What I recall from that time is cuddling with my mother on the living room sofa and resting my head on her swollen belly while she stroked my hair. I would speak to my invisible sibling through her belly button. I imagined Mum's belly button served as a receiver, and my sibling could hear me.

'Ooh!' Mum squealed. 'The baby just kicked!'

'He did?!' I scolded my sibling through Mum's belly button. 'Don't kick Mummy! You'll hurt her!'

Daddy padded across the carpeted floor, watching his expanding family. He pointed to Mum's belly.

'That's your brother.'

Mum shook her head. 'Don't do it, Abram.'

'Well, it's fifty-fifty.'

'What's fifty-fifty?' I liked the sing-song sound of fifty-fifty.

'It means you have two choices,' my father informed me. 'Either the baby is going to be a boy, or it's going to be a girl. But you're going to have a brother!' Mum clutched her belly, and rolled her eyes.

'Either way, it doesn't matter.' Daddy attempted to mollify Mum. 'Even if I have ten sons, I could never love them as much as I love Sharon.'

'Oh, you're an idiot!' Mum blasted Daddy, but couldn't help smiling, all the same.

The next thing I remember is sitting alone on a bench on the main floor of the Royal Victoria Hospital, happily waiting for my brother to be brought to me. (At the time, children weren't allowed onto the maternity ward. Nor on any ward. A toddler could be left sitting alone in the lobby, but could not accompany an adult onto the wards.) I had no idea that, in the process of his delivery, he and my mother were nearly killed.

Michael Lucian (with an eye, not a jay) was a breach baby. Due to arrive on our mother's birthday, he stubbornly resisted entry into the world. Three weeks after his due date,

171

he was dragged out of our mother's womb with high forceps. The obstetrician presented my father with a dreadful choice.

'Your wife, or the baby. We can't save both.'

Abram signed his son's death warrant an hour before he was born.

Despite the best efforts of the attending physician, Michael emerged neither dead, nor brain damaged. In fact, he was perfectly intact. Miraculously, he was physically perfect. He had feathery white hair, eyes the colour of blueberries, and weighed almost ten pounds. When our family paediatrician first saw Michael, he nicknamed him 'Little Lumberjack.' When our father first saw him, he nicknamed him *Bikush* (baby bull). The nickname stuck.

Daddy wheeled Mum out of an elevator and into the hospital lobby. She held a writhing, blanketed bundle in her arms. Despite her ordeal, when she saw me, she smiled. My brother was placed into my waiting arms. Mum's mission was accomplished. It nearly destroyed them both, but now I had a friend who would see me through life. I would never be left alone in the world.

Today Michael Zajdman is a paediatrician and neonatal care specialist. It has been noted, and remarked upon, that the most difficult and dangerous cases arise when Dr Zajdman is on call. It's as if those babies are waiting for him.

***

I was disappointed with my eagerly awaited brother. I was also concerned. 'Daddy, there's something wrong with him.'

'What is it, *shepsaleh* (little lamb)?' Both Daddy and Mum snapped into alert.

'He can't talk!' I was looking forward to having a brother I could talk to, the way I could talk to my Daddy. Mum and Daddy relaxed.

'Don't worry, *shepsaleh*. He'll talk, he'll talk.' Maybe he would, but Daddy didn't tell me when. In the meantime, I found the uncommunicative blob boring. Mum kept referring to Benjamin Spock's bible for mothers, the blockbuster best-seller *Baby and Child Care*. Because of Dr Spock, I was recruited to feed Michael his bottle and burp him over my shoulder, in order to feel neither threatened nor excluded by the presence of a new life in the household.

My mother's fear of sibling rivalry, based not only on Benjamin Spock's warning but also on her painful relationship with her sister Ania, proved unfounded. I felt neither threatened nor excluded. I felt secure. When I didn't have to feed Michael, I ignored him.

While my brother and I were coming to consciousness, our father was struggling to make a living. Three times he went into business with partners, and three times he was swindled. His brother-in-law wouldn't give him a job. Through it all, my mother kept reminding him, 'No one's trying to kill us, we have the children, and we have each other.'

It was bitter, the winter of 1959. An epidemic of Hong Kong flu raged through the city. The disease felled Mum, Daddy and me. We were compelled to quarantine. Who would take care of infant Michael?

Ania and Camille weren't an option. My father's siblings couldn't be trusted with anything. Through a network of neighbours, a woman was located on Goyer Street. Her name was Katarina Trautmann. In an audacious dash for freedom, *Herr* and *Frau* Trautmann, with their two teenage daughters, escaped East Berlin in 1953.

Katie Trautmann was born in Aachen in 1912, one of four daughters. There may have been a little brother who died. In 1916, her father was killed on a battlefield in France. Their widowed mother raised Katie and her sisters. In the 1930s, Katie was working as a maid in a wealthy home in Berlin. Friedrich Trautmann was a guest. That is how they met. In Berlin, Friedrich Trautmann was an engineer and during the war was recruited as an officer into the *Wehrmacht*. According to what he told Mum, during the war Friedrich Trautmann held a position and was posted to a place where he would not have participated in atrocities, but he was aware that atrocities were being committed. After the war he was considered skilful enough to be of value to the Russians, who conscripted and transported him to the Soviet Union where, for two years, he served a form of slave labour. In Montreal, Friedrich Trautmann earned a modest living as a mechanic.

The Trautmanns' eldest daughter, Helga, was born in 1938. Doris was born on 8 December 1940. I always remember Doris's birthday because it is two days after mine.

In the depths of winter, at the start of 1959, the Trautmanns sheltered and cared for my baby brother Michael. Katie Trautmann grew to love my brother like the son she never had. She rocked him and held him to her ample breasts and placed him in a carriage positioned in front of a sunlit window, as though he were a plant. When my parents recovered and were once more able to care for Michael, reluctantly, Mrs Trautmann returned him.

Two years later an apartment across the hall from the Trautmanns' apartment became available, and we moved to 2975 Goyer Street, apartment fourteen, Montreal, Québec! I had to memorise this address in case I got lost. 'If you can't find your way home, then you go and find a policeman,'

Mum instructed. 'The policeman is your friend. He will bring you home.'

I recall our first evening in the new apartment. I was five years old. Mum was on her hands and knees, a large brush in hand, scrubbing the floor of the room that, for the next seven years, I would share with Michael. Mrs Trautmann lugged a mop and a bucket. She was helping; scouring and cleaning the adjacent floors. As I watched the two women it seemed to me that I must do my part, so I fetched my toothbrush, filled a cup with water, sloshed the water onto the floor, plopped onto my hands and knees beside my Mummy and began scrubbing at a floor tile with my toothbrush. As my Mummy would say, 'Monkey see; monkey do.'

Mum stopped scrubbing in mid-scrub. Mrs Trautmann's mop stopped moving. The older German woman and the younger Polish-Jewish woman smiled at each other.

'*Słodka.*' Mum whispered. Then she translated. 'Sweetheart.'

'*Kind.*' Mrs Trautmann agreed. Almost in unison, they appealed. 'Don't help.'

Mum and Mrs Trautmann spoke German to each other, and English to me. They never addressed each other by their first names. Over the course of their decades-long friendship, the two Europeans called each other 'Mrs. Zajdman' and 'Mrs. Trautmann'.

***

While Mum and Dad worked, Mrs Trautmann greeted us at lunchtime with sometimes hot and always lovingly prepared meals. In winter, I recall coming home to steaming bowls of chicken noodle soup. We often had chicken noodle soup because it was Michael's favourite. I also recall sandwiches

175

of linseed bread lined with thin slices of spicy German salami.

After school the door to Mrs Trautmann's apartment was always open to us. Michael grew so attached to Mrs Trautmann that he began telling people she was his grandmother. He felt guilty about doing so, but wasn't sure why. Instinctively, he knew not to repeat this to Mum. Instead, Michael confessed to me. I heard his confession, and then pronounced, 'That's not the way it works.'

'But I want a grandmother! Why can't I have a grandmother?! All the other kids have one!'

'Because! A grandmother is a mother who is either your mother's mother or your father's mother, except that Mummy doesn't have a mother and Daddy doesn't have a mother, so you can't have a grandmother. Anyway, we've got a grandmother.' I contradicted myself, and didn't care. 'She's hanging on the wall.'

'You mean the lady in the picture? But she's not real.'

'Well, she used to be real. In 'Before The War' she used to be real.' The term Holocaust was not yet in common usage, but I had heard of The Land of Before The War. It was a mysterious place my parents returned to when they spoke Polish.

Michael refused to accept a photo facsimile. 'But I want a real grandmother NOW!'

'Look.' My little brother was cute, but he could be exasperating. 'We have our parents but they don't have theirs. So who should cry; them or you?'

'Oh! I never thought of it that way.'

Over Jewish holidays, unless Daddy was called upon to lead a *Seder*[31], we were never invited to extended family, but we always shared Christmas with the Trautmanns. Their Christmas tree was our Christmas tree. On Christmas Eve, Michael was accorded the honour of sticking the star onto the top branch of the *Tannenbaum*.

'Allez *h-up!*' Mr Trautmann would hoist Michael and lift him level to the top of the tree. Nervously, Michael fumbled among the decorations until he managed to insert the star-shaped piece of foil onto a top branch.

'Bravo!' Mr Trautmann would declare, and Mrs Trautmann would applaud. 'You did this *gut!*' Michael would thrust out his little chest and beam with pride. Then he'd be lowered back down onto the ground.

I would profit by this greeting card moment to sneak a piece of chocolate from an open box on the coffee table. Invariably Mrs Trautmann caught me at it.

'Sharon! You will get fat! You want to be an actress! You must have *disziplin!* You cannot be fat!'

'Ach Katie!' Generally silent, Mr Trautmann sprang to my defence. 'It's Christmas! Leave the child alone!' Like my Daddy, Mr Trautmann was on my side.

***

My recollections of Helga are vague. Early she married a German businessman named *Herr* Lothar and returned with him to Germany. Helga looked like a sun-kissed Rhine maiden, but Doris was dark, and looked like Romy Schneider. She had a brief first marriage to a man named *Herr* Apfel. Michael and I called him Mister Apples. Mister Apples worked in a chocolate factory. I thought Doris was

---

[31] The Passover celebratory meal

wondrously lucky to be married to a man who worked in a chocolate factory! He would bring us samples, and Mrs Trautmann stressed their quality. These were no adulterated Oh Henry bars.

'Kinder, das is DEUTSCHE schokolade!' We were in no doubt that it was indeed German chocolate.

I was sad when Doris left Mister Apples. There would be no more *schokolade*.

I was born slightly lame. From Germany Mrs Trautmann imported (or perhaps it was Helga who sent over) Franz Josef *Wasser*. Mrs Trautmann believed this spring water had healing properties. Nightly, either Mrs Trautmann or Mum would massage my feet with the emperor's elixir, and then they had me walk back and forth across the living room floor with pencils between my toes. Each evening I had to walk repeatedly back and forth across the living room floor with pencils between my toes until, for me, from Germany, Mrs Trautmann imported the first of Dr Scholl's arch-supported wooden sandals. In the hours after school, when I finished my homework and before my parents came home, Mrs Trautmann taught me to knit, and later, to crochet. When I asked my mother to teach me to sew she snapped, 'Learn by yourself! I didn't have a mother to teach me!'

In all but name, the Trautmanns became family. They might even have been considered surrogate grandparents, except that I couldn't conceive of the concept, at the time. I couldn't even bring myself to think of Łucjan and Natalia as my grandparents. To me, Natalia was my mother's mother, and Łucjan was my mother's father. It would be decades before I could train myself to use the term in regards to these two lost souls, and even then, it was an effort.

In summer, we were invited to the Laurentian Hills, to a place the Trautmanns called their farm. We were welcome to stay all summer. There were no animals on this farm. It was a primitive property; there was no indoor plumbing, but within walking distance, there was an outhouse. A column of wax paper dipped in honey dangled from a hook on the ceiling over the table used for dining. Flies would die there, but more kept coming through the open door off the porch, heading directly for the honeycombed column, like kamikaze pilots. I was struck by how stupid flies must be.

The bedrooms were located on an upper floor. The room I came to think of as mine had a slanted roof, which leaned in as if wanting to speak to me. On soft summer nights I was tucked in under a light quilt. Outside an open window, jiminy crickets sang in the tall grass. I felt cocooned in a fairy tale.

On the shore of a nearby lake, wearing nothing but a sunhat and an undershirt, Michael would squat, scoop sand into a pail, and then he'd toss it out again. With floating devices strapped to our waists and Michael clinging to my hand, we'd be guided into the shallows, where we'd splash and cool off. In nearby woods, in August, we'd pick berries that Mrs Trautmann baked into late-summer pies. I noted that my little brother's eyes were the same colour and shade as the berries, so I came to call him Blueberry Eyes.

With Michael and I ensconced on this oasis, our parents were free to take a break, even if they couldn't afford a full-blown vacation. One summer they scheduled a three-day getaway, but couldn't see it through. After forty-eight hours alone together my mother wailed, 'Oh Abram! I miss the kids!'

'Okay,' Daddy conceded. 'Let's go.' They got into the family Chevrolet, whose doors against the back seats were sealed so that Michael and I could never fall out, and took off for the Trautmanns' farm.

'Oh. Hi Mummy.' Michael and I were perched on a hill within yelling distance of Mrs Trautmann's country kitchen, companionably sculpting mud pies. 'What are you doing here?'

'Oh!' Mum threw herself on me. Ruefully, Daddy shook his head. 'Oooo Mummy!' I protested and wriggled out of her embrace. 'You're going to make yourself all muddy!'

'*Kinder!*' From down the hill, Mrs Trautmann trilled. '*Kom!* We have lunch!' Michael and I dropped our inedible pies and got up, mud dripping from our fingertips and, in Michael's case, smeared across his cheeks and chin. 'You better wash your face before Mrs Trautmann sees you.' I warned him.

'I have to go inside to wash my face and Mrs Trautmann will see me but it doesn't matter!' Michael responded logically, secure in Mrs Trautmann's unconditional love. We headed down the hill, trailing mud, while our parents trailed behind us. Mum was sniffling. Daddy had his arm around her. 'What's the matter with you, Mummy?'

'Nothing!' Mum blasted. I'm just so happy to see you, that's all!'

The offspring of Holocaust survivors tend to blame their parents for supposedly viewing them as replacements; surrogates for children cherished and lost. As an officer in the *Wehrmacht,* Mr Trautmann didn't see his younger daughter Doris for the first four and a half years of her life. When he returned from the front, he was a stranger to her. As a child, I sensed that Mr Trautmann identified me with Doris. During my formative years, Mr Trautmann seemed to see me as a second chance. For a former *Wehrmacht* officer, it was fitting that redemption should come in the form of a daughter of Holocaust survivors.

Bewildered though he was, my little brother perceived something significant. This middle-aged German couple served as surrogates for the grandparents their war stole from us. Unstintingly they shared their homes, their holidays, and their hearts. Together Mrs Trautmann and I watched and loved Lucy. While massaging my feet with Franz Joseph *Wasser*, Mrs Trautmann sought to encourage me with the tale of Doris Day, whose original name was Doris Kappelhoff and who, as a teenager, injured her leg in a major car accident yet, through exercise and physical therapy, recovered to sing and dance in the movies. Excitedly, she also told me about a hot new German film star who was taking Hollywood by storm. Because this actor had a name that could be played with, I called him Max The Million! (Though he was born in Vienna and raised in Zürich, for Katie Trautmann, Maximilian Schell was German.)

While Katie Trautmann prepared my meals, monitored my intake of chocolates, and focused on strengthening my feet, my Jewish survivor aunts played cards, went to their hairdressers, and bad-mouthed my mother for placing her children in the care of a woman they referred to as 'a Nazi bitch.'

Decades later, shortly after both our birthdays, in front of a downtown Christmas display window, I ran into Doris. She had married again. Her second husband was a Jewish divorcee with five children. Mrs Trautmann was now step-grandmother to five Jewish children.

In front of the Christmas display window Doris stunned me by saying, 'It must've been hard on your mother, having my mother take care of you.' Sincerely, with all my heart, I was able to tell her, 'No. It wasn't. Mum was grateful that we didn't have to become latch key kids. We couldn't depend on extended family. Because of your mother, we had someone to whom we could come home.'

In 1962, after the Eichmann trial – and because of it – Mum applied to the West German government for [32]*wiedergutmachung*. She was one of the last Holocaust survivors to apply for restitution payments, and she did it to put my father on his feet.

By the early 1960s, the West German government had gotten tough with survivors applying for restitution payments. The post-war U.S. government helped the West Germans onto their feet, yet they resented having to do the same for Nazi victims. Their application rules were rigorous. In closed sessions, German psychiatrists challenged survivors' memories, forcing them to recall, recount, and relive horror. One afternoon, having walked home from kindergarten (my elementary school was on the same side of the street as our apartment building), I found my mother sitting on the edge of the double bed she shared with my father. Her eyes were wide with fright, and her face was wet with tears. A telephone stood on the nightstand, next to the bed. Frantically Mum pointed to the phone and then to her throat, which had a pronounced scar on it. She had been waiting for me to come home and call Daddy. Mum had gone mute. Literally, she had lost her voice.

Like my Mum, I was calm and focused in crisis. I understood what to do. Mum wrote down a phone number, and I dialled it.

'Daddy, something's wrong with Mummy. She can't talk. Mummy's not a baby. She's supposed to be able to talk.'

Daddy dashed home. At some point Mum's voice returned, and the episode was never repeated. What I could not know at the time was that, the same afternoon, Mum

---

[32] Restitution payments for Holocaust survivors

endured a brutal interrogation by a German psychiatrist. Did he ask how she had acquired the scar on her throat, which she generally covered with scarves? Mum was accumulating a collection of scarves. A scarf at Mum's throat had become a fashion statement.

After Mum lost her voice, she visited her family physician. Dr Kovacs was a Hungarian Holocaust survivor.

'There's no reason to operate on your vocal cords, and no point.' Dr Kovacs proved a perceptive diagnostician. 'The pain will just move to another place in your body.'

Ultimately Mum received one of the highest pensions granted to a Holocaust survivor. She handed the first cheque to my father. At least, she tried.

'It's not my money,' Dad demurred, feeling guilty at the manner in which Mum acquired it. If I could provide for my family the way a man should, he felt, Renia wouldn't have felt the need to put herself through such an ordeal.

'It's not my money,' Mum insisted. 'It's OUR money. We will use it to build a secure future for our children. This is seed money. With this money, you can start your own business.'

'But you want a house in Outremont.' Still, Dad demurred.

'Silly.' Mum appeared to have inherited her mother's business sense. 'If we build a successful business, we'll be able to afford a house, and then we'll have both!'

This bit of logic convinced Dad. The salesman and the buyer joined forces. They would become a dream team, but not before one final betrayal nearly destroyed them.

CHAPTER TWENTY-ONE

Abram's eldest niece was getting married. Aunt Fela's daughter, born in Radom, Poland in 1935, was twenty-six years old, and nervous about the prospect of becoming an old maid. Quickly she accepted a marriage proposal from a man who had recently immigrated to Canada. Sam Kleiner was a Chilean Jew whose background was murky. He claimed to be some kind of businessman. No one was clear on what he had done, but it would become devastatingly apparent what he was capable of doing.

When it appeared that Abram and Renata's fledgling business was going to succeed, Abram received a call from his sister Fela.

'You have to take Sam into the business. He has capital, but nowhere to invest it. No one knows him here. Sam can't make a living here. He's threatening to go back to Chile. If he does, he'll take my daughter with him. I'm going to lose my daughter!' It was Fela's husband who had refused to give Abram a job when he needed one.

Abram had a bad feeling about Sam. He was so repulsed by his niece's fiancé that, at the engagement party, he retreated with a bottle of wine into Fela's kitchen and got morosely drunk.

'Fela, don't ask me to do this. We're just beginning to get on our feet.'

'You have to, Abram! You can't turn me down. If he goes, my daughter will go with him. You have to help me save my daughter! You have to do this for your family!'

Oh, the siren calls of family. Intuition told Abram he was heading for disaster. Hindsight confirmed it.

Sam Kleiner was not made an equal partner in Abram and Renata's new enterprise. This time, there was no fifty-fifty. Badgered and bullied by an overbearing tribe, Abram and Renata handed over fifty ONE per cent of their business to Sam Kleiner. Within months, the dominating partner stole the rest. Sam Kleiner took it all. Why my parents allowed it, I never asked and will never know. What I do know is that emotional blackmail can freeze the brain of a genius. I also know that Holocaust survivors' greatest fear is the further loss of family. They will submit to almost any form of abuse in order not to lose what passes for family.

When my parents were brought to their knees, my mother took a call from her sister-in-law.

'Why were you trying to make a businessman out of my brother? He's not smart enough to succeed in business. Don't you know Abram's good for nothing except to work for other people?'

'Fela. Please. Let us live. Just let us live.'

Having set up her brother, and overseeing his bid for independence destroyed, Fela delivered the coup de grace.

'Abram's a *goonish*. A nothing! He's good to run errands, that's all. This should be a lesson to both of you. Trying to make a businessman out of my little brother! How dare you. Abram's a *schmatta*. A rag. He's good to wipe the floor with, that's all.'

Unknown to Renata and Fela, Abram had come home early and picked up an extension line. Barely breathing, in stony silence he listened to his sister's rant.

When the call ended, Abram quietly entered his bedroom. Renata was sitting at the edge of their bed, in despair. She looked up. 'You're home early.'

'No.' Meaningfully, Abram iterated, 'I came home right on time.'

'What do you mean?' Renata was bewildered.

'I heard it.' Abram informed her.

'I don't understand.'

'I was listening on the other line.' Abram's chest felt heavy. So did his heart.

'Oh no.' That ugly Zajdman tribe never stopped hurting this sweet and decent man. 'How much did you hear?'

Stoic, Abram responded, 'Enough.'

'I'm sorry.'

'No.' Abram had learned his lesson, though it was not the lesson his sister intended. 'I'M sorry.' He sat at the edge of the bed and wrapped his arms around his wife. 'I'll make it up to you. I promise I'll make it up to you.' After ten years of marriage, Abram and Renata were, at this moment, truly wed.

These were desperate days, not only for our parents, but also for our planet. Missiles were positioned in Cuba. The Americans and the Russians were at loggerheads. The world was a push-of-a-button away from nuclear annihilation.

In November of 1956, in his capacity as a sports editor, Uncle Alek was sent to Melbourne to cover the summer Olympic Games. He liked what he saw, not only of the Games, but also of the South Pacific. From Australia he was able to visit his sisters in Montreal. It would take almost three years and the participation of a senior Canadian government official, but in 1959 Uncle Alek, with his family, was able to defect to Australia. Now, three years later, with global annihilation in sight, Mum wondered if she had found an escape route for us. She had read Neville Shute's apocalyptic novel *On The Beach*. Perhaps my little ones might survive a little longer in Australia, Mum reasoned, before radiation's fall-out reaches them.

'Kang a woo! Kang a woo!' Little Michael's arms were raised and his hands dangled from his wrists, like paws. He was hopping around the kitchen, pretending to be a kangaroo, while Mum sat at the table, crying and listening intently to the news on the radio.

'Hello sweetheart.' Mum greeted me tenderly, as I entered the kitchen. 'How would you like to visit your cousins in Australia at Christmas time?' Clearly, Michael had received the same invitation.

'All of us, or just me and Little Michael?'

'Just you and Little Michael,' Mum confirmed.

The radio was blaring, my mother was weeping, and my little brother was leaping and shouting. Something was seriously wrong with this picture.

I couldn't imagine going to Australia. I had never been further than New York. Certainly, I couldn't imagine going anywhere without my parents. I didn't want to. Why would our mother want to send us away?

'Mummy.' I placed my hands on her lap and gazed at her intently. 'If going to Australia at Christmas is a good thing, then why are you crying?'

As Renata's thirty-fourth birthday came and went, the Kennedy brothers rescued the world. I owe an eternal debt of gratitude to John and Robert. I got to keep my parents, and an encounter with my Australian cousins on their territory could be delayed until I grew older and strong enough to survive it.

CHAPTER TWENTY-TWO

It was a soft summer evening in Outremont's Pratt Park, at a moment in time when the 1960s still felt like the 1950s. My small soft hand rested in my Daddy's large crippled hand. In my other hand I held an ice cream cone.

We had gone to Robil's for ice cream. All four of us. I enjoyed licking sweet strawberry. Strawberry ice cream was studded with real strawberries, then. Little Michael enjoyed smearing his upper lip and chin with chocolate. At the age of two, our merry Little Michael wore a cold Van Dyke beard. Mum always chose green ice cream. She called it pistachio-flavoured. Mum's tongue would catch on the embedded nuts. She'd pull out the nuts, and chew them. I don't know if Mum chose green ice cream for the ice cream, or for the nuts. Daddy stuck to simple vanilla. Daddy considered himself a simple man. He was also visionary.

'Even if we stay here,' Daddy cautioned Mum, 'One day, the children will have to leave. There is no future in Québec for the children.'

By the mid-1960s, separatist thugs had established a bad habit of inserting bombs into Montreal mailboxes, instead of letters. Daddy wanted to move to Toronto, but Mum, who had tossed out her little red suitcase, wanted to stay, so we stayed. In 1965, using savings accrued from accumulated German pension cheques, as well as a loan from the bank, Mum and Dad established Variety Import Export Ltd. They became each other's partners in business, as well as in life, and they would prosper. At first, they worked seven days a week, on their own. I recall Mum spray-painting wicker baskets that were laid out on the kitchen table. Thirty years later, in London, I would see a spray-painted wicker basket holding a champagne bottle at the upscale Fortnum and Mason's.

An extension to the office phone line was installed in our apartment so that Mum could sometimes work from home and so that calls from overseas clients could be taken at any time. My little brother and I were taught how to answer The Office Line. 'Variety Import-Export Limited! 861-615 ZERO!' A child's voice would pipe, reassuring a startled client that he had reached the right party. 'May I ask who is speaking?'

On weekends, Michael and I were brought into the warehouse. We were put to work removing foreign labels from wicker trivets. When our parents couldn't find work we were able to do, I wheeled Michael on a dolly around the warehouse. When we were older, Michael worked on the loading platform, and I typed invoices. Variety was truly a family business.

I believe the import-export business appealed to Dad because he could keep the inventory liquid, while also establishing a nominal head office in Toronto. Memories of his wartime experiences in the Soviet Union kept Dad on constant alert. The establishment of an import-export business would prove a boon to Mum, giving her the opportunity, as a buyer, to travel the world. But not yet. For the moment it was Dad, as a salesman, who did the travelling. His first business trips took him to Toronto.

Whenever Dad was scheduled to return from Toronto, Mum sat by the telephone in a state of high anxiety. When he made a comfort stop, Dad called from a public payphone. The calls would sooth Mum's nerves, but not for long, and not by much. On one return trip Dad failed to call. Mum was frantic. I was weary of these roller-coaster waits.

'Mummy.' It fell out of my mouth. I was unaware of the impact my words would have. 'Why are you always waiting for bad news?' Mum's eyes widened with wonder. Why, indeed, do I do it?

When Dad finally arrived, Mum almost collapsed with relief.

'Daddy.' There were moments when I served as a marriage counsellor. 'You should've called. Mummy gets really scared when you go away.'

Dad understood the origins of Mum's panic, as I could not.

'*Kochana.*' His arms reached out to her. 'Forgive me. The reason I didn't stop to call was so I could get home faster.' From then on, as inconvenient as it was, in the days when cell phones were considered science fiction, Dad would stop several times along the road to reassure Mum that he was safe.

In 1967, after the Six Day War, chalk drawings of swastikas appeared on the sidewalks in our multi-cultural neighbourhood. Mum was having nightmares again. By 1968 my parents had paid off their debts, which is when we moved to a predominantly Jewish neighbourhood. Mum felt less threatened in a Jewish ghetto.

For the first and only time, we moved into a duplex. We lived on the upper floor. Our landlords, an elderly Jewish couple, lived downstairs.

On a weekday morning in early spring, I was in my small back bedroom putting on my school uniform when I heard a siren song emanating from the kitchen. It was just after the eight am newscast on CJAD Radio. Generally Mum kept the volume low on the kitchen's transistor in order not to disturb our landlords, but on this morning she raised it high. I had never before heard such a sound. It was a bouncing, wailing, joyous noise that raised my spirits and blasted me out of my bedroom and into the kitchen.

'Oh Mummy Mummy!' I cried, as I straightened out my tunic.

'This music is so different!' I did not yet know that a sound new to me, for Mum signified the sound of freedom. 'It's so happy!' I continued to gush. 'It's so beautiful! Oh Mummy, Mummy, this music is going to be a hit!'

On the kitchen table Mum set small dishes filled with single scoops of cottage cheese ringed by crescents of orange slices, created to imitate the appearance of a rising sun.

'Well,' Mum smiled. Her smile was wry. 'If it will be, it won't be for the first time.' Then she extended her arms and wrapped me into them. 'Come.' Her feet began to tap in time to the music, and so did mine. 'I'll show you how the G.I.s danced.' Before breakfast, in the kitchen, Mum taught me to jitterbug to the sweet swing of Glenn Miller's In The Mood.

'Hey!' Michael emerged from the bathroom, rubbing sleep from his eyes. 'What's going on?!' It was a question my brother would pose both to himself, and to us, for years to come.

Dad's birthday was in April. Israel's birthday was in May. Dad was turning fifty-one. Israel was turning twenty. Mum bought Dad the best present she could think to give him. She felt they could afford it, now.

'We're going to give this to Daddy together, but don't tell him in advance. It's going to be a big surprise!'

Ceremoniously, Mum and Michael and I gathered in the kitchen one evening after dinner, before Dad's birthday. We were giving Dad his birthday present early, so he would have time to prepare.

'We have something for you, Abram.' Deceptively casual, Mum convened.

'Oh yes? What is it, *kochana*?'

'Guess!' Merry Michael challenged.

'How can I start to guess?' Dad had no clue.

'It's something for your birthday,' I prompted.

'Oh, that's nice. Did you make me a card?'

Dad said he preferred homemade presents to store-bought presents, so we created our own birthday cards. I wrote the poems, and Michael drew the illustrations.

In a way, we would be presenting Dad with a card.

'We're sending you on a trip.' Mum steered the guessing back into the ballpark.

'You are?' Good naturedly, Dad played along. 'Where am I going? Am I going to Toronto?'

Michael and I giggled.

'A little further than that.' Heavily, Mum hinted. Dad's curiosity was piqued. Michael couldn't stand the suspense. He burst, 'Which continent, Daddy! Guess which continent!'

Light dawned. Dad's warm dark eyes dilated. He gazed at Mum. 'No!'

193

Warmly, Mum smiled back. 'Yes.'

Abram's lifelong dream of seeing *Eretz* Israel, so long deferred it was finally denied, was on the verge of coming true, and it was Renata who was making it happen. Solemnly, with her well-honed sense of the dramatic, Mum presented Dad with the airline ticket. She had purchased a two-week stay in Israel, along with a two-week stopover in Paris, the city Dad fell in love with as a young post-war refugee.

'But we can't afford it!' Dad was generous with everyone, except himself. He switched into Polish. 'We need the money for the children! You'll have to give back the ticket!'

Mum had anticipated Dad's response. 'It's a non-refundable ticket. 'If you don't use it, we'll lose the money.'

Dad covered his eyes with his hands, in a failed attempt to hide the tears in them. 'I'm going? I'm really going?' He half-whispered.

'Yes, my darling.' Mum gazed tenderly at her *kochana*. So did we. 'You're really going.'

'To Paris, too?' Dad was having a difficult time accepting such a gift.

'To Paris too.' Mum confirmed.

Dad sniffled. Then he pulled himself together.

'You send me to Paris at your own risk!' Dad began to tease. 'If I go to Paris, I may look up my old girlfriends!'

'Well then you'd better take a shovel with you!' Michael and I were mystified. We couldn't follow Mum's logic, but then, one had to keep on one's toes in order to keep up with these two larger-than-life characters.

'Your old girlfriends are probably dead!' Mum clarified. 'You'll need a shovel to dig them up!'

At the beginning of May, Dad went on his dream trip – without a shovel. After two weeks in Israel, he flew to Paris. It was mid-May. Civil unrest led to wildcat general strikes. France's economy was skidding to a halt. The atmosphere was so volatile that another French revolution seemed imminent. For a frightening few hours, France's federal government was paralysed when President de Gaulle, the wartime hero who had liberated Paris, now felt the need to escape it.

A week into Dad's projected two-week stay in Paris, I woke to a vision of my father coming up the sidewalk of our street with his one small suitcase in hand. That day I had a cold, so I stayed home from school. I was alone in our rented upper-floor duplex. Mum was downtown, in the Variety office, and Michael was in school. It was early afternoon when my early morning vision manifested. There was Dad outside our living room's large picture window, shuffling along the sidewalk with suitcase in hand.

I did not run to greet him. I stood quietly, and allowed Dad to let himself in.

'Och!' Assuming our upper-floor duplex was empty, and planning to surprise us, it was Dad who got the surprise.

'I saw you through the window, Daddy.' Sweetly, I smiled.

'What are you doing home?' I was a stellar student. It would be out of character for me to play hooky.

'What are YOU doing home?' I mirrored my Dad.

'Me? Ha!' Dad snorted. 'I saw a tank on the Champs Elysees, so I turned around, went back to the hotel, picked

195

up *mein* suitcase, and beat the hell out of there!' Before the expression became trendy, Dad was a Survivor with a capital S.

'I'm going downtown to surprise Mummy. Don't tell on me. At least let me surprise one of you!' Having fled Paris, Dad headed to his office.

It was after five o'clock when Dad walked into the warehouse on Dowd Street. The two employees had left. Mum was alone in the back, near the bathroom. She had changed out of her work clothes, and was wearing a party dress. She stood in front of a long and large piece of glass that had been mounted on a back wall and served as a mirror. She was applying mascara. Clearly, she had a special evening planned.

'Aha!' Dad sneaked up behind her. 'I caught you!' Dad's image stood reflected in the glass. He made a lame attempt at scowling.

'Abram!' Mum dropped her mascara wand and whirled around. 'What are you doing here! You're supposed to be in Paris!'

'Is this why you sent me away?!' Ripples of laughter rose in his throat. 'Who's the guy?!'

'Abram!' After fifteen years of marriage, Mum still wasn't sure when Dad was kidding, and when he was not. 'I'm going to the Bonaventure Hotel. My [33]Hadassah chapter is making a party! You know we make a party at this time every year!'

'A likely story!' Dad tried to keep a straight face, but couldn't. He started to laugh, and so did Mum. Then Dad said what he really meant. 'Surpriiiise!'

---

[33] Hadassah-WIZO: Women's International Zionist Organization

Then Mum said what she really meant. 'But seriously, Abram, why did you leave Paris? We've been following the news. Is the situation that bad?'

'I saw a tank on the Champs Elysees. I didn't need to see more.' Dad sighed at the precarious state of his beloved Paris. 'Seeing a tank was enough sightseeing for me.'

'Then it's good you're back, and safe.' Renia hugged her man. Then she manned the telephone. 'Rega! Put another plate on the table. Abram's home!'

Before eleven p.m., Mum and Dad returned from the Hadassah party. Even though it was a school night, Michael and I were waiting up for them. Was there really a revolution in Paris? Our Dad could give us an eyewitness report.

At eleven p.m. Mum turned on the television, and the four of us sat together, watching the news. Orly Airport was shut down. In a cosy corner of North America, with Daddy safely beside us, we discovered that he had caught the last plane out of Paris.

***

Six weeks later, Mum stood in a quiet and respectful crowd at a lunchtime rally in front of the new underground shopping complex Place Ville Marie. She had left her Dowd Street office before noon and was walking up to Dorchester Boulevard. Thirty-five hundred downtown office workers, all with the same intention and destination, did the same.

Standing in the sunshine and nibbling on sandwiches, they listened, enraptured, as the prime minister capped off his Québec campaign.

'Of course one country, one ethnic group, one language, one nation – of course it would be simpler.' Canada's leader, standing on a raised platform, spoke into a microphone held

197

by an aide. With professorial elegance, Pierre Elliot Trudeau countered the opening statement of his argument. 'When we talk of one nation, we are not talking about this kind of nation. We are talking of the Canadian people, the Canadian country, the soil that belongs to all Canadians no matter where they come from. We are in a province and a city with a French majority. We want the English-speaking minority and all the others to be welcome in our province in the same way we want French Canadians to be at home everywhere in the country.' Trudeau concluded. It was 21 June 1968, the longest day of the year, at a glorious high noon.

Less than three decades after she stood with her mother at a rally in the streets of her native city listening to a declaration of war, Mum stood alone in the streets of her adopted city with her hand on her heart and a half-eaten muffin wrapped inside her purse, deeply attentive to the prime minister's every word.

From my cousin Roma I inherited a beaten-up old upright. The battered piano was squeezed into my tiny back bedroom. Late on Friday afternoons, after my weekly piano lesson with Frances Goltman on Girouard Avenue. I would take a bus to the Henry F. Hall Building on Maisonneuve Boulevard. The newly created Conservatory of Cinematographic Art was situated in this building, which doubled as a campus for Sir George Williams University (now Concordia University). Mum would come up from the Dowd Street warehouse which doubled as her office. Weekly we'd meet for the six p.m. screening of an old film classic. Sometimes we attended the second screening too, which was held at nine p.m. During the interval, waiting for the auditorium doors to reopen, we'd fall into conversation with university students, or check for upcoming productions at the D.B. Clarke Theatre, which was located in the basement.

At the conservatory, the first film we saw was Frank Capra's 1939 *Mr Smith Goes to Washington*. It was the first viewing, for both of us... 'Liberty's too precious a thing to be buried in books, Miss Saunders.' Jimmy Stewart's idealistic Everyman pleads. 'Men should hold it up in front of them every single day of their lives and say: I'm free to think and to speak. My ancestors couldn't. I can, and my children will.'

Capra's last pre-war film hadn't reached *Pan* Draber's *kino* before the outbreak of war. At the film conservatory, Mum caught up on a six-year hiatus in movie-going.

After our self-styled Friday night film festivals, whether primavera buds were sprouting on Mont Royal's trees or icicles dangled from the Hall Building's roof, Mum and I took two buses back to Cote St. Luc.

A decade later, at McGill University's repertory cinema, Mum and I attended a screening of Carol Reed's classic *The Third Man*, which was shot on location in Vienna at the same time *I Was A Male War Bride* was being filmed in Mannheim. Because I prodded Mum about her past, her intention in accompanying me to this screening was to show me the inside of a sewer. During the confrontation between Orson Welles and Joseph Cotten in what is, purportedly, the bowels of Vienna, in the darkness of the hall Mum hissed, 'They call that a sewer?! Who are they kidding! That's not a sewer! I know what a sewer looks like! Our sewer in Warsaw was a real sewer! That sewer up there (on the screen) is a luxury sewer! It's a Hollywood sewer! They don't know what a sewer looks like!'

Nervously I scanned the student audience. They were fully absorbed in the film's climactic scene, and paid no attention to my mother. It would be three decades more before Hollywood paid attention. At which point, Mum was recruited and served as historical consultant on a Holocaust-related film.

CHAPTER TWENTY-THREE

As my parents established themselves in business and their reputation grew, my mother, as the company buyer, was sought out by trade commissioners of then-communist countries. When the Polish trade commissioner invited her to open trade routes, Mum balked. She had sworn never to return to the country that had inflicted so much humiliation and pain. In 1973 Mum broke her vow, and that is when her healing began.

By 1973 Variety had acquired a manager and several employees. For the first time Mum and Dad felt they could take a leave of absence and travel together. Not only did they return to Poland, but Dad showed Mum Paris, and Renata explored Italy, the land beloved by her father Łucjan.

Mum and Dad left for Europe from Dorval Airport on a Saturday afternoon in early spring. It was considered a momentous occasion; Renata was returning to her native land for the first time since leaving it. The following afternoon, I would be attending a panel discussion at the Saidye Bronfman Centre Theatre (now the Segal Centre Theatre) entitled *The Jewish Mother in North American Literature*. Irving Layton was scheduled to be on the panel. Mum would miss it, but she prepared me for my first exposure to a man who had become a literary icon. Vividly, Mum conjured up the image of a slim young poet in a rumpled, brown suit, clutching a battered, brown suitcase, dashing into an English-language class on dark winter afternoons. With affection, Mum spoke of the kind and compassionate teacher who demonstrated unfailing patience, especially with older members of the class, who had a hard time learning a new language. As we strolled through the airport lounge there appeared directly in our path, as if on cue, a tanned and burly sixty-year-old hipster with a flowing, white mane, wearing a cream-coloured shirt open almost to the navel of his Buddha-sized belly, a heavy, shiny medallion hanging from a chain around his neck and resting against his bare, white-haired chest. He was flanked by two young female admirers – one on each arm. Without hesitation, Mum rushed to greet him.

'Professor Layton! Oh! I was in your class in the library. I was one of the refugees. Do you remember me?' Layton gazed intently into Mum's face, which was radiant.

'Renata Skotnicka!' Layton bellowed. As the renowned literary figure clasped Mum into his bear-like embrace, twenty-four years fell away.

'Of course I remember you! How are you?!' The two groupies stood mute. The Buddha bear sized her up. 'You look terrific! What have you been doing all these years?' Layton appeared as warm and kind as Mum described him.

'I'm fine. I – I married. I had a family – this is my daughter – and today I'm going to Poland, can you imagine? I came from Europe – and I'm going to Europe!'

'That's wonderful.' I stood shyly, on the side. The encounter with Layton was warm and pleasant. I was impressed, and looked forward to seeing him on the stage of the Saidye the next day.

The encounter sent Mum over the moon.

'Oh Sharon! This is incredible!' Mum gripped my arm, her eyes glistening with tears. 'I'm going back to Poland today, and who do I run into at the airport, but the man who taught me English!'

'It's quite a send-off.' I agreed.

Mum half-shook and half-clasped my arm.

'Oh sweetheart.' She gazed tenderly into my eyes, as if I were the mother, and she, the child. 'I'm so glad you were here with me, to see it.'

Mum and Dad scheduled no more than twenty-four hours to spend in Warsaw. Both were nervous about returning. When Mum woke in the hotel room, she saw Dad sitting in a chair, in his pyjamas, gazing at her with tears in his eyes.

'What happened, *kochana?*' Mum called from the bed. 'What is it?'

In wonder and gratitude, Dad shook his head. 'This was the first peaceful night I've had with you since we've been married. No nightmares, no crying, no screaming. Oh my darling Renusia.' Tenderly, Dad informed her. 'You slept like a peaceful baby.'

Renata had come home.

Mum and Dad extended their stay in Poland. Based on a clue provided by Uncle Alek, Mum traced Agnieska Draber, her childhood friend Irena's younger sister. Agnieska was an entomologist working and teaching at the University of Warsaw. On Friday afternoons, she took a commuter train to Sochaczew. Agnieska's childhood home, the home created by a pre-war Romeo and Juliet, an excluded Catholic youth and the shunned daughter of the town rabbi, had escaped the ravages of war. In a tall curio case, old crockery rested complacently behind glass. On a sideboard draped with old lace sat a silver samovar, its surface warm, its contents steaming, in anticipation of a family gathering. In the kitchen, on a counter, a wide rectangular pan held a square-shaped log of lemon-coloured [34]*sernik* studded with raisins as thick as the flies Agnieska studied under a microscope in the university lab. Outside the picture windows of this Chekhovian oasis, in a private garden, breezes blew through apple blossoms. The cherry trees were not yet in bloom.

Three sisters and their long-widowed mother greeted Mum and Dad.

'Renusia!' *Pani* Draber embraced Mum, and thirty-four years fell away. 'How well I remember Lutek, your father.' *Pani* Draber referred to Łucjan by the diminutive used by intimates. 'In my mind's eye I can see him performing on the stage of the library he built. He played an Apache dancer. Around his neck he wore a bright red scarf. How that scarf flashed! The audience could see it all the way at the back of the hall. Lutek threw back his head and leapt across the stage with such panache! What a character! What a man!'

The three sisters in attendance were Agnieska, Masha, with her much older husband, and Danuta, the youngest, who was born just before the war. Danuta's dream was to taste fresh pineapple. She had never seen a fresh pineapple, except in pictures.

Since there were originally five sisters, there must've been another one, whose name I can't recall, but I know that Irena wasn't there. At least, she wasn't there in person.

---

[34] Cheesecake, Polish-style

'Where is Irena?' To Agnieska, Renata asked the obvious.

Wordlessly, Agnieska pointed to an enlargement of a full-length photograph on a wall. In the photograph stood a serene-looking woman of indeterminate age. Only her face was visible, and that only from mid-forehead to mid-chin. The rest was cloaked in a nun's habit. Agnieska's sister was more than a sister. The granddaughter of a pre-war Polish rabbi was now Mother Superior of the Carmelite convent in Łódź.

Ironically, it was the Jewish Juliet who survived the war, and the Catholic Romeo who didn't. *Pani* Draber remained safe behind her apple and cherry trees. It was *Pan* Draber who died in Auschwitz, as a self-proclaimed socialist and political prisoner, in 1945, close to the end. If the Draber sisters knew how their father died, they didn't say.

In the Draber dining room Mum, Dad, *Pani* Draber and the three sisters sat down to a repast of *sernik* and *chai*. A breeze wafted through the open window. The buds on the apple and cherry trees were primavera green. After they had fortified themselves, the Drabers and their guests headed for Sochaczew's Catholic cemetery where an ornate plaque, with a photograph attached, marked Kazimierz Draber's grave. Danuta, the daughter he barely knew, placed a bouquet of flowers at the foot of the grave. It is doubtful that his remains rested beneath its surface. Perhaps the authorities at Auschwitz sent his ashes to his family if they paid the fee generally demanded, but by 1945 it was likely that this protocol was no longer observed.

Mum could not visit her father's grave because the Jewish cemetery no longer existed. Post-war, it was turned into the town dump. Townsfolk upended the tombstones and used them to pave private driveways. Into the twenty-first century the site was once more transformed, this time into a children's playground. I like to imagine it would please

Renata's pre-war protector to know that modern-day children are cavorting on the surface of his remains.

In communist Poland, it was the clergy who became the underground resistance. When she came back to Canada, Mum wrote to her childhood friend Irena, now known as Mother Theresa of Łódź, asking her to initiate a search for Irena Podbielska of Łomża.

CHAPTER TWENTY-FOUR

In the spring of 1974, Mum returned to Poland alone, in her capacity as a buyer for the import-export company she and Dad built together. From the Hotel Forum she set out for an address given to her by one of Dad's friends. She had American currency stuffed into her purse that, during this period in Communist Poland, was considered contraband. Mum was on a mission. Once more she was serving as a courier. This time, she was delivering precious U.S. dollars to the sister of Dad's friend. U.S. dollars were the preferred currency for the exchange of goods on the black market.

Stepping outside the entrance of Warsaw's best hotel, she refused to hail one of the waiting cabs. One look at her elegant and obviously foreign-bought coat and the cab's meter would become conveniently broken, while the fare would magically rise.

Renata didn't need a map to find her destination. Her native city, destroyed during her adolescence, had been reconstructed according to its pre-war design. Striding determinedly along the wide sidewalks, she passed the queues for food, the weary women patiently waiting, and the shops suddenly closing because they had run out of produce.

'Dolarki! Dolarki! Change money, Mrs! Please!' A desperate local, sniffing a foreigner, leeched onto her.

'Get away!' Mum shooed at the young Varsavian, shaking him off as he were a [35]*szmalkovnik*. He felt like one of the vile scum who exploited desperate Jews during the war. Mum had to remind herself that now it was the descendants of her persecutors who felt desperate and trapped in the dead-end that was communist Poland in the nineteen seventies.

Mum chose to conduct personal business in the homes of the people she was seeing, rather than invite them to the hotel. On the night of her arrival, lying in bed, she gazed up at the ceiling and noticed what looked like a giant fly. At that moment Mum realised that her room was bugged. Mum's pace quickened. She reached the address she'd been seeking, and entered the arched doorway. A tense-looking woman hovered in its shadows.

'*Pani* Zajdman! I've been expecting you. *Prosze bardzo*. Please, do come in!'

Mum stooped to enter the basement apartment. There was a beaten-up sofa in the main room, two wooden chairs, and a frayed area rug. Through a partition Mum could see a pot simmering on a gas stove. The wallpaper was peeling, and the air was dense with the must of years.

'*Prosze Pani*. I have soup for you.' The woman, whose name was Irena and whose married name I can't recall, (her maiden name was Fuerstenberg) served cabbage soup flecked with meat. Mum knew that hours of queuing had gone into obtaining those specks of meat. She sipped the liquid and left the food, knowing it could still be put to use.

Mum pulled out the money and photographs she had brought from Henryk Fuerstenberg in Montreal. Irena devoured the images, pushing aside her bowl of soup. Irena Fuerstenberg was a middle-aged divorcee who lived in this

---

[35] Wartime blackmailer of Jews

hole of an apartment, alone. She had left her Catholic husband years before. Alcoholism was a national disease, and Irena's husband was afflicted. Men used vodka to solve unsolvable problems, and the demons it invoked masked despair. Drinking had also induced her husband's anti-Semitic streak, which was another disease plaguing the Poles. Marriage to a Jewess created a combustible situation, and Irena had bailed out.

Post-war intermarriage was one of the reasons there were still Jews in Poland.

Jews who had survived in hiding during the war found it convenient to continue hiding behind a Catholic spouse. For a Jew hoping to marry another Jew, in post-war Poland, the pickings were slim.

'Tell me, *Pani*. What is your first name?' Irena queried her guest.

'My name is Renata.' Mum responded.

'Really? It's beautiful. But how does a woman born in Poland come to have such a name.'

'My father studied in Switzerland. He brought the name back with him.'

'Such a lovely, musical name. You know, I have a friend whose daughter's name is Renata.' Irena went on to tell Mum all about this wonderful friend. Then she made a slip of the tongue that could bring one to believe in God, if anything could. She referred to this friend by her maiden name. '…and then Irena Podbielska said to me…'

'What? WHAT?! You're lying! I am Irena Podbielska!' Mum flipped out, and into a parallel universe. 'My name is Irena Kystyna Podbielska, I was born in Łomża, and my father is a prisoner of the Germans. Who dares call herself by my name?! This other girl is an imposter, whoever she is! I am Irena Podbielska! I am not a Jew!'

'*Pani* Zajdman!'

'*Ja jestem* Irena Podbielska. I am Irena Podbielska. I am not a Jew! I am not a Jew!'

'Renata!' Irena Fuerstenberg smacked Renata out of her hallucination.

'*Pani* Zajdman. Please! What is wrong? What have I done?!' When she recovered, Mum told her.

'My friend Irena had a father with the border patrol who was taken prisoner-of-war. Her mother died when she was six. She had two stepmothers. The first one died, and the second was deported to Siberia in 1940.' Memories flooded back. 'My friend Irena had two stepsisters. The younger one was deported with her mother, and the other lived in Łomża with their grandparents.'

'It sounds very much like Irena.'

'But it's not possible! I saw the school go up in flames!'

'Neither Stefan nor Irena has ever told me such a story.'

'Stefan?'

'Her husband.'

'Her husband? What is her name now?'

'Weinfeld.'

'But that's a Jewish name.'

'Yes. She married a Jew. Irena has a son named Roman, a daughter named Renata, and she's married to a Jew.' The women shuddered. 'There's only one way to find out. I don't have a phone, but the Weinfelds do. When Stefan retired from the army, he turned to writing. His works of science fiction have become prominent. They're required reading in the high schools. They aren't managing too badly. They're one of the few who have a phone. *Chodź, Pani* Renata. We can call from the post office. We can still get there before it closes. *Chodź, Pani* Renata. Come.'

Irena Fuerstenberg led her guest through the darkening streets. What if it isn't her? Mum thought. Worse, what if it is, and she doesn't remember me? It's been thirty-three years since the morning we lost each other, and we'd been together only eighteen months. Why should she remember me? It was another life.

At the post office, Irena Fuerstenberg dialled and spoke with a man on the other end of the line. Then a woman's voice came on the line.

'Hello Irka. Here is Irena. I have a visitor from Canada who says she has news of a friend of yours.'

'Of mine? But I don't know anyone in Canada.'

'I think you should speak to her.' Irena Fuerstenberg extended the receiver. *'Prosze Pani,* take the phone. Don't be afraid. Take it. Please.'

'Hello. *Pani* Weinfeld?'

'Yes.' *Pani* Weinfeld's tone was familiar. Oh help. How does one do this? *'Pani* Weinfeld, were you born in Łomża?'

'Yes. I was.'

'Was your mother's name Helena, and your father's name Czeslaw?'

'Yes! Yes! But I don't know anyone in Canada!'

'*Pani* Weinfeld. Do you – would you – would you happen to remember a Jewish girl from Warsaw?'

'Why of course.' Irena's recall of Mum was instant. 'Renata Skotnicka. She was my friend. She died.'

'Irka.' Mum slumped against the wall. 'Irka.' She reiterated, using a diminutive she hadn't used in thirty-three years. 'Irka, it's me.'

A scream pierced the receiver. Then there was silence.

'What this? Who are you? And what did you say to my wife!'

'*Pan* Weinfeld? I'm sorry. Is she alright?'

'Is she alright? Is she alright?! She's just fainted! Is she alright? Irena! Irka!' There was a muffled commotion, and then Stefan Weinfeld came back on the line.

'Alright, she's coming to. But who are you? And what did you say to my wife?!'

'I'm sorry. I know it was a shock. It's a shock for me too. I knew Irena during the war. We were roommates in a boarding school in Białystok.'

'Renata? Are you Renata Skotnicka?' Clearly, Mum hadn't been forgotten.

'Yes. I am.'

'But that's impossible. You're not supposed to be alive. You were killed in 1941. The Germans shot you all!'

'Not all. Three of us survived.'

'Oh God. My God.' Stefan Weinfeld, the Polish-Jewish science fiction writer, started to cry. Irena Fuerstenberg intervened. 'I'm sending her over in a taxi. Now you're expecting a guest, so pull yourself together!' Irena sniffled. 'Come. I will call a taxi.'

Irena waited with Mum until the taxi arrived. She gave the driver the Weinfelds' address and added, 'This lady is a VIP from Canada, so if you flick off your meter I'll report you to the militia!' The taxi sped away. It deposited Mum at her destination. Standing on the sidewalk was a woman flanked by two men. They were waiting for her. Mum paid the driver and offered him a tip.

'No *Pani*, no! No want *dolarki*. No want trouble!'

Mum stepped out of the taxi, and it took off. She turned to the trio beaming at her. There was a middle-aged man with a beaked nose, a receding chin, and glasses. There was a pale young man with red hair and his mother's high forehead. Between them stood Irena. She had grown stout and dowdy. Her twinkling brown eyes were hidden behind glasses, and her wispy ash blond hair had turned grey.

It took a moment for Mum to find her voice. 'I wouldn't recognise you, Irka.'

'I wouldn't recognise you, either.' They ushered Mum into their apartment, where another Renata had just arrived. She was sixteen and a senior in high school. She looked like her brother; the same porcelain pallor, the fine red hair, and their mother's high forehead. She was a dreamy girl, sensitive and shy. She had wondered about the lost Renata, and marvelled that she was now meeting her.

Solemnly the Weinfeld family gathered around their guest.

'What happened to you, Irena?' Mum gazed at her rediscovered friend. 'How did you survive?'

'It wasn't our school the Germans set fire to. It was the building next door. I ran back to my home, to my grandparents and my sisters. A few weeks later I met some of our friends who thought they'd seen you, but weren't sure. I'd heard everyone was killed, and even if one or two managed to escape, I was certain it couldn't be you. You were so helpless; you seemed the least likely to survive.'

Sardonically, Mum chuckled. 'What happened to your father?'

'He was shot in the prisoner-of-war camp, trying to escape. I found out through the Red Cross.'

'And your stepmother?'

'She survived. So did my sisters. The younger one died of cancer after the war.' Irena turned pensive, and shy. 'Once, I made a trip across the country and passed through Sochaczew. I remembered you telling me it was your father's home, and that you'd spent your summers there. I couldn't help it. I cried.'

'I was deported to Germany in 1943. I came back here in '45 to look for my brother. I found him. I asked him to help me find you. Alek reinvented himself as a journalist. He worked for a newspaper in Gdansk. He placed an ad in the newspaper, asking for information about you.'

'I heard about that!' Irena erupted. 'Someone who saw the ad told me about it, but I was afraid to respond. I thought, I don't owe anyone money; why should anyone be looking for me?!'

'Oh Irena.' Mum shook her head. By dismissing the miraculous, Irena delayed their reunion by twenty-nine years. Mum gazed at the family of eyes wondering at her.

213

'I survived in a labour camp in Mannheim as a deported Pole. My brother arranged forged documents for me.' Then came the coup de grace. 'I thought you were dead,' Mum confessed, 'So I took your identity.' This revelation was overwhelming. Irena broke down. Her son and husband sat helpless. The younger Renata wrapped her arms around her mother, and held her.

Mum and Irena talked far into the night. No one slept. No one could. As the sun rose Renata turned to Renata, 'Tell me about yourself. What is it you would like to do?'

'I'm not sure. I thought of being a journalist, but in this country one cannot tell the truth. Perhaps I can be an architect. I should like to build something.'

'I'm going back to Canada soon, but I don't want to lose any of you. One day you must come to visit me, and my husband and my children, each and every one of you. In the meantime, I would like you to let me send something. What is there that I can get for you?'

'Well, I know Roman would like a pair of jeans.' Roman blushed and lowered his head. 'And *Tatus* would like books that he can't get here, though I don't know if that would get you into trouble.'

'But what about you? Isn't there anything I can get for you?'

'Well, if it wouldn't be asking too much – could I have a Burt Bacharach record?'

Mum smiled. 'I think that can be arranged.' Then Mum turned to Irena. They faced each other, drained.

'Let me send you something. What is it I can get for you?'

'Well.' Sadly, Irena fondled her prematurely grey hair. 'Do you remember the colour my hair used to be? It wasn't that long ago. If I could have something from Canada, I think I should like…' She gulped, and then pressed on. 'If I could have anything, really anything that I wanted, then I would like to have – a bottle of peroxide.'

Mum didn't know whether to laugh or cry. 'Irka! They don't make peroxide anymore!'

'They don't?'

'No! They don't!'

Irena's face fell.

'Products have improved. Irena. I'll send you something better!'

Once more, Irena grew pensive. She rose from the table. 'Renata. *Chodź.*'

Irena led Mum out of the kitchen and down a corridor, to a back room. The atmosphere grew strangely tense. Stefan, Roman and the teenage Renata remained motionless, and silent.

In this back room, tucked away from the rest of the apartment, a twenty-seven-year-old man squirmed in an armchair. He giggled. He squealed. He rolled his eyes, seeing, and not seeing. Irena introduced him to Mum.

'This is my first-born. Pawel.' Now Mum stood motionless and silent. Irena continued. 'He was born in 1947.'

Like Dad, Stefan Weinfeld survived the war years in the Soviet Union. Post-war, he returned to Poland to search for family. He didn't find them. Instead, he found Irena.

'Pawel was born normal and healthy. He was such a sweet baby. When he was eighteen months old…' Again Irena gulped, and forced herself to continue. 'Meningitis did this to him.' Pawel's body would develop and grow old, but he would be intellectually disabled for life. His mother fed him, cared for him, and daily changed his diapers. She taught the two children who came after Pawel to love, respect and care for their brother. During Poland's most recent surge of anti-Semitism, in 1968, Stefan wanted to emigrate to Israel, but the Israelis wouldn't accept a tragically handicapped young man. Irena offered her husband a divorce, as well as custody of Roman and Renata.

'I will not have my son locked up in an institution.' I told Stefan. 'You can go to Israel and take the other two with you, but as long as I live, Pawel's home is with me.' Presented with these terms and conditions, Stefan chose to stay.

Irena led Mum away from Pawel, leaving the door ajar. The two war buddies returned to the kitchen. Mum was overcome with admiration. As a teenager under siege, Irena refused to abandon her grandmother. As a mother under siege, she refused to abandon her disabled child.

CHAPTER TWENTY-FIVE

The seed was planted for Mum and Irena's reunion seven years before it manifested. When I was ten years old my mother told me the story of her classmate Irena whom, she assumed, had 'died.' Mum didn't give me the context for Irena's supposed demise. She sighed and said simply, 'but she died.'

Innocently, I responded, 'How do you know she's dead, Mummy? Did you see her die?' I don't know why I said it. It just fell out of my mouth. Mum said nothing, but the words falling out of the mouth of her babe planted a seed of doubt. It also sparked a glimmer of hope.

Before breaking her silence in the 1980s, I was the only person to whom Mum leaked messages from behind the barbed wire of her parallel universe, because I was the only one willing to receive them. In our small family circle that was loving and tried to be happy, my parents spoke to each other in Polish. To me, Polish was a secret language in which my parents could say things they didn't want Michael and me to hear. When my parents did speak in English, they would preface their comments by saying 'Before the war,' or 'After the war.' In the world of Before the War, all seemed elegant and gracious and lovely. People were civilised and kind. By stark contrast, the world of After the War was shrouded in mystery and darkness. Between these two worlds lay a forbidden chasm, and when I perceived the ghosts hiding behind my mother's haunted eyes, I knew she had slipped into the Before the War world. I longed to follow her there so that she would pay attention to me too. I gained a foothold into my mother's parallel universe by bringing out old photographs she kept buried in a wicker sewing basket. Under the lid of my mother's basket, memories in monochrome edged each others' images. They vied for my attention, as well as the attention of the woman who preserved them. Mum would pick up a snapshot and tell me a story about the girl frozen in time there. Then she'd picked up another, and tell me the names and stories of all the warm and friendly faces smiling at us out of the moment they were captured in time. A few were not smiling. These would have been images of those captured in wartime. Most of the photographs were taken in the immediate aftermath of the war, when it was possible to preserve keepsakes without betraying one's true identity.

Carefully editing out horror, Mum fudged or omitted the context and, prompted by the photographs, told me stories of war and post-war buddies missing, living, and no longer living except in Mum's prodigious memory and painfully aching heart. So it was that, in 1975, when I received a suspect phone call from a mysterious stranger, I was able to warn my mother, and prepare her.

'Ma? You got a few minutes?'

'Yes sweetheart. What is it?' I was home alone. I called Mum at what we referred to as 'The Office'.

'A man just called, looking for you. There was something creepy about him. He said he knew you in Germany. His English is very good, but I detected a Polish accent. I offered to give him the office number so he could call you there, but he refused to take it. He said he would call back later. He wouldn't leave his number, and he wouldn't tell me his name.'

'Yes, that is strange.' When long-lost friends are on the verge of finding each other, they don't allow formalities to stand in their way.

'Ma, I have a feeling I know who the guy is.'

'You do? Who do you imagine he could be?'

'Well,' I hesitated. As I was listening to the caller, a story Mum had told me surfaced in my mind. It hung there, like a warning lit in neon.

'Well Ma, I have nothing to base it on except a feeling, but remember you told me the story about a guy who sold you a fake contract when you came to Canada? I don't know why, but I have a feeling it's him.'

Mum gasped. 'As far as I know,' she said, slowly, when she recovered her voice, 'Wlodawsky returned to Germany. I heard he made a fortune there. What makes you think the caller might be him?'

'I don't know, but I can't shake the feeling. It's as if he wants to catch you off-guard. There's something slimy about the guy.'

When Wlodawsky called in the evening, Mum was ready for him.

'Hello Renata.' The man who robbed a refugee and then attempted to coerce her into sexual slavery greeted her years later as if they were old friends. 'How have you been all this time?'

'Get to the point,' Mum snapped, in Polish. 'You must want something. What is it?'

'Well! If you put it that way!' What Wlodawsky wanted was Mum's testimony, and he was willing to fly her to Munich at his own expense so she would stand up in a

219

courtroom and state, to the world, and especially to Wlodawsky's son, that he was never the vicious Warsaw Ghetto policeman a German writer was making him out to be. The publication of a German-language book making this assertation drove Wlodawsky's wife to a breakdown, and his son wouldn't speak to him. Wlodawsky was combing the world in search of witnesses who might testify on his behalf.

'I didn't know you were a policeman in Ghetto.' Blandly, Mum admitted.

'I wasn't!' Wlodawsky pleaded.

'I know what you were capable of.' Mum retorted contemptuously.

'So?' Wlodawsky ignored the implication. 'Will you come to Munich to testify? I'll fly you first class! I'll set you up in the best hotel! You'll have royal treatment all the way! I'll pay for everything!' Wlodawsky was desperate. How the tables had turned. Mum enjoyed poetic justice. It was the only kind of justice she had ever known.

'Hmmm. I'll have to think about this.' Wlodawsky's post-war victim was in no rush to rescue him.

'What is there to think about? You have children! You can understand that I'm trying to save my son. He's threatening to commit suicide!'

'I said I have to think about it!' Mum was immovable. 'Come to my home next week. I'll give you my answer then.'

Wlodawsky wasn't interested in socialising. Neither was Mum. She had an agenda, and Wlodawsky had little choice but to follow it.

Dad never ducked a confrontation, so on the evening Wlodawsky was scheduled to visit he must have been instructed to make himself scarce. Michael wasn't there either, so I surmise that Dad removed him. Mum needed to confront her dragon alone, or almost alone. Oddly, I was encouraged to stay. I watched as my mother prepared for her encounter with the dragon. Mum was in her later forties, at the peak of her power and beauty. She was graceful and slim. Her chestnut-coloured hair was luxuriant, her legs were shapely, and her back was strong and straight. Her blue-grey eyes were clear and focused, her cheekbones were high, her smile was radiant, and her pale skin was flawless. On this evening in early June, Mum donned a knitted, pastel-coloured halter top that showed off her well-proportioned shoulders and toned, willowy arms. Mum rarely applied make-up, but on this evening she indulged, highlighting the blue of her eyes and accentuating her full, sensuous lips. She clipped on a set of amber earrings, which she had purchased in Poland, and then awaited the arrival of the dragon. He came precisely at the set hour: a dapper, manicured, white-haired gent in a custom-tailored suit, edging the age of seventy. His shrewd gaze sized up the tastefully furnished and spacious apartment that was now Renata's home. He understood that the homeless refugee had made a success of her life, in the sense a man like him would define success. Having grown shrewd, too, it was what Mum intended him to see, which is why she issued the invitation.

Renata was rich, or felt rich, in other ways.

'This is my daughter, Nadja.' Mum introduced me. 'You spoke to her on the phone. She's nineteen. She's in theatre school.' When I was accepted into theatre school, Mum and I decided that Sharon would become known as Nadja.

Nineteen. My full, sensuous lips curled. The same age my mother was when you conned her out of all the money she had and tried to ruin her, you slime bag.

'Well, she's certainly beautiful enough to be an actress,' Wlodawsky oozed. 'The daughter is even more beautiful than the mother.' Blankly, I stared. What a shithead.

'Oh no.' Mum modified. 'I was never so beautiful, and never could be.' As Mum and her dragon parried, I stood uneasily between them, like a monkey in the middle.

'I'm going to my room.' I announced, heading to the door at the end of the living room, and our apartment. Echoing my father, I addressed my mother, and indirectly warned Wlodawsky. 'If you need me, I'm here.'

I entered my bedroom, and turned on my TV. I kept the volume at a reasonable level, yet loud enough to let the dragon know that Renata was no longer alone in the world.

Through my bedroom door I heard hushed and strained voices conversing in Polish. Wlodawsky pleaded. Mum remained adamant. 'What your son thinks of you is your problem.' Mum spat out her final words on the subject. 'My father had a child he loved, too.'

Wlodawsky's mission failed. He left our apartment and slunk back to West Germany, where the second generation was beginning to confront its parents about the open wounds of what still felt like the recent past.

I emerged from my bedroom. Mum stood dull-eyed and rigid, like a statue.

'You okay, Ma?'

'Yeah, sure.' She retreated to her bedroom, and removed her finery.

Dad and Michael came home. Dad nodded to Mum. 'It's done?'

'Yes.'

'You feel better now?'

'I feel fine.' Mum meant it.

'Good to hear.' Dad opened his arms, and Mum fell into them.

'*Oy yoy!*' Fiercely, Dad hugged her. 'This is a brave lady!'

The days were now long, but as Dad was wont to say, the years are short. Abram picked up his penknife, stuck it in his pocket and took off on one of his solitary walks around our predominantly Jewish neighbourhood. Abram was on a mission of his own. He was in search of a Mercedes Benz. Dad knew the sight of a Mercedes Benz always transported Mum back to Mannheim. Should he find one parked in front of a Jewish home, the car's owner would wake to find that his vehicle needed new tires because, under cover of darkness, a middle-aged prankster, in a gesture of solidarity with his war-damaged wife, grimly slashed them. Mum knew this was done when Dad wandered back late at night, giving her a wink, and flicking his knife.

CHAPTER TWENTY-SIX

In August of 1977 my uncle Alek, with his Jewish companion, came from Melbourne to visit. After sustaining a heart attack, he left Irena Bobinska. Alek put himself through the process of a legal divorce, though he was never legally married. He did it for the sake of appearances, believing it would spare his children embarrassment. After divorcing Irena, Alek entered into a relationship with a wealthy Jewish widow. Sonya was what was finally being acknowledged as a Holocaust survivor. So was Uncle Alek.

Alek's few remaining years were good ones. With his companion as guide, Alek immersed himself in Melbourne's vibrant Jewish community. Sonya's financial resources enabled Alek to reunite with his sisters in Canada.

I wasn't in Montreal when Uncle Alek arrived. I met him a few days later, in his hotel room. Though Mum tried to prepare him, the sight of Natalia's face revisited on mine sent him into mild shock.

'Mama!' He gasped, as tears sprang to his eyes.

'Hi Uncle Alek!' I hailed the relative I had never met, and threw my arms around him. Alek was family.

I discovered my uncle Alek to be the soft side of Mum. He had the same high cheekbones and slanted eyes, but Alek's eyes were brown. He spoke English with a half-Polish and half-Australian accent. Alek hovered over me like a mother hen, studying my reactions and anticipating my desires. When he saw that I enjoyed the freshly squeezed orange juice I was offered in his hotel room during our first encounter, freshly squeezed orange juice awaited me each morning. My uncle gave me a watch, which he said would never stop ticking. The watch stopped ticking the day Alek died.

For my part, I wasn't used to having a relative treat me so well. Only Daddy indulged me the way Uncle Alek did. How wonderful it would've been to grow up with a loving uncle.

I knew Alek but briefly. His manners, as well as his attire, were immaculate. He took several showers a day, and frequently washed his hands. In the final days of the '43 uprising, Uncle Alek survived Warsaw's burning Ghetto by hiding in a pile of excrement. Since then, it seemed, he could never get clean enough.

In post-war Poland Alek made his mark as a sports broadcaster, sports writer, and ultimately as a sports editor with a newspaper. In November of 1956 he was sent to Melbourne to cover the summer Olympic Games. Reluctantly he returned to Poland. With the help of Mum, Dad, and others who cannot be named, with his wife and children Alek was able to defect in 1959.

Alek's first son died tragically in 1955, and his last son was born in 1958. In 1952 his only daughter was born. She was given the names Hania Natalia, in honour of Alek's sister and mother. His children did not know Alek was Jewish until the eve of their emigration, when he took his son Andrej to the Jewish cemetery in Warsaw and introduced him to 'family'.

In Melbourne Alek ran what the Australians call a 'milk bar,' and did his best to raise his children. In effect, he did it alone. Irena Bobinska's tenuous hold on reality was reflected in physical attacks on her husband as the symbol of her hatred for, and seduction by, 'the Jews'. She came to believe the death of her first child was God's punishment for having carnal relations with a Jew. Repeatedly she screamed at her children, 'That Jew isn't your father! Don't call that Jew 'Daddy'. You call that Jew *Pan* Skotnicki!' Not *Pan* Mlynek, which was Alek's name, but *Pan* Skotnicki. In post-war Poland Alek adopted his stepfather's name. Irena's children inherited it, never knowing it wasn't their own.

Shortly after Alek and Sonya arrived, Mum, Michael and I set off on what could be considered A European Grand Tour. Our first stop was London, where Alek and Sonya joined us. I now imagine how surreal it must have seemed to my mother and uncle, in the year of Queen Elizabeth's Silver Jubilee, to whisk off to a West End theatre in a rotund, black taxi cab on a soft September night, our first night in London. It certainly seemed dream-like to me. Life had given brother and sister a second chance, and they seized it.

I said goodbye to my uncle Alek in London. I would never see him again.

In Paris, in a cave-like bistro called *L'Apostrophe,* Mum, with her sketchy French, ordered what she believed to be pork chops. In the progressive and secular home of her childhood, Mum enjoyed pork chops served with apple sauce.

When the waiter placed the dish in front of her she screamed, 'Take it away! Take it away!' The startled waiter removed the plate. Michael and I were mystified. Mum explained. 'It was pig's knuckles – and it still had hair on it!'

'How do you know?' Logically, we responded.

'Because I worked in a slaughterhouse in Germany! I recognised it!'

'Oh yeech! That's grooooss!' Michael and I groaned. When we were sufficiently recovered, Mum related her experience with the butcher and his wife in Vernheim.

In Budapest I clasped my mother in my arms and waltzed her along the Danube, whose waters were brown, not blue. In Ljubljana, which was still a part of Yugoslavia at the time, I wanted nothing except to eat its buckwheat bread.

It was in Warsaw that I watched Mum come into her own. Haughty, with aplomb, she marched us past the airport's armed guards.

My exceptionally tall, blonde and big-boned brother could pass as a Slav, but my dark and delicate features, as well as my Wetherall coat, bought at Liberty in London, marked me as a well-to-do Westerner. In the autumn of 1977, Warsaw was grey, grim and corrupt. Mum chased away women who, literally, tried to buy the coat off my back. Before entering taxi cabs, Michael and I were instructed to keep our mouths shut. Mum sat up front with the driver, masquerading as an aunt who was showing the city to a niece and nephew visiting from Chicago. (Isn't that where all migrating Poles go?) That way, the cab's meter would function, and the fare wouldn't rise into the stratosphere.

In the bathroom, in our hotel suite, I discovered Mum and Stefan Weinfeld. Mum was perched on top of the toilet's lid, and Stefan balanced on the bathtub's rim. Stefan was running hot and cold water in the tub, and Mum kept flushing the toilet. As bath water ran and toilet water gushed, Mum and Stefan conversed in stage whispers.

'What on earth are you doing?!' I erupted. Mum brought her hand to her mouth, motioning me to shut up.

'But what are you doing?!' I mouthed exaggeratedly, as though trapped in a silent movie. Just as silently, but without my (and her) histrionic flare, Mum led me out of the bathroom and pointed upwards, to what looked like an oversized fly embedded in the ceiling. Because we were foreigners, our hotel room was bugged.

***

On our first evening in Warsaw, I was innocently picking apples from a barrel in what passed as a grocery store, when I sensed something amiss.

In a store that contained nothing but apples, onions and lemons, customers were staring at me. The cashier was glaring daggers. She muttered something to the customers, and my mother spat out a response. Then Mum came over, ordered me to drop the apples, and hustled me out of the store. 'Ma? What happened?!'

'In a communist country you don't pick your own apples.' Mum's tongue dripped acid. 'They sell you what they want to sell you, and half of what they sell you is rotten. The manager was incensed that what she called 'a foreign bitch' dared to pick her own apples. She told the customers she was going to charge us ten times the price of the apples, before she realised that I know Polish. She found that out when I told her to go fuck herself and her rotten apples.' Then Mum trilled, 'Welcome to Warsaw, kid!'

It would be in Warsaw's Jewish cemetery where the ghost of the teenaged Renata rose from the body of my middle-aged mother. The day we visited the cemetery its gates were closed for, of all reasons, a Jewish holiday.

'It's a communist plot, but a good communist keeps going.' So saying, Mum, or Renata, or both, grabbed my hand and pulled me through brambles and under bent and barbed wire fences, until we reached the enclosure of the dead. Then the hunt was on for the grave of Natalia's father, who died in 1923, early enough to have a recognisable grave. When we found the burial plot of the philanthropist who, according to the inscription on his stone, 'clothed the naked and fed the hungry,' we also found the neighbouring grave of Ludwig Zamenhof, the doctor and writer who invented Esperanto. How fitting that it was a Jew who created, or tried to create, a universal language.

It was only in the home of Stefan and Irena Weinfeld that Mum felt she could relax, and when she did I saw a woman I had never seen before. My anxiety-ridden mother morphed into a warm, witty, and delightful companion. She seemed like a fish floundering in extended death throes suddenly thrown back into water. What surprised me even more was that I became the same way. High wire anxiety was so much part of my mother's being, and mine, that I hadn't known we could function any other way. It seemed complicated then, but it doesn't now. What Mum and I felt was safe.

In 1980, Mum and Dad brought Stefan and Irena for a visit to Canada. Dad developed a special fondness for the quietly dignified Polish Jew. A year later, at the height of civil unrest and the birth of Poland's *Solidarity* movement, Stefan came to visit us again, this time on his own.

Through his wife's reclamation of her lost friend, Stefan Weinfeld found an escape route for his children. In 1939 his father led him to the Soviet border, promising to follow with Stefan's mother. The father knew such a promise, whether he would be able to keep it, or not, was the only way he could convince his son to leave them. The eighteen-year-old boy never saw his parents again.

Now, in middle age, Stefan's frequent bouts of depression were mitigated by Renata's promise to bring his son and daughter out of Poland. Forty-two years after Stefan left his troubled country he would leave it again, for a visit to Canada, and return to it, again, because of family.

On a cold and clear Hallowe'en, Dad, Mum and I drove Stefan to the port in Montreal's Old City. We sat quietly, in an almost empty waiting room. A Polish sailor approached.

'You'll have to take your meals at the first seating, sir; the second one is fully booked.'

'Fully booked?' Mum hissed at Dad, in English. 'Or cancelled!' The ship's departure was further delayed because five more shipmates had defected.

'Looks like you'll be having tête-à-têtes with the captain, Stefan,' Dad cracked. We walked Weinfeld to the gate, and he broke down in Mum's arms. Then he pulled himself together, shrugging like Chaplin's Little Tramp. Painfully, he lifted his valise.

'*Do widzenia,* Renia! *Do widzenia* Abram!' Having said his goodbyes, he padded up the gangplank of the Stefan Batory, his narrow shoulders bent under the burden of his destiny.

Sadly, Dad watched as the diminutive man in his faded suit and out-dated glasses disappeared through the entrance of what was rapidly becoming a ghost-ship. Dad, as well as Mum, felt he had found a brother in the gentle spirit who had been unable to travel as far, nor as fast, as he. Dad sensed, rightly, that he would never see him again. Dad's talent for turning heartbreak into dark humour did not fail him.

'*Nu?* The Poles are jumping ship, and the Jew is going back.'

In care of my parents, Stefan left a letter for his son. 'Don't look back.' He wrote to the future. 'Forget the Old

World, and forget the old. Build your life anew in the New World.'

Ten days after Stefan's departure, martial law was imposed on Poland. By the time exit became possible, Roman had married and attached himself to his wife's family. Stefan then transferred his dream of escape to his daughter, but Renata married and settled, like her brother. It was only with the collapse of the communist stronghold that Renata the Second, as we called her, with her husband and baby in tow, approached her father and told him they were ready to leave.

With the transformation of Poland into a democracy, Poles attempting to enter western countries could no longer claim refugee status. Ironically, entry into the newly united Germany, with its vistas of economic opportunity, became the goal of many disgruntled Poles, as they took to misrepresenting themselves as persecuted Jews. When Renata the Second declared herself ready to emigrate, my brother Michael, who by then had relocated to Toronto, approached the local [36]J.I.A.S. office with a letter from Mum, and with money. It was decided that Renata and her family would settle in Ottawa. Mum cautioned Irena and Stefan not to send their daughter to Québec.

Renata the Second, with a husband and two small children in tow, arrived in Canada's capital during a deep freeze in January. Mum took a bus to Ottawa and, in a temperature of minus thirty-five Celsius, met them at the airport, led them through government offices in order to secure their landed immigrant status, and then oriented them. 'It's a communist plot, but a good communist keeps going.'

---

[36] Jewish Immigration Aid Society

CHAPTER TWENTY-SEVEN

During the first week of the new year of 1981, I took a call from relatives in Melbourne. Uncle Alek was dead. On New Year's Day, on the anniversary of Natalia's death, a heart attack, his second, sent him to hospital. On the fourth of January, as he was being discharged from hospital, (and why was he being discharged so soon?) a third attack killed him. Because he was an officer in the Polish Air Force during the early days of the war Alek was considered a veteran, so his coffin was draped with the Australian flag.

When I took the call, Mum and Dad were vacationing in Florida. I made a point of contacting Dad directly. It fell to Abram to deliver the heart-breaking news to Renata. He invited her for a walk along the beach, draped his arm around her, held her close, and gently informed her of her brother's passing. I was three thousand miles away, yet I could imagine my mother's wails breaking with the ocean waves.

Renata lost Alek too soon after finding him again. Once Irena Bobinska and her pathological possessiveness no longer stood between them, brother and sister were able to resume their relationship unimpeded. Renata had visited Alek in Melbourne the year before. They planned to meet in Jerusalem in June, for the first International Gathering of Holocaust Survivors, a seemingly impossible undertaking brought into being by the American organiser and activist Ernest Michel, a native of Mannheim who had worked alongside Mum in American Military Government headquarters, thirty-five years before.

It would never happen now. Instead of meeting Alek in Jerusalem in June, Mum flew to Melbourne the following January for the unveiling of his tombstone. The traditional Jewish ceremony denoting closure was almost hijacked.

In a replay of the war's aftermath, Renata heard Alek calling to her in dreams. His nocturnal appeals became so disturbing that Renata called Alek's eldest son Andrej, who was now Andrew.

'*Ciocia* Renia! Did you get our letter?'

'What letter?'

Alek's three surviving adult children had jointly written to their *ciocia* (auntie) in Canada, appealing for help. Within three months of Alek's passing, Sonya became involved with another man, and decided to arrange the unveiling at an obscenely early date so she could introduce her new love interest socially. It was the wealthy Jewish widow who was paying for Alek's stone. His three Catholic offspring seemed neither willing nor able to pool their resources and shoulder the responsibility of marking their father's grave.

'Tell Sonya I'll pay for my brother's stone!' Renata shouted over the overseas line.

Ciocia Renia could always be counted on to cover the bills.

While my Australian cousins were still children in Poland, their Canadian-based aunt sent oranges and medication. Instead of resuming her education, Renata kept working to fill the flow of orders emanating from their mother. She couldn't escape the thought that this woman saved her brother's life. Irena Bobinska constantly reminded her of it. From the first month of Renata's arrival in Canada, shopping orders arrived. The first was an itemised list of Elizabeth Arden cosmetics. Coyly, Irena Bobinska wrote, 'I want to look attractive for your brother.' Working as a cleaning lady,

Renata scavenged in her employers' garbage cans, pilfering the residue of rouge in a discarded stick so she could smear it on her lips, but she managed to scrape up enough from the sixty dollars earned each month to send Bobinska top-of-the-line cosmetics.

In winter, the refugee in Canada ate twice a day, subsisting on donuts and peanut butter, while buying and shipping citrus fruit to her brother's children. While their schoolmates half-starved, Alek's children thrived on Floridian oranges, courtesy of *Ciocia* Renia.

In the autumn of 1949, Renata received a letter from Irena Bobinska, frantic with fear that there wasn't going to be enough fuel to heat the house in winter. Renata wrapped the fur-lined coat she brought from Germany, went to a bazaar and bought a second-hand cloth coat, and shipped the fur-lined treasure to Poland. She instructed Bobinska to sell the coat and use the proceeds to buy coal. After surviving her second Canadian winter in a cloth coat, Renata received a cheerful letter from Bobinska reporting how she had sewn pretty trimmings onto the cuffs and the lapel, how she enjoyed wearing it, and how much the neighbours admired her in it.

After conning Renata out of the coat on her back, Bobinska went to work wheedling money out of her for abortions, or so she said. Supposedly Renata and Abram footed the bill for four abortions. Alek never knew, because, for reasons that seemed obvious, and probably were not, Bobinska warned Renata not to tell him.

Decades later, Renata learned that Irena Bobinska lived sumptuously in communist Poland, throwing lavish parties, holding open houses and entertaining scores of guests. She also discovered that Alek had been neglected. He was constantly hungry, and always cold. Fastidious about his grooming before the war, in communist Poland Alek's appearance grew shabby. His one good suit was threadbare. There were visible holes in his socks. Without Bobinska's knowledge, Alek managed to purchase a new pair of socks. Afraid to return home with the purchase, the journalist ducked into an alley and, hiding behind garbage, removed his shoes and his torn socks, and put on the new ones.

Irena Bobinska resented the sacrifice she believed she made by emigrating to Australia. She was bitter towards the Jews because they were unappreciative of all she had done for them. She felt she should be honoured as a Righteous Among The Nations, and could not fathom why Melbourne's Jewish community shunned her.

Bobinska's shopping orders to Renata stopped when Alek, having sustained his first heart attack, walked out on his ersatz marriage thirty years after entering into it. When his heart broke beyond repair, Renata paid for his funeral and burial, as well as his memorial stone.

CHAPTER TWENTY-EIGHT

In November of 1981, Ania Młynek Hoyos was dying. In an eerie replay, Renata would lose both siblings within the same year, just as she had lost her parents.

Both Ania' s children pre-deceased her. During the four years of her protracted illness, my parents took care of my difficult aunt. My brother and I helped out. Michael accompanied Ania to early morning chemotherapy treatments before attending classes at medical school, and I ran errands, directed by my mother. Ania directed Mum to a safety deposit box in a bank vault.

'It's everything I have, and it's a lot. Use what you need to pay the expenses, and keep the rest for yourself.'

When the box in the vault was opened, Mum stood aghast. One shiny copper Canadian penny winked at her, in mockery. Camille had reached the box first. The penny he left was his message to the two Jewish sisters.

Mum never told Ania of the theft. She assured her sister she had retrieved the money, and then paid all the expenses herself.

During the last stage of her illness Ania entered hospital, but then screamed to be released because the doctors and nurses were bullying her, or so she charged. After several days at home with her husband, Ania begged to be returned to hospital. The doctor in charge of the palliative care unit refused to allow her back, so Mum hired a private nurse, wining and dining her and lavishing gifts on her, including Ania's fur coat, so she would treat her dying sister well, and ignore the menacing presence of her brother-in-law. After accepting all the perks, the nurse stole Ania's jewellery, anyway.

As Mum sat vigil by her dying sister, Ania gazed up at her and implored, 'Finish it. Please finish it.'

'What do you mean?'

'You know what I mean. There's no point in prolonging the agony. Please, Renusia, help me to finish it.'

As the full import of Ania's request registered Mum recoiled and exclaimed, 'No!' A part of her, the deepest part, questioned the extent of her love for her sister. Did she love her enough to help her die? If she were to honour her sister's request, might she be doing so from motives she didn't dare acknowledge, even to herself?

Ania overrode her sister. 'Cyanide. You can get cyanide.'

'No! I can't. We're not In Ghetto. There's no cyanide available here.' A quick and easy death was the best one could hope for in the Warsaw Ghetto. Cyanide became an expensive and sought-after luxury. Ania managed to acquire cyanide capsules for herself, but she would not share them with her little sister. Though her feelings for Mum were ambivalent, Ania was determined that Renata live.

'There must be a way,' Ania pleaded. 'Camille trips me when I get up to go to the bathroom. He's lacing the food with morphine.'

'We'll find a way to keep you comfortable,' was as much as Mum could bring herself to say. 'But don't ever ask such a thing again!'

'Abram, I want to get Ania out of her apartment. I want to bring her to us, to die.'

'Absolutely not!' Dad unstintingly supported Mum during the ordeal of Ania's illness, but now he was drawing the line. 'You will not bring Death into this house!'

'You're selfish!' Desperate to protect her sister, Mum reverted to the dirty street fighter she was compelled to become during the war. The accusation was unfair, and she knew it. Dad always placed family first, and himself last.

'Oy chameleh mamaleh!' Daddy switched into Yiddish. The words he used translate into 'little donkey mother', in reference to Mum's stubbornness, but when Dad used it, it became a term of endearment.

'I will do everything I can to help, but we cannot have the children disturbed. We have hurt them enough. They need peace and quiet to concentrate on their studies, especially Michael. He's going to be a doctor; he cannot be made upset by sickness.' As soon as the words tumbled off his tongue, Dad recognised their irony. Mum smirked. 'Oh come on! You know what I mean!' Feeling frantic and overwhelmed, Mum burst into tears. Dad wrapped his arms around her. *'Kochana.* This is what I will do.' Dad negotiated. 'Every day after work I will go to your sister's apartment. I will stay with her and make sure that animal doesn't go near her. She won't be left alone for a minute. I will sleep there, right beside her, on the floor in her bedroom, whether the nurse is there or not. Once the nurse is awake in the morning, I will come down to the office.' It was a remarkable offer. No one would have made such an offer, except Dad. What Mum had known for a long time, and Dad never divined, was that Ania was in love with him.

Always a man of integrity, Dad kept his word. Each afternoon after closing the office, he went directly to Ania's apartment. As soon as he stepped in, Camille recoiled and kept his distance, eyeing his brother-in-law like a wary fox. Dad was tender with women and tough on men, and Camille knew it. As long as Dad was on the premises, Ania was safe. Each evening Dad lay on a mat, on the floor, next to the bed where Ania lay dying. He joked with her and sang to her and told her stories that were almost bedtime stories, like he did with me when I was a little girl. When the time came he said the *kaddish* for her, the year-long prayers for the dead. In the meantime he served as her guardian and angel, until the Angel of Death came to release them both. The dying woman was able to sleep peacefully beside the man she loved, because her sister gave him to her.

CHAPTER TWENTY-NINE

By 1982 and into 1983 my parents had reached a new level of contentment, seemingly at peace with themselves, and certainly at peace with each other. They were worried about me. I was floundering, hanging back from full entry into adulthood, though Dad seemed to understand that I needed to lose my way in order to find it.

'You will go through the hard part now,' he reassured, and prophesised, 'Then you will wind up on top, just like me!' Michael was a straight arrow; confident and popular and Dr President of Everything. When I grumbled about our Golden Boy, Dad admonished me, giving me a piece of advice that would reverberate down the decades. 'Don't be jealous from your brother. For him, the hard part will come later, and when it does it will be really hard because he won't be used to it. He's going to need you.' To Michael he said, 'When I'm gone, you will be the man from the family. You will have to protect the women.'

In the autumn of 1982 I initiated a weekly Friday night date with Dad in a restaurant in Chinatown. Mum joined us on the Friday evening of 1 April 1983. Three weeks later she was scheduled to fly to Warsaw for the fortieth anniversary of the Warsaw Ghetto Uprising. A week later, Mum had arranged to take me to Washington, for the second International Gathering of Holocaust Survivors. Dad declined to come along.

In the restaurant, Dad made a crack about needing to 'put salt on Mummy's tail,' a reference to Renata's love of – and newfound freedom to – travel. Mum rebuffed the remark, and Dad huffed, mock-offended, 'Well, I can disappear!' I shuddered. Dad was as effervescent as ever, but he didn't look well. Though it was cold and rainy, he was sweating, and his skin had taken on a strange greyish tinge. The change in Dad's appearance was visible enough for me to remark upon it to my mother.

'Oh Daddy's fine. He's just tired. He had a check-up with Dr Amdursky two weeks ago and got a clean bill of health. In June we'll go to Florida, and he'll take a rest. Don't worry. Daddy will be okay.'

Michael was accepted as an intern at Hadassah Hospital in Jerusalem for the summer of 1983. Michael inherited his father's Zionist dream, and the internship was a first step in what he hoped would be making [37]*aliyah*. For several summers Michael worked as a [38]*madriach*, leading student tours to Israel. He was so identified with this role that a friend bought him a shepherd's staff, and we took to calling him 'Moses'. When I heard that Dad was going to join him in Israel during the upcoming summer I fretted. 'You're going to drag Daddy around in the heat? You know he has high blood pressure.'

'Don't worry about it.' Michael scoffed. 'I'll rent an air-conditioned car!'

Overhearing our exchange, Dad piped up, 'I hope Moses doesn't take me through the desert. I won't make it.'

***

---

[37] Emigration to Israel
[38] Group leader

Wednesday, 6 April promised to be a special day. Michael, at the top of his class, was also president of McGill University's Medical Students' Association. He had just been awarded The Scarlet Key for outstanding student leadership, and in the evening was scheduled to be feted in the home of the medical faculty's Dean.

Mum and Dad went to work, as usual. In the early afternoon, at the office, Dad took a call from Mrs Trautmann.

'You must be so proud of Michael!' It was Mrs Trautmann who was proud of Michael. The infant she had sheltered and protected, the toddler who had been hoisted to ceiling-height in order to stick a foil star at the top of her Christmas tree, was now an award-winning university student about to become a doctor!

'Big deal!' Dad blasted the simple *frau*. 'He's just a lucky guy. I wish his sister would have some of his luck.'

Dad's secretary glanced at him.

'Don't worry, Mr Zajdman. Sharon will settle down. She'll find a husband and give you grandchildren.'

'Oh I don't care about that!' No one recognised how advanced Dad was. 'Better she should live alone for the rest of her life than to live at the mercy of some sonofabitch who doesn't deserve her. All I want is for *mein* daughter to be happy.'

It turned out to be Dad's dying wish.

At three in the afternoon, Dad went for his daily swim at the Bonaventure Hotel. He returned to the office at five, drove home with Mum, and carried her bags up the stairs, into the elevator, and down the corridor to their third floor condo apartment.

My parents never bought a house in Outremont, or anywhere else. Dad did not trust Québec politics. When he turned sixty-five the old socialist reluctantly became a man of property, buying into the first condominium project in Cote St. Luc. By securing a roof over our heads, Dad believed he was protecting family.

For the evening of 6 April, as a gift, Dad was given two tickets for a hockey play-off game. Since Michael was having dinner with Dean David Johnston (the same David Johnston who would later become governor-general), Dad elected – or threatened – to take Michael's girlfriend to the game.

'If he won't take her out, I will!' Gleefully, Dad informed Mum. 'I'm going to play a trick on both of them!' Then he got back to business. 'Call the Forum and check to see if the game starts on time. I'm going to take a shower.' When I was a child, whenever Dad rose to leave a room without explanation, I was gripped by panic and would shout, 'Daddy, where are you going?!' If Dad's destination was the bathroom, he would smile and explain, 'I'm going where no one can replace me.'

After calling The Forum and putting away the contents of the bags Dad had carried for her, Mum sensed something amiss. The apartment was too quiet. Abram said he was going to take a shower, but she didn't hear water running.

Quelling a rising sense of anxiety, Mum headed to the back of the apartment, to the second bathroom off the master bedroom. What she found sent her screaming into the hallway.

'Help my husband! Help my husband! Please, somebody help him!'

I was alone in my downtown apartment. I was scheduled to attend a French class at McGill that evening but depression, like an invisible chain, held me back, so I was in when the call came.

'Something's happened to your father.' I recognised the voice of my mother's next-door neighbour and heard Mum shrieking in the background. The neighbour stated grimly. 'Come home.'

Before calling a cab, I had the presence of mind to turn off the burner under a pot of lentils simmering on the stove. To this day, I can't stand the smell of lentils.

There was an ambulance parked in front of my parents' condo complex. The door to the third-floor apartment was open. Michael was already home, bearing down on Daddy's chest and exhorting two lethargic paramedics to do the same. For two hours Michael pounded frantically on Dad's uncharacteristically unresponsive heart, but Dad detested doctors and hospitals, and decided he wasn't going.

For years I accepted that a massive coronary killed Dad instantly. Like the form letters sent to families of fallen soldiers, I was told and wanted to believe, 'He didn't know what hit him.' Near the end of her own life Mum confessed she had seen signs of distress.

'His clothes were tossed around the bedroom. That wasn't like him. He was always neat. Everything had its place.' Mum sighed, and surmised, 'He seemed to have stripped quickly, in an effort to get to the bathroom. Perhaps to splash water on his face? The way he undressed and seemed to race to the bathroom tells me he wasn't feeling well. Still, he didn't call for help.' Mum attempted to console herself. 'If I hadn't been in the apartment, I would never have believed I couldn't save him.'

At 10:30 in the evening Michael wearily shook his head. Dad was laid out on a sofa in a small spare room.

'Would you like to say goodbye to Daddy?' Michael led me into the room, and averted his gaze. I didn't. Because tubes had been forced into his mouth, Dad's cheeks were distended and bruised. Michael and Mum couldn't bear to look at him, but I refused to leave Dad's body unattended. I sat silently beside him until suddenly, horribly, I felt my arm being raised, and turned to see a long and large needle about to be inserted into it.

'Get away from me!' I screamed at the paramedic. There were two of them, like vultures, hovering over me. One held something that looked like a blanket, and the other waved the terrifying instrument in his hand.

'Let her be. Leave her alone with her father.' Michael hustled the paramedics out of the room.

After a time that seemed like an eternity, Michael gently led me away, and Dad's body was removed.

Without sedation, without alcohol, with only shock as a shield, we three lay down together in our parents' double bed. I lay on one side of Michael, and Mum lay on the other. Michael lay flat on his back and spread his arms, like the branches of a tree. We curled into them, and huddled against the pillow-like pads of his massive shoulders. Then my little-big brother said something I've never heard him admit to before or since. 'I'm afraid.' Overwhelmed, he stared at the ceiling as Dad's mantle descended upon him. 'What's going to become of us?' Michael was all of twenty-four, and in the course of an evening he had gone from being a carefree golden boy to self-anointed man of the family.

PART III
GOING PUBLIC

CHAPTER THIRTY

The trips to Washington and Warsaw were cancelled. I went to work in the family business in order to ensure that Michael stayed in medical school. Like his father before him, Michael buried his Zionist dream. He continued living at home longer than he liked. I lived alone in a downtown apartment. Irena Podbielska Weinfeld was flown in from Warsaw on a special three-month 'Visa of Compassion' in order to tend to Mum, who was wild with grief. Mum had a past she avoided, a present she detested, and thoughts of the future filled her with dread. She'd fly into terrifying rages, aimed mainly at me.

'You're young. You'll have a man. My life is over!' She didn't seem to remember that the moment she lost her husband, I lost my father.

In the midst of his own grief Michael was struggling to complete his medical degree, appease a girlfriend resentful of his new responsibilities, and lend support to his devastated mother. There was no support, no comfort, and no consolation for me.

The family business became a battle zone. The increasingly dangerous manager Dad had been too tender-hearted to fire began manoeuvring to take over. When his attempt was thwarted, he entered into a conspiracy with Dad's chief competitor. Most of the employees took advantage of our vulnerability, except for Dad's loyal secretary, who fed me information she was too frightened to convey directly to Mum. She also taught me to administer the office's daily affairs. When not under attack at the office or by my mother, I turned to doing what my English teachers insisted I was destined to do: I began to write.

In 1986, my first story was published in *Viewpoints,* the now defunct literary supplement of The Canadian Jewish News. It was a fictionalised account of Mum's reunion with Irena Podbielska Weinfeld. The publication of *The Return* made a local celebrity of Mum. A woman in Toronto read it and thought we might be related. She contacted the Montreal editorial office. The office contacted me. I instructed the editor to forward my address to the woman in Toronto. A week later I received a self-addressed, self-stamped envelope from the Toronto reader. Her name was Grace Spiegalman. Her maternal aunt, in Warsaw, was married to one Zygmundt Skotnicki. In *The Return* I used my mother's maiden name and characterised her as 'a lawyer's daughter from Warsaw.' In its editorial notes The Canadian Jewish News described the story as being based on true events. Could we possibly be related? In her letter, Mrs Spiegalman gave a detailed list of the names and occupations of her first cousins from Warsaw, whom she had last seen in London in 1938.

I did not write to Grace Spiegalman. I called Toronto Information, got her home phone number, and telephoned immediately.

'I am Nadja Zajdman. I just got your letter.'

'Oh!'

'I'm not able to answer your questions, but I suspect my mother can. I'm on my way to the office. I'll take the letter with me.'

When the woman in Toronto retrieved her voice, I found it to be the voice of a cultured Englishwoman. Grace Spiegalman was a native of London who married a Canadian soldier and came to Canada as a war bride in 1946.

'But I thought you had written your own story. How old are you, my dear?'

'I'm thirty. How old are you?'

'I'm eighty.' (Grace was lying. She was older.)

'The 'Renata' in the story is my mother. It's her real name.'

'That's what my daughter said. She said it was the daughter who was writing her mother's story, but I didn't believe anyone could write such a story without having lived it. The emotions are so real. How could someone as young as you understand what these people were feeling, and portray it so vividly?'

'Well,' I was embarrassed. 'I'm kind of on the sensitive side.'

After ending the call with Grace I called my mother at the office, read her the letter, and gave her Grace's phone number. Mum was on the line with Grace before I reached the office.

It was a Tuesday in early September. I was scheduled to fly to Toronto at the end of the week, where I would be joining my brother. In June, Michael had graduated from medical school, and was now doing his residency at the Hospital for Sick Children in downtown Toronto. We were planning on driving to Niagara-on-the-Lake's Shaw Festival in order to take in plays. Mum bought an airline ticket, told Grace to expect us, and on Sunday afternoon we gathered in Grace's apartment.

In her youth, Grace listened as avidly to family stories as Mum had done. As I would do. Being a generation older, she was able to supply Mum with missing information. It turned out that Grace and my mother were not directly related, but fell on opposite sides of the same family tree. Armed with information supplied by Grace, Mum reactivated contacts in Warsaw. Four years earlier, she was asked if she might be related to one Barbara Skotnicka, who had married a Frenchman and moved to Paris.

'Not Jewish, and born after the war? Impossible.' Mum made the same logical assumption, and jumped to the same wrong conclusion as her war buddy Irena Weinfeld. 'We can't be related.' Now Mum remembered the exchange, and tracked down the woman who had given her the lead.

In late October, on the weekend of Mum's fifty-eighth birthday, a Paris phone number was forwarded to Mum. Nervously, she made the call.

Barbara and Francois Kern, a childless couple in their thirties, lived in a suburb of Paris. Barbara's father was Łucjan Skotnicki's cousin. In the 1930s Barbara's father served as personal physician to the Shah of Persia. ('I tried to tell my children that my uncle served in the Persian court,' Grace wailed, 'but they just laughed and made fun of me!') Barbara's father left both the court and his Bette Davis look-alike wife when he caught her in flagrante with a foreign diplomat. After the war he married Barbara's mother, a much-younger Catholic woman who sheltered him during the wartime horrors and hunts for Jews. Barbara was born in 1950.

While at university, Barbara worked part-time as a tour guide in Auschwitz. Francois Kern was a university student from Paris who, as part of a student group, came to visit Poland and the camp site. Barbara and Francois met in Auschwitz.

Through Barbara, Mum and Grace learned the fates of the Skotnicki clan. Grace's first cousins were gone now, but their children and grandchildren were scattered across Europe and in Israel, and Barbara was in touch with them all.

As a result of Mum's call to Paris, letters and phone calls flew across three continents. In the summer of 1987, the scattered Skotnicki clan gathered in Paris to reclaim their lost cousin Renata. Grace was too frail to attend the family reunion, so Barbara and Francois flew to Canada to meet her.

In the spring of 1988, the Toronto branch of The Canadian Jewish News ran a feature story about the chain of consequences triggered by the publication of a short story in their literary supplement. Grace was interviewed, and her picture appeared in the paper. Mum sent the editors a floral bouquet. The story's author went unacknowledged.

CHAPTER THIRTY-ONE

In 1983 the Auschwitz survivor Sabina Citron, residing in Toronto, took publisher Ernst Zundel to the Canadian Supreme Court for distributing propaganda purporting the Holocaust to be a hoax. Inconceivably, within the lifetime of its survivors, the Holocaust was on trial. Citron's courage in publicly confronting a neo-Nazi galvanised Mum. She recalled the vows made by the dying and doomed. 'If one of us survives we must tell the world what was done to us. If you live, you must tell.'

In the late 1980s I was training as a docent at Montreal's recently established Holocaust Centre, and joined a group consisting of the sons and daughters of Holocaust survivors, which called itself Second Generation. In the group I met a man whom I brought home to Mama. Technically, he didn't belong in the group, and knew it. Yehudi Lindeman was born in Amsterdam in 1938, on the street where the German refugee family Frank lived, with their daughter Anne. Lindeman felt too old to be among us, yet too young to be with the bona fide survivors. He had attended a conference in Vancouver, where he first heard the psychiatrist Robert Krell, who was born in The Hague in 1940, use the term 'child survivor', denoting European Jews who were under the age of majority during the war. During a break at a meeting, he spoke to me of wishing to start a group for what he considered a sub-section of survivors.

At a documentation workshop I listened to interviews Lindeman had recorded with survivors, and felt he was the right person to interview Mum. I had tried to interview Mum, but the attempt failed because I was trying to protect her from reliving horrific memories, while she was trying to protect me from hearing them. We needed a neutral third party and Lindeman, as a European and professor of literature who approached the subject as story, seemed ideal. Thus began, in the late winter of 1989, an extraordinary series of taped interviews recorded on successive Sunday afternoons in Mum's living room. Lindeman introduces what is to come. 'It's March the fifth, nineteen hundred and eighty-nine. It's a Sunday. (It was also fifty years to the day of Alek's engagement party and his ill-fated fiancée's 21st birthday.) We're in the home of Renata Zajdman at 6795 Korczak in Montreal.' In Canada, from 1982 until the end of the millennium, Mum lived on a street named after her childhood hero Janusz Korczak.

Revealing the details of her traumatic past to a sympathetic third party seemed to burst a dam in Mum. Once she began to speak, she seemed unable to stop. We didn't want her to stop. As a storyteller, Mum was mesmerising. She was also a living witness to the greatest cataclysm of the 20th century. In the late winter of 1989 Mum was a woman of sixty, with total recall, who spun her grim tale like a traumatised Scheherazade. Lindeman and I listened, spellbound, until a click on the tape recorder signalled it was time to insert a fresh cassette.

The trap door to memory was sprung, and after the sessions Mum stayed up half the night doing something she hadn't done since she was a schoolgirl: she wrote. On the nights I stayed in her apartment I found Mum sitting up in bed, the lights in her room blazing, with sheaths of paper filled with her handwriting, strewn across the blanket.

'I remember! I remember! I'm remembering so much more!' These nocturnal notes would form the basis of a private memoir intended 'as a reference for my children and grandchildren'. (A copy of this work is now archived with the United States Holocaust Memorial Museum in Washington.)

While Lindeman was teaching during the week and interviewing Mum on Sundays, he was also using his connections at McGill University to create an audio-visual documentation centre that would film interviews with Holocaust survivors. Mum was one of the first interviewees in a project called Living Testimonies.

Lindeman's dream of creating an association for European Jews who were children during the war was about to be realised.

'Oh Nadja, your mother has such a nice, big, comfortable living room.'

'Don't be coy.' I saw through Yehudi. 'Just ask her.' The Montreal chapter of the International Association of Child Survivors was born in my mother's living room.

***

'…I never thought that I would be able to sit here and talk about these things. I never had the courage to do it. And then I saw other people coming out… and then, a few times, I heard people say, about people like me, you are actually an endangered species, because after you are gone there will be nobody else, there will be no one else left to tell the real story. And my children really wanted me to do it. And maybe because it is fifty years now, 1939-1989, I feel that everything is coming full circle, that I have to do it, that maybe my time is running out.'

Renata Skotnicka-Zajdman speaking to Rabbi Grafstein
in the McGill film studio, 6 June 1989

On the morning of 6 June 1989, Mum entered a small studio located in Montreal's McGill University. She was ushered onto a platform, seated in one of three chairs, and a body mike was attached to the inside of her brightly-coloured top. Seated across from Mum were Yehudi Lindeman and Sarah Leah Grafstein. At the time, Grafstein was one of Canada's six ordained female rabbis. She was also an amateur filmmaker. It was Rabbi Grafstein who taught Professor Lindeman how to use a video camera. During this session she would serve as co-interviewer. Lindeman had succeeded in realising his dream of an audio-visual project whose mission and mandate was to film and preserve the oral histories of Holocaust survivors. The project, which he called Living Testimonies, predated filmmaker Steven Spielberg's Shoah Foundation by five years. If Mum wasn't the project's first interviewee, then she was its second.

On this bright day in June, Mum is visibly nervous. Her hooded eyelids and the expression in her eyes suggest that she has barely slept. She had grown accustomed to speaking to Lindeman in her living room, on her territory, and by extension into a cassette recorder that she often forgot was there. But she is intimidated by the prospect of performing in a formal studio setting. She knows she must distil the telling of her epic tale to fit the confines of a four-hour interview. For the first time Mum is about to undergo what she came to call 'my open heart surgery', exposing her wounds and telling her traumatic tale to those who not only have never heard it before, but are unfamiliar with its background. She senses the significance of the occasion and is determined to get it right.

At first Mum is so tense and disoriented that she addresses the camera directly, until her interviewers gently correct her. Because Lindeman already knows Mum's story, he is able to lead her into it. Mum met Grafstein several times before this interview and has developed a warm and friendly relationship with her. Together the professor and the rabbi relax Mum and guide her until she gets her grip, sheds her self-consciousness, and mesmerises her audience.

The highlight of this interview is a consistent lie. Mum's year of birth is given as 1926. In fact, Mum was born in 1928. Mum began lying about her age in order not to be taken for a child and not to be taken with the children. On official documents her year of birth is listed as 1925, which is the year Irena Podbielska was born. Post-war, Mum perpetrated the lie in order to maintain her new and desperately won independence. Having inadvertently evaded the sheltering umbrella of the Canadian Jewish Congress's War Orphans Project, her first years in Canada were harder than they needed to be.

During the interview, whenever Mum is asked how old she was at a certain point in time, she responds instantly with a two-year mark-up. She never trips up and never gets it wrong. When Grafstein mentions how young Mum was to have witnessed and endured so much horror, the rabbi's expression of sympathy is met with stone-faced silence. Only Mum knows that, as young as her audience believes her to be, she was even younger.

Though her official documents state Mum's year of birth as 1925, when Mum met Dad she gave her year of birth as 1926. Mum led Dad to believe she was nine and a half years his junior. In reality Mum was eleven and a half years younger than Dad, but she was afraid that confessing to an age gap of more than ten years might make him uncomfortable, so she foisted upon the love of her life what was likely an unnecessary lie. Because Dad believed the woman he married was born in 1926, not only their children but also their entire social circle had to be convinced of it, too. It was only near the end of her life that Mum set the record straight so that the date on her gravestone would be the right one.

Within a few years of this interview, Rabbi Grafstein emigrated to the United States, and Mum took on the role of Lindeman's co-interviewer. At McGill University's Living Testimonies oral history project Mum would serve as researcher, co-interviewer and, ultimately, its associate director, for the rest of her life.

CHAPTER THIRTY-TWO

Early in 1990, in *The Canadian Jewish News*, Mum read a book review of a memoir written by an American army veteran.

At war's end, a thirty-four-year old Jewish lieutenant from Chicago named Albert Hutler was appointed displaced persons' officer for a three-hundred mile region of southwest Germany. Educated as a lawyer and trained as a social worker, Hutler balanced military demands with the exigencies of traumatised people. Though Jewish survivors were not the only DPs in his charge, they were his main concern. In his efforts to restore their health and dignity, on their behalf he and his staff requisitioned office buildings, apartment complexes, private homes, and at least one castle. Then they confiscated every useful article found on the requisitioned premises. They organised medical facilities, soup kitchens, nurseries, and sponsored religious services. They even supplied a keg of wine as a gift on every railway car transporting French returnees. (When Hutler learnt that repatriated Frenchmen were demonstrating in the streets of Paris because the government subsidies being given to help them rebuild their lives were also being granted to their fellow French Jews, the wine stopped flowing.)

Jewish survivors were given work as translators on Hutler's staff. When he discovered that 249 Polish Jewish survivors of a death camp, 'liberated' in the French sector, were placed in a Polish DPs camp, the lieutenant risked court martial by arranging to have them transferred to his sector in the American zone. He signed passes and identifying papers on American Military Government stationery, enabling survivors to move freely as they searched for loved ones.

As word of the guardian-angel-of-a-Jewish-officer-with-the-name-that-sounded-like-Hitler spread among the survivors, they descended on his office. In Hutler's office, Wednesday was 'Jewish Day.' On Wednesdays, displaced Jews gathered at American Military Government headquarters to tell their stories to Lieutenant Hutler and the Jewish chaplain. He did what he could to ease their transition into the post-war world. In his memoir, called *Agony of Survival*, Hutler relates his own anguish in the face of their tragedy, and his awe at their resilience. In a letter to his wife he wrote:

> *'At yesterday's meeting, a man with a record of six years at Buchenwald, with its 'standing room', its 'incinerator', the 'small camp', a man broken in body and yet with hope – hope because he has a sister in England and a cousin in America – came to the office. He talked of his own daughters who he heard are in a camp in the Russian area. His eyes glow as he speaks, and yet he does not know whether they are alive or dead. He speaks gently of his wife, whom the Nazis murdered. What can we do for him? A pair of shoes, a suit, a few suits of underwear, and a shirt – we can give him these. But can the Germans be made to give him back his wife, his girls, or even his healthy body? America just won't believe…'*

Albert Hutler was awarded the Bronze Star for his work with French refugees and DPs in Germany, and decorated by the Dutch government with the Order of Orange-Nassau with Swords – their highest honour – for helping refugees from Holland. He formed lifelong friendships with several of the survivors who settled in the United States. Then he received a call from Renata.

'Are you Lieutenant Hutler?'

Taken aback, the veteran responded, 'Well, I WAS! And who are you?!'

Mum choked up. 'I was one of the DPs under your protection in your sector. I passed as Polish Catholic during the war. You wrote and signed a document restoring my true identity. I still have it.'

'Lee!' Al shouted. 'Pick up the extension line!' Al's wife Leonore quickly picked up the line.

Lee choked up. Al choked up. Listening on an extension line in Canada, I was close to tears, too. Then the old soldier called us to order by announcing, 'I didn't remain a lieutenant. By the time I was demobilised, I reached the rank of captain!'

Mum sent Hutler a video of the four-hour filmed interview she gave for Living Testimonies. Hutler sent Mum a copy of his memoir, which he inscribed 'To Renata Zajdman, who belonged to Hutler's Jews in Mannheim, Germany when both of us were living under the American flag'.

I had long been fascinated by a photograph in my mother's possession. It was taken in Heidelberg within two weeks of VE Day. It was a wedding picture, but this wedding was unlike any wedding I had heard of, or attended. It was the first Jewish wedding held in Germany after the war, and Mum was the bridesmaid. Between Mum's vivid storytelling and background information culled from Hutler's memoir, I was able to write the story of this unique historical event. *A Wedding in Heidelberg* was first published in *Viewpoints,* the same literary supplement which, in 1986, published my story *The Return.* It would subsequently appear in the Canadian Jewish anthology *Parchment* and in my first short story collection, *Bent Branches.* After Mum's death, the story resurfaced in *The Saturday Evening Post.*

Figure 7: The first Jewish wedding held in post-war Germany on Sunday afternoon, 13 or 20 May 1945. It was organised and attended by U.S. Army personnel. Post-war Jewish weddings were small gatherings consisting of the young. Parents and grandparents were noticeable by their absence. Most of them were dead.

Before submitting the story for publication I sent it to Hutler for feedback.

'You've got the period and atmosphere right. You've also portrayed Colonel Winning well. He was a great guy. He was a colonel with heart. Now let me tell you a story about Colonel Winning!' Thus began a correspondence that continued for over a year, until Mum and I flew to San Diego.

'Rise and shine!' Mum sang out. 'It's three o'clock!' It was three o'clock in the morning. I stumbled into my clothes. On the frigid street outside Mum's window, the blaring siren of a rolling snowplough ensured I stayed awake. A pre-arranged driver arrived at Mum's door and put our suitcases into the trunk of his car. The windshield wiper clicked rhythmically, like a metronome, batting aside the lace-like flakes which were dropping softly in the pristine, pre-dawn world of a Victorian snow-globe.

On board our flight, I watched drowsily as ice was melted, as if by unseen angels, on the great metal wings of the plane. Mum was worried we might miss our connecting flight. In Toronto we discovered our connecting flight held, if not for us, then perhaps for the television actors I spotted entering Business Class for the day-long flight to California. I settled into my seat, accepted a cup of complimentary wine, and wrapped my ears in a headset. Flying across the continent above frozen clouds, I was lulled by a score of melodies half-a-century old. In my overheated imagination, trombones slid over the airwaves of the BBC. Glenn Miller's rich sweet swing, which Mum called 'freedom music,' heralded the approach of the American patrol. The St. Louis Blues marched across the combat zone. Moonlight cocktails mixed destruction with stardust; sunrise saw devastation, and broadcast serenades. Dreamily I sipped on a California rosé.

In a bathroom at San Francisco's airport, I removed my long johns.

We sat in a lounge, waiting for the commuter flight to San Diego. Mum fumed.

'What's holding up that goddam plane?!' It was the last lap of our journey before the reunion with the officer Mum hadn't seen in forty-five years. For Mum, the delay was maddening.

Playfully I suggested, 'Maybe they have to de-ice the wings.'

'Hmmph.' Mum was ready to detonate, and I knew it. Pressing my luck, I pressed on. 'He won't show up in a jeep, you know.'

'Oh shut up!'

Despite the photographs they had mailed to each other since Mum initiated contact, she still pictured Hutler as a young and angry man perched on a jeep, ordering Germans out of their homes, requisitioning castles, and supervising the repatriation of human masses. I pictured him in black and white, a cross between Richard Widmark and Richard Basehart, a straight-shooting Yank with his helmet cocked rakishly at an angle, alternately storming villages, liberating concentration camps, and handing out Hershey chocolate bars. I giggled at the image.

'What's so funny?' Mum charged.

'Nothing.' I leaned my head on one of Mum's hiked-up shoulders. *'Fraulein.'* Suggestively, I crooned. *'Voulez-vous schlafen mit mir?'* It was the pick-up line Mum had overheard used by GIs; a tangle of German and French.

'Goddamit Sharon Nadja! You're just like your father!'

'Thank you.' I batted my eyelashes. 'I take that as a compliment.' Pecking Mum on the cheek, I took her hand, and held it. 'This is exciting.'

'Yeah yeah.' Mum acknowledged, and relaxed. A little.

The commuter flight arrived. Boarding was announced. Mum jumped. I continued holding her hand. That's what I was there for.

It was a cloudless morning. The towering palm trees lining the sidewalks waved like giant fans. Bougainvillea, scarlet hibiscus, violet irises and velvety birds-of-paradise bloomed exuberantly outside a back window overlooking a subtropical garden. The tranquil, wealthy enclave curved around a bay. A car pulled up in front of the bungalow at the top of the hill and a reporter, an Orson Wellesian figure with a smoker's cough and a limp, squeezed out of it. He was a friend of the Hutlers, and was invited to interview the woman who had risen out of the ashes. The interview seemed to serve everyone's purpose. It would help sell Hutler's book, and it was a great scoop for the reporter.

Within minutes, it became appallingly clear that the reporter was historically illiterate. The interview devolved into a form of interrogation. I intervened, but Mum brushed me off, believing she had to endure abuse in order to be a good guest. Whatever her host Hutler felt, like a good soldier, he kept to himself.

In years to come Mum learned to deflect attacks by journalists and even to turn the tables on them, but this was her first exposure to what I came to think of as Shoah Business, and she was unprepared.

For the rest of the week, reporters and camera crews invaded the bungalow at the top of the hill. Mum was interrogated, and her memory of historical events challenged. She was instructed to smile adoringly at the embarrassed veteran while he reluctantly held up his book. I went into hiding, going for long melancholy walks on the aptly named Shelter Island. Unable to rescue Mum because she refused rescue, I brooded. The more Mum felt compelled to perform for the press, the more I withdrew. By the time we returned home, we were barely speaking to each other.

'Do you want me to come over?'

'No. I'll take an aspirin and try to sleep.'

'I'll keep the ringer on in case you change your mind.' Mum reached for me in the only way she knew; by making herself sick. Protective of Mum since childhood, I mothered my mother to the point of being a nag. However, since returning from San Diego I had become distant.

Half-heartedly, I glanced at a late movie. Before it ended, the phone rang again.

'I feel horrible. Please come home.'

I called a cab, grabbed my bunch of Mum's apartment keys, slipped mild herbal sedatives into my purse, and packed oranges. Mum's fridge was generally empty; she never cared to cook. Now widowed and living alone, she saw no reason to.

On entering the apartment I found Mum trembling at the edge of her newly purchased queen-sized bed, like a terrified child.

'My arms and legs are burning! I feel like I'm on fire!'

'Do you want me to call an ambulance?' I couldn't think what else to do.

'No!' Mum's nursing training came back to her. 'Anyway, I know it's not my heart. It's my arms and legs. I can't move them! I can't take off my nightgown, and the material is burning me!' I lifted the flannel nightgown and tried to remove Mum's arms from its sleeves. Her hands and feet were truly twisted, and her extremities were startlingly gnarled. Propelled by instinct, I fed her a herbal sedative. As it took effect I soaked cloths in warm water, and applied compresses to her hands.

'Did you have a bad dream?'

'Not that I know of. I didn't have any flashbacks today. A few hours ago, I was fine!' As she felt my hands on hers, Mum's breathing eased. Staring at the ceiling, she wiggled her fingers. 'How do they look?'

'Like you're playing the piano.' Desperately Mum gripped my hand. 'I don't want to die alone. Don't leave me!' I continued applying compresses. Mum gulped. Her eyes pleaded. 'My throat is dry. I'm very thirsty.'

I peeled an orange. Just as when Mum lost her voice after being interviewed brutally by a German psychiatrist in the wake of the Eichmann trial, the San Diego reporter's rough handling amounted to violation. Mum seemed capable of surviving everything except social embarrassment. In order to perform for the Hutlers and appear a good guest, as in wartime, she suppressed her visceral response. But the Holocaust is obsessed with its survivors, and the subconscious will not be long denied. In the form of a psychosomatic inflammation, repressed rage was rising to the fore.

I coaxed, 'Do you think you can feed yourself now?' Reassured, Mum cooperated.

'I'll try.'

Mum sucked on the flesh of the orange. Insistently she clung to my hand, and finally fell asleep.

Shards of dawn slit the vertical blinds. I scanned the gallery of ancestors living on my mother's bedroom wall. There was a faded-looking Sarah Leah, in her dark wig and high-collared coat, her tired eyes gazing resignedly from behind tiny round spectacles. A picture of the grey-bearded patriarch Michal who, mercifully, had been taken early, hung on the wall alongside Leah as her husband never lived to see her.

Their youngest son Abram was part of the gallery, now. His image was everywhere. In one photograph he was an open-shirted, bare-footed jester on a Florida boat, cocking-a-snook at the camera; in another he was a loose-limbed, warm-eyed, beautiful, young man idling in a Paris doorway. Then he became the sardonic, overweight, middle-aged businessman, uncomfortable in a suit, out-of-character in a tie, triumphing over these impositions by tipping his yarmulke at an irreverently lopsided angle. Snapping back to a remote past, he was the lanky, intense, grieving youth in knee pants, standing guard with his grandmother at his father's freshly covered grave.

I shut my eyes and spoke to my father. 'I'm tired, Daddy. I don't know how I can carry Mum's suffering anymore.'

I opened my eyes and looked down at my mother's face. Her luxuriant hair, shot through with silver threads, fell against the pillow in dark waves. Her pale, translucent face revealed nothing of what she had endured. It was in my mother's eyes that I saw the outlines of her history, from the orphaned waif wandering the streets of the Warsaw Ghetto, to the toughened teenager hiding in the open, to the young refugee, aged beyond her time, scrubbing the floors and toilets of wealthy Montreal matrons. I could remember the devoted wife working slavishly in a home-grown family business. Now, I cradled an ageing widow in my arms.

As I studied my mother's face, tears coursed down my cheeks. Would I ever resolve the conflict between pride at being born to such a courageous and resilient woman, and resentment at having this same tortured soul as a mother? I am part of that history, and its victim, as well.

Figure 8: Abram in June 1968

I watched over Renata all through the night. Her features softened. She rested.

The family of ancestors pressed in upon me. I surrendered to the hold of my mother's hand, and all the photographs of my father on the walls and the dresser and on my mother's nightstand, smiled down upon us both.

CHAPTER THIRTY-THREE

'The Polish policeman had a brother (in-law.) He looked like a vicious hoodlum. We'd walk through the streets of Warsaw and onlookers thought he was an informer taking me to the Gestapo. I felt so safe with him... He died in the Uprising. Not the Jewish uprising; the uprising a year later...'

Renata Skotnicka-Zajdman speaking to Rabbi Grafstein in the McGill film studio, 6 June 1989.

Into the 1990s, Mum became increasingly active in Holocaust Education. She trained as a docent at Montreal's Holocaust Centre. She worked as a researcher, interviewer, and served as associate director on McGill University's oral history project Living Testimonies. She attended international conferences. She lectured to students in schools and on group tours, both at home and abroad. She reunited long-lost relatives and rescued the lost identities of hidden children. She also confronted the former classmate who betrayed her in the Polish hamlet in the winter of 1942. Mum became a wounded healer transforming lives.

Each spring Mum travelled to Poland, spending an average of three months there. She became the North American liaison for the Association of Hidden Children in Poland. In Warsaw Mum roomed with friends, and worked in an office located on the street where she had lived as a child.

Some of those in Poland hidden during the war when they were children came late to the recognition of their Jewish roots. Those who married mostly inter-married, and their children were raised as Catholics.

At least one became a priest, and several became nuns. Some were still too frightened to acknowledge their antecedents. Many lived in poverty. Mum lobbied for the establishment of pensions for those robbed of their parents and inheritance. Łucjan's daughter won her case. She was also integrating her many identities and becoming the Holocaust educator and activist Renata Skotnicka-Zajdman.

What she was doing for others, Mum was about to do for herself. In 1997, during a search to discover the fate of another child hidden in wartime, Mum stumbled on clues suggesting her wartime rescuer Janek Bartczak might be alive.

During a time of war and in a place of horror, friendship flourished between two young men wooing two Jewish sisters. One of the men was a Polish Catholic, the other, a Polish Jew. The Catholic youth became a smuggler. When Warsaw's Jews were walled into their ghetto, Janek's business activities allowed him daily access to the girl he loved. Unknown even to the members of his immediate family, he joined the underground resistance movement.

Janek Bartczak was generally perceived as a dandy. His brother-in-law, a policeman who patrolled outside the Ghetto gates, dismissed him as a spiritual lightweight. Janek strutted through the streets of the Ghetto in knee-high black-leather boots, a black leather coat, and a Tyrolean-type hat. His hair was flaxen and his features Slavic-sharp. His intimidating appearance made a powerful impression on his Jewish friend's teenage sister Renata. His phantom would swagger through the back alleys of her memory for the next fifty years. Trying to transmit his image as vividly as she could, Renata came to call her ghost 'Richard Widmark', after the sinister-looking film star.

During the height of the deportations in the summer of 1942, Janek's brother-in-law arrested Renata at the Ghetto gates. The arrest was pre-arranged. Pawel Golombek used his position to lead to safety the Jews he was supposed to be shutting in. His apartment became a safe house. He and his family supported not only themselves, but also the escapees they sheltered, by the smuggling activities of his wife's two brothers, and by selling moonshine manufactured in their kitchen, as well as his policeman's salary. An unquestioned arrest, a child snatched from *Umschlagplatz* (the central train platform where Ghetto Jews were collected and carted off for mass murder), hidden under his coat, and delivered to the sanctuary presided over by his wife and mother-in-law – Golombek committed these audacious acts under the noses of the Germans and his anti-Semitic neighbours, acts which, had they been discovered, would have led not only to his execution, but to the execution of his entire family.

***

During a brief and unhappy return to Poland in 1945, Renata's brother led her to believe that Janek Bartczak was killed on the Warsaw barricades during the second uprising in August of 1944. She mourned him, and in her mind, she buried him. Over fifty years later, in her capacity as an activist in an international network developing among Jews who survived genocide, my mother Renata decided to find out what happened to the child with whom she shared sanctuary in the Golombek household. Ultimately, she would. But first she would make another discovery.

While searching for Isabella, the child hidden and raised by the Golombeks, Mum stumbled upon an old address for one Janek Bartczak. Like many Poles, it appeared he had gravitated to Chicago.

My mother considered me her memory keeper, and regularly ran spot-checks. As she got older, the imperative to impart the legacy of her spectres grew increasingly intense. Deceptively casual, she queried, 'Who was Pawel Golombek?'

Innocently, I answered, 'He was a Polish policeman.'

'Correct,' Mum pronounced, like a schoolteacher who was satisfied, but only for the moment. 'And who was Janek Bartczak?' The bar was raised higher. 'Ahhh – Richard Widmark?' Mum smiled. Close enough.

'What happened to Bartczak?' The interrogation was relentless. I had gotten away with the doppelganger analogy; now I knew I'd better get this one right.

'He was killed in the August '44 uprising.'

'Not necessarily.' Mum was savouring the moment when she could deliver the punch line. She then called a member of her network in Chicago, a woman for whom she'd been instrumental in reuniting with a twin brother in Poland. The woman went to the address the next day.

'He doesn't live there anymore. The neighbours say he retired and moved to Arizona.' Within the week Bartczak resurrected, metaphorically enough, in Phoenix.

'I have to go and see him.' Mum stated the obvious, and immediately began to plan. 'I've got enough flight points on my Visa card to make the trip, but where would I stay?'

Instantly I turned to the telephone and called Rabbi Grafstein, whom I'd met when she helped to establish Living Testimonies. At the time of Mum's first interview, Rabbi Grafstein signed a contract with a Canadian synagogue. The synagogue's board of directors broke the contract when they discovered they had hired a woman. Rabbi Grafstein sued the synagogue, won her case, then applied and was accepted as a prison chaplain in Phoenix, Arizona.

Along with changing her country, Rabbi Grafstein changed her too-Jewish-sounding first names to the Hebrew Ayla. After serving her term as prison chaplain, Grafstein was hired by a Reform synagogue. To her American congregants she was known as Rabbi Ayla. Rabbi Ayla would marry an American businessman ten years her junior, and together they adopted a half-black boy. Only in America.

'Your mother will stay with me.' Rabbi Ayla responded as I hoped she would. 'Meeting Renata changed my life.'

'Janek's story must be told.' Mum moved into crusader mode. 'But who can interview him? Regina says his English is poor.'

'Are you kidding?' Incredulous, I stared at the woman who was missing the obvious. 'You will!'

'Me?' Mum was overwhelmed by the suggestion.

'Who could do it better? You'll conduct the interview in Polish. Everything you've done has led to this.'

As I became aware of the obvious, my breath caught. 'You appear to have been chosen.'

'Oh my.' As the import of my words sunk in, Mum shuddered. 'But who would set it up? We have cameras and a technician in the studio here, but how would we do it in Phoenix?'

Once more, I called Rabbi Ayla, who then placed a call to California. Mum was officially registered as an interviewer for Steven Spielberg's recently established Shoah Foundation. Technicians and equipment were expedited to Arizona.

Mum flew to Phoenix at Easter. The metaphors were becoming outrageous.

When Mum and Janek reunited, she fell into his arms.

'You're alive, you're alive.' She huddled against the older man's chest, the way she had on the night of the bombardment. 'I still can't believe it.'

The elderly gentleman held her close. 'So are you,' he whispered. 'This is even harder to believe.'

Janek was now in his mid-seventies. His flaxen-coloured hair had thinned out, and what was left of it was white. He was still vigorous and strong. Living in freedom and peace had allowed Janek to shed his tough persona, and his natural sweetness shone through the features of his broad Slavic face.

As they got their bearings, the rescued and rescuer updated each other on what had turned out to be their lives. 'My brother and I accepted that you were trapped and killed on the barricades during the '44 uprising.' Mum gazed at her wartime rescuer, in wonder. 'How did you manage to escape?'

'The same way you did, *moja kochana*.' Janek gazed tenderly at the woman, now in late middle age, whose fate he had accepted would forever remain a mystery. 'I escaped through the sewers. Unlike you, however, once I got out, I didn't have far to go. When I hauled myself out of a manhole I looked up to see a policeman staring at me. It was Pawel, my very own brother-in-law!'

'*Mój Boże!*' Mum erupted, unconsciously shifting into her wartime Catholic persona. 'My Lord!'

'Oh yes!' Janek agreed. 'Can you imagine? I was starving. I was stinking, I was wet and I was filthy, and I resurface in downtown Warsaw like a vision out of hell!'

'What a shock for Pawel,' Mum gasped, 'But a happy shock!'

'Oh, I'm not sure he recognised me right away, but I recognised him! I think the shock for Pawel was discovering that I had joined the Underground and fought in the second uprising. He didn't think much of me, until then.' Janek was obviously proud to have earned the respect of his heroic brother-in-law.

Continuing to fight in the underground resistance movement, Janek was captured by the Germans and sent to a prisoner-of-war camp in Germany. He escaped, made his way to Italy and joined the Polish army-in-exile under General Anders's command. Before war's end, Polish warriors were shattered by the news that the dream of an independent Poland was lost; betrayed at Yalta by Roosevelt and Churchill. Janek's unit was transferred to Britain. Like many Polish soldiers and sailors and airmen who helped to save the country that ultimately betrayed them, Janek felt he couldn't go home. While still in power, Churchill offered British citizenship to displaced Polish servicemen and women. After he was ousted from power, the new Labour government tried to scare displaced Polish military personnel into leaving. Like thousands of Polish refugee servicemen and women, Janek decided his future lay elsewhere. He emigrated to South America. Only in 1947 was he able to notify his family in now-communist Poland that he was alive. In time, he married an Argentinian woman. Janek's wife was now serving coffee and cake. In awe, she watched the woman who had risen like a phoenix from the ashes. So did their son, Antonio, with his Jewish wife and their two young boys. Their grandfather had never spoken of his wartime exploits. True heroes are silent, or dead.

Unlike most subjects interviewed for Holocaust oral history projects, Janek was relaxed. He told his tale as if holding a long-overdue conversation. He was almost gleeful as he recounted how often and how well he outwitted both the German occupiers and his treacherous Polish neighbours. When Mum asked why he behaved as he had, Janek responded by placing his hand over his heart. His testimony was a gift to both of them. The woman whom he rescued as a child was now a rescuer of Memory.

When Mum returned home, she made it her mission to have Janek officially recognised and honoured by the Israeli government as a member of an elite group known as Righteous Among The Nations. Israeli law stipulates that at least two living witnesses submit depositions in order to validate the nomination of a candidate. Having yet to locate the hidden child Isabella (though they would), Mum's network launched a search for Janek's wartime Jewish lover. She was traced to New York City. In the intervening fifty years, Ada had been twice divorced and recently widowed.

'You've got to do this,' Mum commanded.

'Of course I will.' Ada was in a daze, reeling from the news that her wartime lover was alive. Ada and Janek reunited over a telephone line, but they would never set eyes on each other, again.

Before leaving for her annual stay in Poland, Mum called Janek to say goodbye. He was a widower, now.

Three days after Mum's departure, Antonio called me.

'Oh gosh! I'm so sorry. I'm so very, very sorry.'

'Will you tell your mother?'

'Of course I will.'

Calculating the time change between North America and Europe, I estimated that I could still reach Mum in her Warsaw office.

'Sweetheart! This isn't our usual time to talk. Is something going on? What's up?'

My silence sent Mum into alert. 'Something is wrong. What is it?'

Sadly, I told her. Janek Bartczak suffered a stroke and died a second and final time. He was seventy-nine years old.

'No! Oh no! I'd only just found him and now I've lost him again!' Mum was grief-stricken.

'No Mum.' My voice was soft with sorrow. 'You haven't lost him. Antonio told me his father died at peace because he finally found out what happened to you and to the other child sheltered in his home. Who he was and what he did won't be lost because you recorded it. The Shoah Foundation will keep Janek's story and memory safe. He's safe now, Mum. He's safe. Janek will never be lost again.'

Mum was in tears, and I was near tears. Yet, despite her grief, my mother recognised the truth of my words. Not only had she taken the time to say goodbye, but Renata, the wild orphan of war, also found a way of saying Thank You.

Since Janek was no longer in a position to receive it, a notice was sent to Antonio, summoning him to an Israeli consulate. In a desert city in the American Southwest, in a ceremony witnessed by his Jewish wife and their two sons, Janek's son was presented with a certificate and medal for his father's part in providing a safe harbour during a violent storm, and for his magnificent, and now-stilled heart.

CHAPTER THIRTY-FOUR

At a conference in Israel, Mum met a woman from Warsaw whom she came to consider one of her best friends. When she was six months old, Bieta Ficowska was smuggled out of the Warsaw Ghetto in a wooden crate. Holes were punched in the crate, to give her air. She was sedated and asleep when the stepson of the woman who became her adopted mother removed her from a world on the verge of annihilation. A silver spoon engraved with her birth date and first name was placed beside her. The Catholic midwife who took her in worked with the social worker Irena Sendler.

In the summer of 1942, Bieta's birth mother telephoned from behind the walls of Warsaw's Ghetto in order to listen, through the receiver, to the babbling of her baby girl. At the time Bieta's mother, Henia Koppel, was in her early twenties. Her husband Josef was significantly older. Before the war he was a financier. Henia kept, concealed, a cheque book from a Swiss bank, which she expected would enable the family to begin life anew, once the Nazi madness passed. In the meantime, her consolation was that her child was safe.

Bieta was placed in the care of a Catholic nanny. She was scheduled for baptism. The nanny arranged to meet with Bieta's grandfather when he emerged on the Aryan Side in a work detail, under German guard. In tears, the observant Jew handed the Catholic nanny a tiny white dress and a solid gold cross.

Before boarding the train that took her to Treblinka, Henia Koppel heard the voice of her child one last time.

***

During the war, the social worker Irena Sendler headed the children's section of Zegota, a clandestine organisation created to rescue Jews. Working with Warsaw's social welfare department, Sendler held a special permit allowing her entry into the Jewish ghetto in order to check for signs of typhus. The German occupiers feared that recurrent epidemics of the disease would spread beyond the ghetto walls. It was under the pretext of conducting inspections that Sendler and her associates, consisting of nurses and social workers, smuggled out infants and toddlers. Sometimes the children were whisked away by ambulance. Sometimes they were carried out in suitcases or, as in Bieta's case, a simple crate. In this manner Sendler and her associates managed to rescue 2,500 Jewish children, placing them for protection in orphanages, convents, and private homes. Since it was necessary to supply these children with new names and identities Sendler, with the intention of returning these children to their parents after the war, kept an unofficial record by writing down the children's original names on slips of paper, placing the slips into a jar, and then burying the jar underground.

Eventually Sendler was discovered, arrested, tortured and sentenced to death. She was already in a prison yard, on the verge of facing a firing squad when, in an audacious raid, comrades rescued the rescuer.

In 1965, Sendler was one of the first Polish wartime rescuers to be recognised and honoured by Israel's Yad Vashem. Her fellow Poles were not impressed. By the 1990s Sendler was an elderly widow, permanently crippled due to the torture she endured in wartime, and living in borderline poverty. Bieta was taking care of her.

It was through Bieta that Mum would be introduced to Irena Sendler. Mum was with Sendler in Warsaw when word came that a group of American teenagers were about to call on her. In February of 2000 they wrote Sendler a letter, and Sendler wrote back.

'I have no idea what this is about. You'd better stick around, Renata. You speak English. I'm going to need a translator.'

Three high school girls from the hamlet of Uniontown, in Kansas, discovered the identity of Sendler while researching material for a high school history project. They assumed she was dead and were searching for the site of her grave, only to discover that Sendler was alive. The teenagers from Kansas wrote and performed a short play about Sendler's wartime exploits. What began as a high school history project led to media attention and a ten-year North American tour. The kids from Kansas also presented the play in Poland. When Mum met the kids from Kansas she also met their teacher, Norman Conard.

Mum established a pattern. In spring, she would leave for her annual three-month stay in Poland. I was always glad, and even a little relieved, to see her go. I felt like I was sending a kid to summer camp. As much as I loved the woman who was my mother and often felt like my child, as long as I knew she was having a good time, I welcomed the break.

Still, when Mum left, I went through a form of withdrawal. I'd move into her apartment on Friday evenings and stay over the weekends; cooking in her kitchen, sleeping in her bed, wearing her nightgowns, cocooning under her blankets, and sensing the ancestors watching me from the walls.

While Mum was in Poland, we remained in touch. I wrote long and discursive letters giving her news of home and sent them, first to Bieta's fax machine and later, to Bieta's computer. They were delivered during the week and by the time I called on the weekend Mum was up-to-date, and filled me in on news from her end.

Into the third month of Mum's overseas stay I would get signs that increased in quantity and intensity as her arrival date approached. I missed her and she confessed that, into the third month she was beginning to miss me and felt ready to come home. In July Mum would return to an apartment freshly cleaned, the air-conditioners recently installed, the pantry stocked with bottled water, the refrigerator filled with yoghurt, berries, orange juice and bagels, and the embrace of my open arms.

One morning, the day after her arrival, she confessed to an acquaintance, 'My real friends are overseas. If my daughter wasn't here, I wouldn't come back at all.'

CHAPTER THIRTY-FIVE

The day after Christmas of 2004, an earthquake in the Indian Ocean set off a tsunami that drowned 230,000 people in fourteen countries. It was one of the deadliest recorded natural disasters. The year 2005 began with international mourning.

I was always with Mum at the start of the year. Her mother died of typhus in a Russian hospital at six p.m. on New Year's Day in 1940. For Mum, the first day of the year was always the hardest day of the year. On New Year's Day of 2005, Mum lay on her bed under a portrait of her mother, listening to the news on the radio. She cocked her head.

'Do you think I'm going to die this year?' Mum posed the question as if asking if I expected to see rain.

'No.' I lied. Both of us were absorbing morbid vibrations. The news ended. Mum remained silent. Chillingly, an instrumental of Swing Low, Sweet Chariot played on the radio.

Invariably Mum and I went to the movies on New Year's Night. At a friend's recommendation we went to see the recently released Finding Neverland. The story behind the creation of J.M. Barrie's classic Peter Pan was enchanting. It also felt ominous.

'Why did she have to die?' The real-life Peter asks Barrie, after the funeral of his mother, who has passed from cancer.

Barrie opens a copy of the book he has just written.

'Your mother will live forever in the pages of this book.'

Mum did not die in 2005. By winter's end, she was belatedly diagnosed with the cancer that would kill her.

When Mum turned seventy, she began having what are referred to as 'health issues.' She developed erratic blood pressure.

'I used to be able to get upset without having a problem!' She wailed.

'Perhaps.' I acknowledged. 'But you gave everyone else a problem.' In this case, 'everyone else' meant me.

As we spent more and more time on emergency wards, I changed my mother's doctors as rapidly as I would have changed her cleaning ladies, had she let me. Replacing a doctor is no mean feat in Quebec's medical care system. Still, in the summer of 2003 Mum did not return from Poland on schedule, because she had such a dangerous episode of fluctuating blood pressure that she was deemed unfit to travel. Private doctors called in by Bieta patched her up and got her well enough to return home despite the fact that, before leaving, Mum said to me, 'If I die in Poland, don't bring me home.'

Mum was vague about her dealings with doctors. What I saw was that she was taking more and more medication, and it was constipating her. She developed haemorrhoids. She was sent to, or referred to, or asked to be seen by a colorectal specialist, my brother's former classmate. Dr Stein kept cutting out the haemorrhoids, and they kept growing back, or appeared to. On her 76th birthday, in 2004, Mum had another appointment with Barry Stein. In 2004 Mum's birthday fell on a Saturday.

'Dr Stein is seeing me on a Saturday as a favour, because I'm Michael's mother.' She preened, proud of her special status.

'But it's your birthday. Is that how you want to spend it?'

'It's only for an hour, and then I'll spend the rest of the day with you. Going to see Dr Stein is a gift I'm giving myself. I want to live, and be healthy.'

At eight am on the morning of 23 October 2004, I turned on my television, and was confronted by what appeared to be the face of my father. It was a close-up of Fredric March, in an old film. I called Mum.

'Daddy says Happy Birthday.'

'Oh? How did he communicate with you?'

'Through Fredric March, in an old film.'

'Oh!' My father's resemblance to the American film star was so startling that, as a child, I mistook him for March when I saw a classic still in a movie magazine.

Mum went to hospital to keep her appointment with Barry Stein. He examined her. 'I don't see any more haemorrhoids.'

'But I'm still bleeding.' Mum insisted. 'Maybe you should do another test.' The voice of guardian angels spoke through my mother.

'What for? You had your test two years ago.' Stein dismissed what might have been a life-saving suggestion. Not an army of angels, not the watchful presence of my father's spirit, not God himself, if such an entity exists, is a match for such a doctor.

Mum reported the details of her appointment with Michael. Instead of calling for a second opinion, Michael sent his former classmate a fruit basket, as a form of thank you for taking care of his mother.

Over the course of the next six months, I noticed uncharacteristic fatigue in Mum.

'What is making you so tired?' That much, I asked.

'I guess I'm getting old.' Mum shrugged off her symptoms.

Mum's increasing flatulence could not be easily dismissed.

'What are you eating?' Mum's diet was always good. She enjoyed fresh fruit and stir-fried vegetables. She did not have a sweet tooth. She was not a heavy meat eater.

'I haven't changed my diet. The pills they're giving me make me constipated. And I think I must still be developing haemorrhoids, because I'm still bleeding.'

On 11 March of 2005 Mum saw her GP, who insisted she receive 'another test' in a situation he considered an emergency. On the morning of 16 March, I accompanied my mother to hospital. Deep in her heart, she later told me, she already knew.

As I sat in the waiting room while Mum underwent a colonoscopy, I heard nurses referring to her.

'That one gave us a rough time. But she's come back from the other side.'

On Wednesday, 16 March 2005, our lives changed irrevocably. That day, for the first time, I heard the words 'mother' and 'cancer' coupled. We had entered CancerLand. Mum wouldn't leave it alive.

I did not return to my apartment that evening. I stayed overnight with Mum, and contacted Michael. I caught him on a ski hill. For some, it was March Break.

Michael flew into Montreal the same evening. Within a month, Mum was scheduled for surgery.

'Do you trust Barry Stein to do the operation?' I asked my brother.

'I trust Barry Stein to do the surgery.' Bitterly, he added, 'Barry Stein knows how to cut.'

Michael took charge of post-operative procedures. He got down on his knees and scoured Mum's private hospital room. He hired night sitters, but stood on guard all day, not leaving even to pee unless I was there to watch over Mum. Still, I could not protect her from a bullying nurse, so Michael quietly had the nurse dismissed, which put hospital staff on alert. Older nurses with children were impressed by Michael's vigilance. Younger nurses and orderlies felt threatened. I heard their comments, and repeated them to him, which is when Michael began bringing gifts for the orderlies and younger nurses.

Several days after the surgery, from her hospital bed, Mum began to shout.

'Get me onto the balcony! I need air!' There was no balcony in the hospital room. Mum was hallucinating. She had been overdosed. I watched in awe as Michael, quietly, always quietly, summoned the young doctor on call and cajoled him into reducing Mum's medication.

From then on, except for the multiple rounds of chemotherapy endured over the course of the next eight and a half years, whatever procedures Mum underwent were performed in Toronto.

***

In the summer of 2006, Mum was in her first remission and back in Poland, doing the work she considered her mission. I was home alone, listening to CBC Radio. A woman in her forties was being interviewed. She was a cancer patient who had a projected six months to live. Four years earlier she had undergone testing for lung cancer. She never received her results. She called the hospital requesting them. In effect, she was told that no news is good news, so she did not pursue the matter. Now she was dying, and had come on radio to warn the public about the pitfalls of our medical system.

Generally, when Mum went on her extended trips to Poland, besides checking and handling her phone messages, I picked up and checked her mail. I had instructions to open mail that looked important. This time Mum had the post office hold her mail, so she did not receive the letter from the hospital until she came home, and she came home early in order to undergo testing. According to the letter, her test was being postponed by a month. Had the hospital called, I would have received the message and relayed it to her.

'Goddam it! I could've stayed longer in Warsaw!'

At that moment I recalled the interview with the dying cancer patient. 'Mum, you've got the requisition. Don't wait. Go anyway.'

Mum gave me a searching look, but did not protest. She had no visible symptoms, but she took herself, along with the requisition, to hospital. The markers were up.

According to the results, two tumours had entered Mum's liver. Left untreated, she would be dead within three months.

Michael flew into town. Dr Zajdman found himself on the other side of the system he had given his life to. He was presented with several options, all of them terrifying. On his way back to Toronto he called from the airport. Out of our mother's hearing, he wept into the receiver. As my younger brother cried, I heard our father's voice emerge from the ether. 'Don't be jealous from your brother,' Dad had admonished. 'For him, the hard part will come later, and when it does it will be really hard because he won't be used to it. He's going to need you.' Heeding Dad, I suggested to Michael, 'If they can operate, why don't they?' To me, the choice seemed straightforward.

Michael's sobs subsided, and he came to attention. 'I don't know.' He was truly mystified. 'But I'm going to find out.'

Michael's colleagues in Toronto sprang into action. 'Bring your mother here.' I imagined I heard a sigh of relief as Daddy's spirit receded into the ether.

Surgery in Toronto was scheduled for early October. An Ontario cancer specialist Michael trusted urged him to get treatment started, so on the Friday before the Labour Day weekend we returned to hospital for a round of chemotherapy.

Before moving into Mum's neighbourhood in 2010, I would move into her apartment for several days after each round of chemo, in order to watch over her. Mum lay on a hide-a-bed in the living room, because that is where the balcony was located. In clement weather, we kept the balcony door open. On the Labour Day Monday after this round of treatment, Mum raised her head off the pillow and pleaded, 'Help me! I need to throw up. Give me the garbage can. Quick!' I grabbed a nearby pail and placed it under her chin but before Mum could vomit she fainted, rolling onto the thickly carpeted floor before I could catch her. Horrified, I grabbed the portable phone Mum kept beside her and, instead of dialling 911 I punched in my brother's home number. Because it was a national holiday, I expected him to be home.

My brother's wife answered the phone. Early in their marriage, my sister-in-law let me know she would be one more relative to steer clear of, so I did. At this moment, I had no choice but to deal with her.

'Put Michael on the phone.'

Though Ann is a doctor, I knew not to ask anything of her. 'Mum's just fainted. She's lying unconscious on the floor.'

Icily Ann responded, 'I'm on the other line with my mother. You'll have to wait.'

'Ann! Please! She's lying unconscious on the floor!'

Ann's response was diabolical. 'I said I'm talking to my mother. I'll give the message to Michael when I'm finished.' Spitting out each syllable, the doctor reiterated, 'You'll just have to wait.'

Instead of dialling 911 and ignoring my brother's call when it finally came, I sat on the carpeted floor paralysed by terror, cradling my unconscious mother's head in my trembling hands. Five weeks later, in Toronto, Mum underwent surgery for the removal of two tumours in her liver.

While Mum's cancer was beaten back, one of her hips began to grumble. Hip replacement surgery was deemed too drastic for a patient in Mum's condition. I had heard of gels, given by injection, which could cushion and alleviate the pain of arthritic hips. In the dead of winter, during a blizzard, the Montreal haematologist we were referred to refused to treat Mum, condemning her to sedatives and a wheelchair. Michael arranged an appointment with a haematologist in his hospital in Mississauga, and in the interim sent his best friend Howard to Mum's apartment bearing a walker, as a New Year's gift. How depressing it was to see that walker sitting in the back room of Mum's apartment. The only accoutrement more depressing than a walker is a wheelchair. We would have a wheelchair on the premises too, before Mum not only received a series of injections, but ultimately, a new hip.

CHAPTER THIRTY-SIX

Mercifully, the first injection Mum received in Mississauga worked, and she was out of immediate pain. Still, it was not a permanent solution. I had seen several of Mum's neighbours transformed by hip replacement surgery, and despite her condition, urged Michael to explore the option.

It would not be until June of 2010 that Mum and Michael met with a surgeon in Toronto. 'If the injections are working, stick with them. Hip replacement surgery is dangerous.' The surgeon rammed home his point. 'You could die. If you were my mother,' he looked pointedly at Michael; I would tell you, 'Don't do it.'

Her hopes dashed by the surgeon, Mum limped along, aided by intermittent injections, each one entailing a trip to Toronto.

The leg extending from Mum's arthritic hip dragged, her knee hurt, her back ached, her shoulders slumped, and she sat on a tilt in order to avoid her failing hip. The imbalance set up Mum for injury. A time came when she stumbled on the thick living room carpet and would have fallen and smashed her hip if I hadn't been there to catch her. 'I gotcha Ma, I gotcha.' She trembled in my arms and buried her head in my shoulder, shuddering for a long while before feeling safe enough to continue moving on her own.

Medically, this situation was considered acceptable.

Hauling around her lopsided carcass exhausted Mum. With the loss of energy and mobility, she became increasingly shut in. I would show up with groceries, or I would just show up, to see her sitting forlornly by her bedroom window, waiting for me. Her friends, and Michael's Montreal-based friends, abandoned her then. No one came to visit, and no one wanted to deal with the handling of a walker, and later a wheelchair, which is what was entailed in taking her on excursions.

Early in the dismal winter of 2009, an injury rendered Mum disabled. She was shut in, shuffling around her apartment with the aid of a walker. It was precisely at this low ebb that Mum received a call from the screenwriter and film director John Kent Harrison. He was hired by the Hallmark Hall of Fame film company to write and direct a movie about Irena Sendler, who had recently died, in 2008, at the age of 98. Fittingly, Sendler died on Mother's Day.

The ensuing relationship was a gift to both of them, though neither recognised it at the time. Harrison was filming in Poland when he was given a copy of Sendler's biography and became smitten with the tale of the diminutive and indomitable wartime heroine. Initially Bieta was contacted. Through an interpreter she told Harrison and the Hallmark producers, 'I was just a baby. I don't remember anything. There's a woman in Montreal you should be speaking to. She's my best friend. She was older. She remembers everything.'

'How old is this woman?'

'She's eighty.'

Harrison was sceptical. According to Bieta, he appeared to doubt whether a woman of such advanced age still retained her marbles, let alone her memory. Mum had a lethal memory, and her mind was laser sharp to the end.

The writer/director sent Mum a Polish version of his first draft. Mum's reaction was swift, and succinct. She tossed the script on her dining room table. 'This thing is a piece of shit!'

I smiled. Mum was never wishy-washy. 'You know Ma, if you were in my writing workshop, you'd have to find another way of saying that.'

'Oh yeah? Like how?'

'Well, how about, 'The way it's written now, the script doesn't tell the real story.'

'Hmmph. Maybe I'll ask to see an English version. They're making this movie in English. Why would I want to read it in Polish? I'm in Canada sixty years! Like I didn't have time to learn English?!'

Upon request, Mum received and studied the English version. Again, the verdict was rendered. 'This isn't much better.'

'Well Ma, it seems you're in a position to help the writer improve his script.' Defensively guarding sacred memories, Mum didn't recognise the opportunity at hand.

'Aw, you remember what happened with that other script I was asked to help with! They turned it into a travesty! I worked with those people and they did what they wanted anyway! They offered to put my name on screen in the credits. I told them, 'If you dare put my name on that piece of trash I'll sue you!' And they were Jews! This guy is a *goy* [39] from Ontario. I looked him up on the internet! They gave him this movie to make because the last movie he did was about the Pope! A Polish Pope; a Polish heroine – close enough! How could he possibly understand the Warsaw

---

[39] Gentile

Ghetto! And Hallmark is producing it! Hallmark?! Achhh! They'll turn it into syrup!' I understood my mother's fears.

'The man's a writer, Ma, and you're a resource. If he has integrity, if he cares about what he's doing, he'll be smart enough to listen to you. And you know,' I warned my traumatised mum, 'This movie will be made whether you participate or not, so you may as well get involved. You can only help to make it better. 'Besides,' I reminded this fierce, formidable, profoundly damaged woman, 'It's your duty. You owe it to Sendler's memory.' That did it. Thus began what would develop into a special working relationship between two people who would not meet face-to-face until the film's Hollywood premiere, a relationship that grew into feelings of mutual affection and respect.

I spent a lot of time with Mum that winter. I was often on the premises when Harrison called, from his cell phone on location in Latvia, to consult with Mum on historical details. It was a good sign.

The opportunity to be of service lifted Mum's spirits. She was doing meaningful work again, and knew it. At the same time Mum was undergoing intensive chiropractic treatment for her injury. 'Mark my words, Ma. On the night of the Hollywood premiere you'll walk down the aisle of the Zanuck Theatre with your arm linked in mine, using nothing more for support but a cane.' Hallmark invited Mum to attend the film's premiere as their guest. Mum responded that she would come only if they included me.

CHAPTER THIRTY-SEVEN

We stepped out of a limousine donated by the town's funeral home. We stepped onto the red carpet donated by the town hospital. The searchlights, donated by a branch of the McDonald's hamburger empire and set up on a residential balcony adjacent to the town's one theatre used for stage shows and live events, were not yet in operation because it was still daylight.

Mum and I were in Fort Scott, Kansas, for the world premiere of Hallmark Hall of Fame's *The Courageous Heart of Irena Sendler*.

Mum was their guest of honour. I served as a kind of aide-de-camp. As we made our entrance, one of Mum's arms linked with mine, the other, gripping the handle of a cane, we were confronted by the local paparazzi. A slew of digital cameras snapped at us like the jaws of baby crocodiles. Our image was published on the front page of the *Fort Scott Tribune* the next day.

The repeatedly renovated Liberty Theatre was built in the 1880s. On the parterre, special attendees were seated at round tables. John Kent Harrison, the writer/director of the film, looking far more relaxed than he had in Hollywood two nights before, sat down next to me before noticing his name was written on a card on a table behind us, together with a group of Hallmark executives. 'Oh no, I have to go and sit there.' Throughout the screening of the film I felt Harrison's eyes burning my back, as he watched me watching his film.

At the private screening for 500 on the lot of the old Twenty-Century Fox studio, Harrison sat three rows behind Mum and me. When Mum was introduced and called to the stage, I stood with her. As we rose, she brushed me aside. 'I'm going by myself!' Mum began her descent down an inclined aisle. I walked several steps behind her, like a parent anxiously guarding as its child crosses the street for the first time. The audience noticed. 'Who is that elegant woman?' Someone whispered. Down front, one of the young Kansans, seeing me hover, leapt up, raced to my mother, and escorted her onto the stage.

At six p.m. we were picked up by limousine in the boutique hotel Hallmark had housed us in, and driven to the Fox studio. With the aid of a walker Mum moved down the long city-like blocks of the studio lot, while I carried her cane. As we approached the entrance of the Zanuck Theatre, we noticed a set of stairs. While I wondered how Mum would negotiate them, a moving platform rolled in front of us, and its driver instructed us to climb aboard. A switch was pulled and the platform rose skyward. As the movie stars took the stairs we floated above the stars and the stairs; Mum, her walker, her cane, and me. That's Hollywood, Baby.

The day before we left for Los Angeles, Mum called. 'I have a favour to ask you.' Coming from Mum, a request was considered a command. 'They're probably going to ask me to give a speech. They usually do, at these things. I've written something, and I want you to read it.' I thought Mum was asking me to proofread and edit her speech. It turned out to be more than that. 'I'm going to be too emotional to deliver it. I want you to read it for me.'

'You want me to stand on a stage in front of 500 invited guests in Hollywood and deliver a speech in your name?'

'Yes.'

My mother was a Holocaust star; she knew how to deliver a speech. 'What are you up to, Ma?'

'I want Hollywood to see what a gorgeous daughter I have. I want to see you back in the limelight.' Mum was referring to the fact that I began my professional life on the stage.

The prospect was tempting; it was also terrifying. I worked on my mother's speech, and then, in a moment of panic, e-mailed the Hallmark representative I had been in touch with while making travel arrangements, asking if a speech was expected. 'No. We're all going to just sit back and enjoy the moment.' Before leaving the boutique hotel for the Hollywood premiere, half-heartedly I looked for my copy of the speech in my suitcase. I couldn't find it.

When the moment came, Mum was asked to 'please say a few words.' She demurred. Mum was the greatest actress I've ever known. Her performance was so pitch perfect that it almost convinced me.

At the reception, one of the Hallmark executives lauded her decision to remain silent. 'You were right. Always leave 'em wanting more.'

My mother eyed me ruefully. She hissed, 'Do you feel as frustrated as I do?'

'Yes and no. I may have missed the moment, but it just didn't feel right. It's Harrison's night.'

At the reception I entered into conversation with Harrison's assistant editor. I confessed my dilemma. 'Oh! I'm so sorry you didn't! I would've loved to hear the speech! I would've listened to you and seen you as a conduit for your mother. Even a truncated version would be worth listening to. Perhaps you can cobble together something for the premiere in Kansas on Wednesday night? And hey, this is

Hollywood. Everyone's looking out for their next job. There is nothing wrong with being ambitious and wanting to shine.'

I was staggered by the audience's response to my mother. At the reception, actors and screenwriters and directors and producers insisted on paying homage to her for no reason other than she had survived which, for Mum, didn't seem reason enough. In Mum's mind, the real heroine was dead, and she was only a piece of living history connected to her. As she perched on the seat of her walker, Hollywood luminaries moved in. 'Tell me your story! I want to shake your hand!' Some just observed, as if Mum were an artefact. I recognised one of them. She was a mature, ageing woman; still classy, still attractive. Silently contemplating Mum, she stood apart. For me, she stood out.

Fifty years earlier, this actress incarnated Margot Frank in one of the first films dealing with the Shoah. Forty years earlier, she played Maximilian Schell's love interest in an adventure epic. I remembered watching it on television and thinking how lovely she was. Now here we were at a reception on the lot of the studio where she began her career, our shoulders draped in glittering shawls, in concession to the cool California evening. She, now a seventy-one-year-old film producer whose once-raven hair was highlighted an artificial gold; me; an obscure, fifty-three-year-old writer from Canada whose chestnut-coloured hair was streaked with God-given silver.

On what was she reflecting as she regarded Hallmark's poster child for the Holocaust? Was she remembering Otto Frank, who wept when he met the dark and wholesome beauty who bore such a startling resemblance to his dead daughter Margot? As she stared at my mother in the midst of Shoah business, she caught me staring at her. 'Are you Diane Baker?'

'Yes, I am.' An infinitesimal lift of an eyebrow betrayed her surprise at being recognised. Her close-mouthed smile mirrored mine. What else could I say? There was nothing more to say. All I could do was savour the moment.

When Mum and I returned to our executive suite, we went to work on reconstructing the speech. Just before two a.m., when I could do no more, Mum found a copy of what she'd originally written, tucked away in her suitcase.

We left the smog-choked Hollywood hills at nine the next morning, for an 11 a.m. flight to Kansas City. We were travelling with the executives from Hallmark, and the troupe from Fort Scott. The four high school girls who created the original production of *Life in a Jar* were young married women now. As an airport official snaked my mother's wheelchair through a serpentine route in Los Angeles' vast airport, we followed behind like ducks in a row; the Hallmark executives, me, and the young women, with one of their husbands in tow. I had negotiated a Business Class ticket for Mum on the Montreal-Los Angeles flight, but now we were all flying Economy. On a midget airline called Midwest, we even had to pay to check in our bags. (It was the first year airlines were charging for the transportation of passenger luggage.) As we scrunched into the cramped seats, Mama Duck turned to one of the Hallmark executives and quacked, 'I'd think you guys would have private jets!'

'We do,' he admitted. 'But we're not using them this year.' I would later learn that Hallmark was in the process of purging 750 employees. In the wake of a global economy gone into cardiac arrest, those who survived the purge were grateful to be able to travel at all.

From the Emerald City, we were airlifted to Kansas. We arrived in The Heartland along with spring. Tender primavera leaves peaked through their buds. The air was dry and crystalline. Farmlands shimmered under wide prairie skies. Shadows fell disconcertingly early, because we had lost two of the three hours gained on going to California.

We reached Fort Scott after six p.m. Main Street was deserted, except for the warm and welcoming presence of Norman Conard. Norman was a multiple-award-winning teacher who was the inspiration and catalyst for the high school history project that rescued the legacy of the rescuer Sendler. No longer in the classroom, he was now the director of The Lowell Milken Education Center in Fort Scott. While his former students, founders of the *Life in a Jar* project, travelled to California, Norman remained behind in order to finalise arrangements for the local film premiere, and our stay. I had met Norman several times, briefly and on the fly, but it was on this trip, for the next two days, that I discovered why his protégées, as well as Mum, adored him.

It was Norman who arranged for the two limousines, the red carpet, the klieg lights, and the theatre. Creative, dynamic, and surprisingly sweet, the beloved 'Mr. Conard' was a middle-aged Andy Hardy who involved the whole town in putting on a show. While it hosted the world premiere of a film, Fort Scott's esprit was reminiscent of Frank Capra's cinematic American towns. Hollywood fever had hit the Midwest, and its inhabitants seemed high on helium.

During our stay in Fort Scott, Mum and I were housed in The Pink Cottage across the street from The Big House. The Big House was one of a twin of Victorian mansions operated by the Lyons family as a guest house. Harrison and the Hallmark executives were housed in The Big House, and Mum and I were sheltered in a dream cottage, which we had to ourselves. We assumed Hallmark was sponsoring our stay, as it had in Hollywood. We would later learn that the use of this romantic abode, built in 1930 and lovingly restored, was also donated.

After a day of travelling, Mum and I dropped onto our ergonomically designed four-poster beds, overwhelmed. Mum said it for us. 'There are hidden treasures in this country.'

The anachronistically fresh air of the flatlands knocked out Mum like a drug. I sleepwalked through this living dream. A bathroom with black-slate tiles led into a walk-in overhead shower that mimicked a rain shower. It was augmented with strategically placed horizontal jet streams. Off the bathroom, there was a room-sized soft beige-toned boudoir for m'lady. The fully-equipped kitchen, its window overlooking a back porch and small garden, had a digital oven and stove top, and under the silent ceiling fan there was a counter bar flanked by leather-covered stools. On the edge of the kitchen counter, as an accent, sat a cowboy-boot-shaped crystal mug. In what might have been a dining room, there was a long desk with a globe perched on its edge. The desk was positioned in front of an electric fireplace. In the darkness, against the mahogany panelling, I could envision one Samuel Clemens (AKA Mark Twain), an extravagantly-moustachioed riverboat captain, dipping a quill into an ink pot and composing another tall tale destined for publication in a newspaper across the state line.

It was 'Miss Pat,' a glamorous, saucer-eyed grandmother, who watched over The Twins and The Pink like a guest-house goddess. She was assisted by her son Nate, who resembled a younger George Clooney. 'For anything simple, call me,' she instructed as she taped phone numbers next to the wall phone. 'For anything technical, call Nate.' Miss Pat carried a dish of fresh fruit salad, yoghurt mixed with nutmeg and vanilla, and a baggie-full of homemade granola studded with walnuts and pecans harvested from a local farm. 'For breakfast, so I won't disturb you in the morning.' Nate showed up after I sent an SOS, when unable to activate the digital oven.

After feeding myself and my drowsy, contented mother with baked potatoes and kefir purchased during a quick stop at Woods grocery store, I fell into my four-poster. The whistle of the trains broke the stillness of the night. Behind my eyes I could see the statuesque Harvey Girls in their long aprons, cinched shirtwaists, World War II coifs, dazzling MGM smiles and sizzling MGM tans. Echoing through the ether like a lullaby came the voice of the golden-throated Garland crooning 'All the way to Califor-nii – ayyy on the Atchison, Topeka, and the Santa Fe!'

I turned to the night table. An ornately carved tray rested on its edge. There was a colourful slip of paper inserted into the tray, and in elaborate calligraphy it read, *It is 1876. Fort Scott is the Rail center of the Frontier, bringing supplies to fledgling mercantiles, loading precious coal, paint, cement and flagstone, and heading WEST! Thus began the romance that exists today between Fort Scott's citizens and the railroads. We locals consider the long whines and whistles from the Burlington-Northern music to our ears. If you are not quite as enamored, here are earplugs to ensure your uninterrupted night.'* Miss Pat had thought of everything.

'Oh! What a beautiful morning! Oh! What a beautiful day!'

Wednesday, 15 April glowed in living Technicolor. There were no locked doors in CapraLand. Before we noticed a need, a friendly soul would poke her face through the door, and just happen to be able to supply it.

In a phone call to the Milken Center, I informed an assistant that Mum was prepared to give the speech she'd refused to give on Monday evening in Hollywood. A few moments later, the wall next to the Mark Twainish desk vibrated, as the phone rang. 'Ahh, Brent said there won't be time for speeches, so you don't have to bother. You can relax.' I was hearing echoes.

'Ma, who was it asked you to give a speech on Monday night?'

'Brent.'

'That doesn't make sense.'

'Then maybe it was Brad. I get those COEs mixed up.'

'CEOs. And there's only one of them.'

'What?'

I sighed.' 'Never mind.'

Brad was the president of Hallmark; Brent was the producer of the film. Tweedledee was saying yes; Tweedledum was saying no.

Mum and I looked at each other in consternation. 'Fool me once, shame on you; fool me twice…' At the same instant, we reached the same conclusion. 'Get it ready. Prepare the speech.'

My mother was trundled off for another round of media interviews. Hallmark was getting its money's worth. As the self-styled aide-de-camp, I had little more to do than enjoy the almost impossibly perfect day. I took my notebook, the speech, and several miniature, red mugs filled with mint tea outside. There was a small running fountain on the porch. A fully stocked fish pond nestled underneath. The enclosed yard contained patio furniture, a grill, and a fire pit. All was sheltered by an old oak tree.

I sat in the sun, editing my mother's speech. Despite what I had told the assistant, I expected to be delivering it that evening. When done I luxuriated in the private rain shower, stretched on a rug in front of the electric fireplace, and then took the speech across the street to The Big House, to type and print on Miss Pat's computer. When I got there, a photographer was taking pictures of a family of children on the steps of the Lyons's mansion. I took a few moments to swing on the front porch swing, like a frontier gal waitin' for her fella to come a callin'. I borrowed a 1948 edition of Life magazine, which lay on the coffee table in the front parlour. After placing it on the quilted spread of my mother's four-poster, I took a stroll along the tree-lined, shady streets of this sparkling Capraesque town.

At the cocktail hour, one of two limousines drove up to the entrance of the cottage. (The other drove back and forth from The Big House, chauffeuring Harrison and the group from Hallmark.) The driver emerged, and waited on the sidewalk. Becky Halsey and her husband came to the door to fetch us. Becky Halsey, henceforth to be referred to as 'Jellyshot Becky', designated herself our official escort for the evening. She told Norman as much. She insisted on it.

A showdown between Jellyshot Becky and my Pistol-Packin' Mama took place at the turn of this century, when Mum was brought to Fort Scott for the first time, as a living example of a rescued child; an added attraction to the Life in a Jar student play. Norman held a party in his home. Becky was one of the guests. Like many Midwesterners, she bubbled with friendliness. What the townsfolk knew, and Mum did not, was that Becky's culinary speciality was Jell-O Shots, which were cubes of Jell-O laced with vodka. Bubbly Becky approached the stranger, aiming a tray upon which was balanced slippery red gelatinous cubes. 'Jell-O SHAT!' She eyeballed my mother. Becky knew the older woman had been born in Europe. 'Jell-O SHAT!' She nodded emphatically, raising a spoon.

Instantly, my cosmopolitan mother understood what she was dealing with. Mischievously she widened her eyes and slowly, hesitantly repeated, 'Jeeellow SHAAAWT!'

'Very good!' Becky was pleased with how quickly the foreigner was learning. She dropped a cube down her gullet, handed my mother one of the spoons lying on the tray, and motioned for her to do the same. Gleefully, Mum played her part. She picked up a spoon and scooped up a cube. She batted the eyelashes shading her steely blue-grey peepers. Becky missed the glint in them. 'Jello SHAWT?'

Becky was impressed. 'Yes! Yes! Jello SHAT!' Becky made the rounds of the room, and kept circling back to Mum. 'Jello Shat!' She coached her protégée. 'Jello Shat!' Mute, Mum would nod, and scoop up another cube. This pattern continued for several rounds. The Pole in my mother was familiar with the effects of vodka. When she began to feel them she erupted, 'Goddamit! What the hell's going on here?! Norman!' Mama wailed across the room. 'This woman is getting me drunk!' Becky reeled. So did my mama, but for a different reason. The joke was on both of them.

Now Becky, her husband, and the senior partner of the funeral home brought us to a wine and cheese reception at the Milken Center on Main Street.

I wound my way to the back of the crowded office, where the fruit and water were located. In the small, tight space I knocked against the back of a gentleman, and we turned to face each other. His small round eyes flashed, and his big round face broke into a wide, delighted smile. It was John Kent Harrison. We hadn't seen each other since the premiere in Hollywood two nights before. To my surprise, the director of the film flung his arms around me. On this soft spring evening, he was expansive and relaxed. After a year of intense and focused labour, Harrison knew he had birthed a success.

Though the Liberty Theatre was one block down on the other side of the street, we VIPs-for-the-evening were bustled back into the limousine and driven around the corner and beyond in order to make the ride appear longer. Our chauffeur was the father of a father-and-son-run funeral home, a white-haired gentleman by the name of Jerry Witt. Indeed.

In front of the theatre, Mercy Hospital's red carpet was slung onto the sidewalk like a bolt of scarlet laid out on display in a material shop. The sight of townsfolk and local paparazzi lining the pavement startled Mum and me. Their cameras were aimed and ready to shoot. We stared at the crowd, glanced at each other, and then grinned in conspiracy. Our chauffeur stopped, emerged, and opened the back doors. I stepped out. My amber earrings danced as I slung my lime-coloured scarf across a shoulder of my emerald fake-fur jacket, clutched my shimmering chocolate-coloured, egg-shaped evening bag in one hand, and offered my free arm to Mum. We strolled down the scarlet bolt, playfully deigning to the crowd. One of many pictures snapped at that moment appeared on the front page of the Fort Scott Tribune the next morning. When I saw it, I screamed with laughter. My glee turned bittersweet on noticing the date at the top of the page: 16 April is my father's birthday. One doesn't need a passport to come from The Other Side. But of course, I reflected, and realised, his blithe spirit would hover over such an event, watching over his two stars.

In the photograph I am smiling sweetly, and move with my head held high. Mum is wielding her cane and leering at the camera, those steely blue-greys proclaiming, 'Bring it on!' This photograph was later placed on Hallmark's website.

As we passed the buffet laid out in the outdoor courtyard at the back entrance to the theatre, our escort Becky offered me a drink. 'I wouldn't accept anything from you that wasn't labelled and sealed,' I deadpanned. Becky blinked, and then handed me a bottle of Ozarka spring water.

Inside the theatre, Mum was corralled for yet another interview; this time, with NBC. I marvelled at how skilfully Mum steered clear of personal questions, and kept refocusing the spotlight on the subject at hand.

After Harrison reluctantly vacated the seat next to me in order to sit with Tweedledum and Tweedledee, it was filled by the ubiquitous Becky. As the lights dimmed and the film unfolded, her cheerful visage turned dark with distress. Tears tumbled into sobs that cascaded into waterfalls of weeping as the misery and horror of the story took hold. By the time the film ended, our little round table was studded with balled-up wads of tissue. I was seeing the film for the second time. As my mother's daughter, I was infinitely better prepared for the material than Becky, but still there were moments when I looked away from images too harrowing to confront head on and when I did, its creator leaned over to stroke my back. 'It's even better the second time,' I whispered. When the film ended and the houselights were switched on, I signalled Harrison and pointed to the bouquet of tissues on our table. One writer smiled ruefully at the other. Becky was a quivering wreck. It was a supreme compliment to the film's creator.

After preliminary speeches on stage, Tweedledee announced, 'I have known Renata for only two days, but in that time I have learnt that this spunky lady will do what she wants to do, and will not do what she doesn't want to do. And so, I ask that she say a few words. Please.' The president of Hallmark almost pleaded. This time, we were ready. I expected to receive the speech from Mum's hand and deliver it for her, but as I rose she hissed, 'No! I have to do this myself!' Leaning on the cane, she ambled her way to the stage. Norman called, 'Sharon! Help your mother!' Well, really.

I stood off to the side while Mum delivered her speech; then helped her off the stage. Mum headed into the courtyard with Harrison, where there was an al fresco buffet. Before joining them, I took a moment to collect myself. How had it come to this? I marvelled, as I watched the audience, in their finery, celebrating the event. A rejected and reviled war orphan, a homeless and displaced waif, was now a Holocaust star. I have never been able to reconcile the need to educate society about what happened in that time and place with the fear that this knowledge would become sensationalised and exploited.

I thought of the missed opportunity in Hollywood, if it really was an opportunity missed. Except for the inspiring orations of great political leaders, my dad detested speeches and those who made them, and my dad's opinion, dead or alive, was paramount. Yes, I wanted to shine, but not over the shot and burnt and mutilated corpses of Holocaust victims. A time would come when I would serve as my mother's conduit, speaking for a woman no longer able to speak for herself, but as long as she was able to convey her message, it was her place to do so, not mine.

CHAPTER THIRTY-EIGHT

'Find me someone connected to the film, and find me someone connected to the story,' the billionaire instructed his assistant, Lou Ann. Lou Ann Lindblade ran an internet search and came up with the name of one of the writers listed in the film's joint credit for screenwriting. Then she found my mother.

On 12 April 2010, a year to the day since we flew to Hollywood, Mum and I were once again in the air. This time, we were on our way to Sioux City, Iowa.

The Jewish philanthropist was the son of a Russian immigrant who, because he couldn't speak English, worked in Sioux City's stockyards hauling dead meat. Annually, Gerry Weiner sponsored an event he termed Tolerance Week, because he didn't want to alienate his Christian neighbours by calling it Holocaust Week. During this week singled out for Judaeo-Christian brotherhood, Weiner sponsored the screening of a Holocaust-related film. In 2010, he intended to present *The Courageous Heart of Irena Sendler*. Having read about Hallmark's poster child on their website, Weiner's Girl Friday launched a search for Mum. Lou Ann located her through Montreal's Holocaust Centre. Despite her chronic cancer and dodgy hip, Mum was still working there as a speaker and volunteer guide.

An invitation was issued to Mum and an escort of her choice to fly to Iowa for the event, all expenses paid. To accompany her, Mum chose the woman she deemed her memory keeper: me.

The invited writer received screen credit. His name appeared under John Kent Harrison's name as co-screenwriter. Larry Spagnola flitted on the margins of Hollywood's film industry for years and, before the creation of *The Courageous Heart*, earned a screen credit for co-writing one horror film. Hallmark cut him out of the screenwriting process when its producer brought on board the more experienced John Kent Harrison.

In retaliation, Spagnola took Harrison to arbitration at the Screenwriters Guild. As a result, the producer listed Spagnola's name among the credits in order to avoid a lawsuit. When Mum asked why Harrison had not been invited, she was told he was invited and then uninvited when he demanded more money for making an appearance than Weiner's organisation was prepared to pay. In fact, Harrison hadn't been approached at all. Lou Ann hadn't done her homework. Weiner's organisation would get what they paid for, and then some.

On the morning after our arrival in Iowa, Mum was escorted to a press conference with Spagnola, who was not only introduced as a screenwriter, but also an historian. Inaccuracies in his comments disturbed Mum. Privately, she corrected him. The screenwriter-cum-historian did not take kindly to what he perceived as an old woman's interference.

The same evening Spagnola, Mum and I gathered in the lobby waiting for Weiner and his entourage. The driver who met us at the Omaha airport pulled up in a stretch limousine. Weiner's entourage included a psychiatrist from Florida and a survivor of Auschwitz, now retired and residing in Florida. Both gentlemen were flown in annually, and the Auschwitz survivor had become the poster child for these events. The camp survivor was a patient of the psychiatrist. They appeared to be almost a couple, except that the psychiatrist didn't hold the survivor's hand. Or maybe he did, metaphorically.

Our party climbed into the air-conditioned limousine, with its fully-equipped bar, for the two-minute ride to the Orpheum Theatre. Spagnola ogled me. As he leered and suggestively waggled his head, his toupee slipped.

Before the screening, a gala dinner was held in the theatre's lobby. Mum and I were seated with the philanthropist at the table of honour. A special meal was prepared for him. The son of a man who hauled cow carcasses in Sioux City's stockyards was a vegan.

Weiner's second wife, who wasn't Jewish, was in attendance. Kathy wore hair that didn't move, a mask of make-up, glittery shoes with spikes verging on the dangerous, and kept alkaline strips in her purse.

'We have five homes,' Kathy informed me. 'We have a ranch here in Iowa, but our main house is across the border, in South Dakota, because the state is tax-free. Gerry keeps an office in Toronto and wanted to buy a house there, but I scotched that idea. 'Are you kidding!' I told him. 'And run the risk of tripping over the homeless?!' So we bought a house in that suburb which sounds like Mississippi. As a Canadian, you probably know what I mean.'

'Mississauga.' I was starting to choke on my salad, and reached for a glass of water.

'Don't touch that!' Kathy commanded. 'Not yet.' She reached into her purse and pulled out alkaline strips. 'The water is acidic. This will alkalinise it.' Kathy dunked a strip into my glass of water, and then passed strips around the table, insisting her guests do the same. 'Gerry, honey. Would you like me to alkalinise your water, too?'

'No, baby. I like my water acidic.' Gerry winked at me and turned to the town rabbi, who was seated on his other side. 'I'm an acidic Jew!'

Realising I had been lifted into the stratosphere of the stinking rich and lyrically ludicrous, I adapted quickly.

'Do you have a private plane?' I attempted small talk with Gerry.

'I used to, sweetie, but I gave it up. The upkeep on those things is expensive!' There really is a limit to everything.

After dinner the guests were invited to adjourn to an adjoining lounge, where the local media interviewed Spagnola. My mother grew agitated at the inaccuracies in his answers. Then the guests and the audience settled into the main hall of the theatre. The hall was packed. Thanks to the philanthropist, admission was free.

The Courageous Heart is a powerful film, and the audience sat hushed. Kathy was deeply disturbed by one scene.

'When the baby is sedated and put into a box that's taken out of the Warsaw Ghetto, why did her parents put a silver spoon beside her? I know they engraved her name and birth date on the spoon, but silver is a metal, and metal contains toxins!'

After the screening of the film, both Spagnola and Mum were invited on stage to answer questions from the audience. A local radio talk show host served as the evening's master of ceremonies. Mum and Spagnola were positioned in front of a podium that held a microphone, and expected to share it. Some questions were addressed to Spagnola: some questions were addressed to Mum. Bizarrely, without warning, Spagnola turned and left the stage. Mum was left standing alone. She grew confused. Assuming the Question and Answer period was over, she limped down the set of stairs placed in front of the stage, supported by her cane.

When Mum vacated the stage, just as suddenly as he vanished, Spagnola reappeared. He bounded onto the platform, installed himself behind the podium, and held centre stage. Since questions were still being addressed to Mum, the master of ceremonies was compelled to run back and forth with his microphone, between Mum and members of the audience. Mum, increasingly confused, stood leaning on her cane near the bottom of the stage. When Spagnola was questioned, it was obvious to Mum and me that he didn't know the answers. To us, it was also obvious that the audience was even more ignorant than Spagnola, and accepted his answers as fact. Promoting himself on the back of Harrison, who had done the work and the homework, Spagnola invented answers. He couldn't be accused of lying because he didn't know what the truth was. Mum's distress escalated as a Hollywood hack hijacked the Holocaust. When questions were addressed to Mum she appeared calm and her words were coherent and clear, but I noticed she was angling the microphone away from herself. As a pioneer in Holocaust Education, Mum knew how to use a microphone.

In an attempt to rescue her, I signalled the master of ceremonies, and he positioned his microphone beneath my lips.

'Mum. I have a question.'

Mum looked dazed. She seemed unable to decipher where my voice was coming from.

'Mummy, I'm here!' I shouted. The forthright declaration and amplified sound of my voice re-focused my mother. 'Mum!' I let the audience know – I let Spagnola know – that this old woman wasn't alone. 'When you and Bieta – who was the baby that was sedated and smuggled out of the

Warsaw Ghetto in a box – ' For the audience, I identified the Polish woman whom Mum considered her best friend. 'When the two of you petitioned the Polish Pope in your campaign to have Sendler nominated for the Nobel Peace Prize, what was his response?'

Mum snapped to attention. 'He helped, of course!' Forcefully, Mum addressed the citizens of America's Heartland. 'The Pope pitched in and together we succeeded in having Sendler nominated. She didn't win the award. The year she was nominated, the Nobel Peace Prize went to the man who was then your vice-president, Al Gore.'

The Midwestern audience was gobsmacked. It took the master of ceremonies a moment to retrieve his voice. Pensively, he spoke into his microphone.

'Does anyone else have any other questions – if you can top that!'

Alone in our room at the Holiday Inn, Mum was exceptionally quiet. I was at her feet, helping her out of her shoes and stockings. Tenderly, she gazed at me. Without assistance Mum lifted off her dress, and then undid her bra. She had to drop its straps below her shoulders and twist the back to the front in order to undo the hooks. I watched sadly, remembering when she could easily wrap her arms around her back to undo a bra. Mum had grown stiffer, and her range of motion increasingly limited.

I helped Mum into bed, removed the cane to a safe corner, and tucked her in. Then I got into my own bed on the other side of the nightstand, and switched off the bedside lamp. I began drifting into sleep. Mum tossed and turned. 'Are you awake?' She asked, hopefully.

'Mmmmm.' Drowsily, I muttered.

'I can't sleep,' Mum confessed, redundantly.

'I know.' I sighed, knowing I wouldn't get much sleep either. Wordlessly Mum hauled herself out of bed, limped over to where I lay, climbed in with me, and curled into my waiting arms.

'Why did he do it?' Mum whimpered, feeling weakened and defeated by the evening's events.

'Who knows.' I sighed.

'Is that what the Americans call a 'Hollywood hack?"

'That guy,' I snapped, 'is what the Americans call an asshole!'

'What a phoney.' Mum pouted, like a petulant child. 'Even his hair is fake!'

I stroked my mother's hair. It had recently grown back, after the latest round of chemo treatments. Mum's virgin hair was lovelier and even more luxuriant than before.

'Well Mum, that phoney is going back to Hollywood tomorrow, and you're not. You've got the rest of the week to turn this around. Make the most of it.'

Mum rolled to remove the pressure from her hurting hip. She pressed her back against me. I wrapped my arms around her. In response, Mum latched onto my hands and held them in a tight and desperate grip.

The next day, speaking to a group of students at a Christian fundamentalist college, Mum, still smarting from the debacle of the previous evening, unleashed. Generally when lecturing to students in her capacity as a Holocaust educator, she gave sanitised versions of her victimisation in wartime. Not this time. This time she did not spare the young people details of horrors and atrocities she witnessed and suffered when she was younger than they. When asked by a fresh-faced girl if she drew comfort from religion Mum blasted, 'No! I don't believe in God. If I did, I'd take him to court! When innocent men, women and children were ordered, at gunpoint, to strip naked and then shot into the pits they had been forced to dig in order to create their common grave, the last thing they saw before being murdered was the inscription on the belts of the Germans – not the Nazis, which was a political party – but the Germans – and it read 'God is with us.' If God was with the Germans, then God is the Devil!' The students were galvanised. One black student slumped glumly, in the back. Mum's eyes caught his, and held them. 'You have a history of slavery and oppression in this country, too.' The black student perked up. 'You're not responsible for what your grandparents did.' Fiercely, Mum eyeballed the white students. 'But you must accept that they did it.' The black student smirked. His classmates gasped. 'Now remember me.' My mother's medical prognosis cast a constant shadow. 'When I'm gone, you will be my witnesses.' The students leapt to their feet and rushed the stage, swamping the sick old woman in bear hugs, kisses and tears.

For the rest of the week, Mum lectured to electrified crowds in America's Bible Belt. At the end of her stay, the philanthropist offered her a thousand dollar honorarium. She refused to accept a personal cheque.

'I don't make money off the Holocaust. If you want to make a donation you can send a cheque to the Association of Hidden Children, in Poland. They are taking care of elderly Poles who rescued them during the war. A few of these rescuers are still alive.'

Mum and I sat side by side in the back seat of the limousine chauffeuring us to the airport in Omaha. The large, thick windows were tinted. Like local celebrities who had ridden in this vehicle before us, we could look out, but no one could see in. Mum was at peace, satisfied with another mission accomplished.

I gazed at my mother's profile, which had once been chiselled, and now was beginning to sag. A woman who survived three wartime invasions and the infamous Warsaw Ghetto was slowly and inexorably being destroyed by medical negligence. To me, my mother's final victimisation was beyond tragic; it was absurd. To avoid becoming engulfed by grief, I trained myself not to look too far ahead.

I lifted my mother's wrinkled and liver-spotted hand, pressed it to my cheek, and kissed it. Then I followed her gaze to the view of the foothills and cornfields and cottonwood trees whizzing past. For the moment, Death could wait.

CHAPTER THIRTY-NINE

In November of 2010, I moved into Mum's neighbourhood in order to live in close proximity to her. She lived on one side of the neighbourhood mall, and my apartment was located on the other. Taking a short cut through the mall, I could walk to Mum's apartment in fifteen minutes. If there was an ambulance waiting and I dashed, I could reach both Mum and the ambulance in ten minutes.

Earlier that autumn, Michael bought Mum a mobility scooter. It was a top-of-the-line model, with strong and sturdy tyres that kept her mobile in winter. When Mum discovered that rain deterred her from scooting outside, she had a roof installed. She tooled around the neighbourhood on her luxury scooter with the roof that protected her from rain and hot sun. Attached to the scooter, a bright orange flag proclaiming PRIDE fluttered in the breeze. Mum enjoyed her scooter. 'I love the way the wind hits my face when I take off! Och, that fresh air! I feel so alive!'

After I signed the lease on the new apartment, in the summer of 2010, the City of Cote St. Luc proceeded with plans to demolish half the mall and build townhouses on the reclaimed site. During the demolition period a large section of space resembled a bombed out war zone. As I watched my eighty-two-year-old mother whizz past the ruins of what was once the Cavendish Mall, superimposed in my imagination I saw a teenage girl on a motorcycle 'requisitioned' by Russian buddies, vrooming through the ruins of post-war Germany. As Mum zipped along she surveyed the rubble and declared, 'There goes the neighbourhood!' The destruction of a section of the mall allowed Mum an unimpeded view of the building where I now lived. 'I scoot along, I see that building and know you're there. It's wonderful!'

At home, Mum excavated a painting she had stored away. It was a painting of a girl on a regular scooter, given to her years before by a family friend. 'He was right when he said this girl represented me. This is me! This is me again!'

On winter's milder days Mum rode her scooter to my apartment. I went downstairs to hold the doors for her, and she parked her machine in the lobby. On winter's bright and icy days I worked in front of the sunlit windows in the back room of her apartment. Mum's modest apartment was serendipitously situated so that it seemed to contain a built-in solarium. Sunlight flooded the rooms during winter's shortest and coldest days. I taught Mum to sunbathe on her bed when the sun kissed it, at noon. 'But the sun gets in my eyes!' She protested.

'So put on sunglasses!'

One brilliantly-lit January day, at noon, I walked into my mother's apartment to find her lying on her back on her bed, the radio on the nightstand turned to a classical music station, wearing nothing but a pair of sunglasses. I gaped. Mum grinned. Her mischievous grin seemed to say, 'You see, Kiddo? You think I don't listen to you, but I do.'

Mum's reconstituted mobility allowed her to do her own shopping again, whether it was arranging a home delivery, or picking up a bag of sesame seed bagels and a carton of unsweetened orange juice and bringing home her purchases in the scooter's basket. Once more she was able to go to the movies on her own. I bought her ticket in advance, and arranged with cinema management at the local mall's

Cineplex for doors to be held open so Mum could drive her scooter directly into the screening room. Knowing she would be dependent on an usher to hold open the large double doors in order to let her out, I came to the cinema lobby when the film was scheduled to end, so Mum would not have to wait nor be dependent on the kindness of strangers. Cinema staff and management developed affection for us. Mum would drive out of the screening room flashing a radiant smile. 'The usher told me you were here, waiting for me!' (During my second Renata-less year I dreamt she was driving through the wide glass doors of the cinema lobby. In this dream, Mum wasn't alone. She was emerging from the movies with a crowd. As in life, I sat waiting for her, but in the dream she was surprised, yet pleased to see me. Again Mum flashed her high wattage smile, waved at me, and drove on amidst a crowd of souls. The glass doors of the Cineplex morphed into the glass doors of an airport, and Mum was in transit, moving to another plane. When I awoke from the dream, I understood I would not be hearing from her for a long while.)

Once a week, a woman from the [40]CLSC came to the apartment to help Mum take a shower. On the other six days, Mum waited until I was on the premises before taking a shower on her own. 'I can do it by myself, sweetheart, I just feel safer when you're here.' The bathroom door was open and, echoing my brother as a child, Mum called, 'Sharon, are you there?' Only when Mum heard my voice would I then hear the water running. Mum managed to take a shower sitting in a shower chair and using a detachable hose. Still, I washed her back and dried her off with a large beach towel while she quivered like a happy puppy. Wrapped in a

[40] *Centre Local de Services Communautaires,* local community service centres: Quebec's medical clinics

bathrobe Mum returned, refreshed, to bed, and groaned contentedly while I massaged her feet.

Medication was arranged over the phone, and delivered. The ring of a phone for the hearing impaired rattled the walls, and me.

Since I now lived in the neighbourhood, Mum received requested library material within hours of placing an order. She e-mailed to me a list of books she wanted to read and films she wanted to see. I retyped the ad hoc list and sent it to the reference department. The material was gathered, and within an hour I was notified that it was waiting for me at the front desk. I'd wheel my shopping trolley to the library, pick up the material and pull it through the snow, like a sleigh, to Mum's apartment. Like my mother before me, I became a courier in a 'walking library.'

When I relocated to Mum's neighbourhood I spent every evening with Mum, unless she was picked up and driven to a meeting at the Holocaust Centre, the Jewish Genealogical Society, or to a group with the misleading moniker The Polish Jewish Heritage Society.

On the evenings Mum was out, I sat reading in an armchair in front of the fireplace or in the oversized rocking chair in the children's section of the neighbourhood library. Whether I was walking home late at night from Mum's place or from the library, I was expected to check in when I arrived. Mum could not rest until I did. 'Okay. Now that I hear your voice and know you're safe, I can go to sleep.'

When spring came, in the afternoons we'd meet at the truncated mall and head for a local park. Sometimes Mum got into a near-collision with a kid on a bike. Both would brake just in time and the kid, whether out of deference to Mum's age, or because he had quicker reflexes, rode around her.

As Mum drove home I trailed behind her. She'd drive through the garage of her apartment building, where she had permission to park the scooter. Several times a week I'd stop by to pick up the electrical charger, take it down to the garage, and charge the scooter.

After our excursions in the park Mum called and confessed, 'I had a good time this afternoon. I love you!'

We were enjoying our simple pleasures and each other. As with my father, Mum learned to trust and rest comfortably with me. By default, we became each other's partners. By default, our relationship became the longest, the most intense and most intimate of our lives.

CHAPTER FORTY

On Mother's Day of 2011, Michael stopped in on his way to his friend Howard's second home in the country, along with a colleague. Gerry O'Leary, Chief of Anaesthesia at the Toronto General Hospital, was instrumental in organising Mum's second and third operations in Toronto, even postponing an appointment with Ontario's Ministry of Health officials because he promised to put her to sleep on the operating table. He also postponed a trip in order to attend her 80th birthday party, a milestone we celebrated in Toronto.

As Mum limped to the door to greet her guests, Gerry's observant eye examined her gait.

'Come.' He offered his arm. 'We're going for a walk.' Without hesitation Mum linked her arm with Gerry's, and followed him into the hallway.

Slowly Gerry strolled with Mum along the corridor, the leg from her hurting hip jutting outward. They re-entered her apartment five minutes later. Mum was winded.

'This is awful!' Gerry proclaimed. 'If I had to walk on a tilt, I'd be exhausted after five minutes too. I'm going to stick out my neck here,' Gerry addressed Michael. 'Your mother needs hip replacement surgery.'

'Finally!' Mum felt vindicated by Gerry's support. 'Finally somebody believes how tired I am!'

Frightened by the ramifications of hip replacement surgery, Michael balked. 'You could die!'

Mum looked him straight in the eye. 'I'd rather die than live like this!'

Silently, I agreed.

'If your mother doesn't have the surgery,' Gerry warned, 'her situation will deteriorate. She could fall and break her hip, and then she'll be bedridden.'

With Michael by her side, Mum revisited the Toronto surgeon who dissuaded them from surgery a year before.

'How do you know Dr O'Leary?' Gerry's intervention, rather than Mum's need, seemed to change the surgeon's mind. In Toronto, hip replacement surgery was scheduled for September. The surgeon would be on vacation in August and so would Michael, who had arranged a two-week private bus tour of Spain for his family, along with Howard's family.

Though she could barely walk, Mum was determined to travel to Poland. In Warsaw, in August, a network of world Jewry known as The International Child Survivors' Movement planned to hold their annual conference. It was the 20th anniversary of their association, and for ten of those twenty years Mum lobbied to have a conference held in Warsaw. Her dream was coming true. Her nightmare was unending.

At the end of June, Mum developed a raw, body-rattling cough. We recognised the signs. We went to hospital. Pneumonia had set in. The markers were up.

Test results were sent to Michael. We understood that cancer had re-entered Mum's lungs, and were expecting she would undergo another operation. We were expecting Michael to call, but he didn't. Mum called Michael's office.

'Isn't he there yet?' The secretary seemed surprised. 'He flew to Montreal this morning. He's on his way to you.'

Mum lay on the closed hide-a-bed in the living room. I lay on the floor next to her, like a loyal dog. Sounds from the street penetrated the thin windows. The sun's glare was relentless. The day refused to end.

Michael arrived and stood in Mum's doorway like The Angel of Death. He said nothing. His tear-stained face spoke for him. The devastated expression on my brother's face sent me racing to the back room. I collapsed onto the futon and curled into a foetal position. The Angel of Death followed.

'I'm not ready for this.' I croaked out the words in a husky whisper. My throat muscles had shut down.

Wearily Mum called from the living room. 'Leave her be. She'll come back.'

When I returned to the living room Michael was beside Mum, on his knees.

'It's inoperable,' he confessed. 'But it is treatable.'

'How long have I got?' Mum's eyes were dry and blank.

'Oh we can give you lots and lots of time!' Michael chirped, unconvincingly.

'Come here, you two.' I knelt beside my brother, and Mum rested her hands on our heads, like a priest giving benediction.

'Michael, promise me you'll take care of your sister.'

'He can't take care of me!' My throat muscles opened. The words rushed out before I could stop them. 'He's not his own man!'

Ann's man remained silent. The next day Michael brought Mum back to Toronto for consultations and further tests. Gerry was there.

'I guess I'll die limping.' Mum greeted him in the hospital cafeteria.

All Gerry could say was, 'Don't think about it now.'

Hip replacement surgery was cancelled, and it was agreed that cancer treatment needed to start as soon as possible. In the meantime, Mum's oncologist alerted Michael to the existence of an alternative drug. It was one of the new generation of cancer drugs targeting the sick cells while leaving healthy ones relatively intact. The drug was approved in the United States and Europe, but not in Quebec, because the provincial government balked at paying for it. In order to promote the drug the company that manufactured it was administering treatment, at its own expense, in selected clinics across the province. Only patients testing positive for a specific genetic mutation were eligible for treatment. Mum was tested in Toronto. The results would be known in two weeks. In the meantime, it was deemed imperative that some form of treatment get started, so Mum returned to Montreal, and conventional chemotherapy began.

Mum was treated with a drug that she tolerated well in the past. This time, it made her violently ill. Before she recovered and test results came in from Toronto, a second round of treatment loomed. Depleted and despairing, she appealed to Michael, 'I can't go through that again. It will kill me before the cancer will.'

'Do what you want!' Michael snapped at his mother. Dr Zajdman was beginning to crack.

'Sharon.' Mum turned to me. I was by her side. I was by her side all the time, now. 'What should I do?'

I had developed tunnel vision. I refused to believe Mum would not test positive for the new drug, because she needed the new drug to live and I needed my mother to live.

'Rest, and wait. Save your energy so you'll be strong enough to respond to the new drug.'

Mum tested positive. Under the circumstances it was considered a miracle, or a miraculous reprieve.

In order to receive treatment Mum had to travel to a clinic outside the city limits once every two weeks, for the next six months, at least. There was a time when we had two cars. Mum gave Ann the better and younger car as a wedding present, and drove the older car until it was good for nothing but the scrap heap. Now we had no car.

At first Michael's friend Howard sort of kind of said he would drive Mum to the life-extending treatments. Then Howard's wife Lynn sort of kind of said she would do the driving, but the private bus tour of Spain intervened, and the Jewish holidays were coming up, and there were the monthly breaks in the Bahamas, unless they booked another cruise. A search for professional drivers turned up characters who, in order to chauffeur a cancer patient back and forth and wait two hours in between, would do so only if they could financially exploit a desperate situation.

A friend of mine stepped in. She was a Polish Catholic woman I met through Mum. This woman said she could and would drive Mum to treatments during the week on her day off, so treatments were arranged around her work schedule. When our friend's schedule was suddenly changed, she called in sick in order to keep her commitment to Mum. Having used up her allotted sick days, when she really fell ill she vomited, dragged herself out of bed, and went to work.

The new drug was not without side effects. It ravaged Mum's lovely skin, and cut deep cracks into her fingers and feet. While the new drug took effect, the first drug continued wreaking havoc. Three weeks after receiving it, Mum's hair blew out.

Still, Michael insisted Mum proceed with plans to travel to Poland. He bought two airline tickets; one for Mum, and one for himself. Before joining his family and those he considered family on their tour of Spain, he accompanied Mum to Warsaw.

The day before the conference, Mum was invited to a reception held by the Polish government's foreign ministry, where an outstanding schoolteacher was to receive an award as Best Teacher of the Year for Holocaust Studies. As Mum sat in the audience, flanked by Michael and Norman Conard, her name was called. She was instructed to approach the podium. In a daze, she struggled to her feet. Despite the air-conditioning, her auburn-coloured wig itched. The eighty-two-year-old chronic cancer patient limped to the front of the hall with the aid of cane. She supported herself, standing on her severely cracked feet, while a representative of the foreign ministry read out a list of her achievements, and bestowed upon her a medal for the Order of Merit.

A hall filled with a hundred people consisting of teachers and their families, government officials, diplomats, and the Chief Rabbi of Poland roared their approval and applauded. Michael and Norman Conard sat stunned.

Mum grew confused. Through her partial deafness and the static of tinnitus caused by *Herr* Phenning's attack on her skull in the Rosol factory during the war, Mum managed to decipher that she was receiving this award for her part in having her wartime Polish rescuers honoured as Righteous Among The Nations, and for her ceaseless activism in building bridges of understanding and forgiveness between Polish Catholics and Polish Jews.

Still, Mum could not process the meaning of the award. 'This can't be for me,' she thought, growing haunted. She felt tugged by the memory of a doll-like young woman, perfectly formed, who seemed to have been created in miniature. She hovered in Mum's heart and mind for seven decades, refusing to leave. Perceiving her own approaching end, Mum feared the story and memory of the woman she considered her surrogate mother would die with her. 'This isn't for me.' Mum was already distanced from the proceedings of the present, and slipped into the parallel universe of her past.

'This award,' she told herself, 'No. All of it. My whole life, the lives of my children and grandchildren, all of it, I owe to my Janka.'

When Mum returned from Poland, she asked me to write Janka's story. I wanted to give her what she wanted, but didn't feel equal to the task. I believed that it would take a Dickens to do justice to Janka's story. To ease my way into her parallel universe, Mum handed me pages from her private memoir, a few at a time.

'Have you got questions for me?' Mum queried, after I perused the pages in privacy. When my questions were answered Mum handed, or electronically sent me more pages.

Considering Mum's prognosis, I decided to self-publish a manuscript completed just before she fell out of her final remission. The text would become a book called *Bent Branches*. It was the narrative of a family bent, but unbroken.

CHAPTER FORTY-ONE

There was another, unforeseen effect of the new drug. In fifty per cent of patients who received it, this drug leeched alarming amounts of magnesium out of their systems. The imbalance rendered Mum irritable, sleepless, seized with cramps, and dangerously weak. Now, along with trips to the clinic, we spent several days a week on the cancer ward of the Jewish General Hospital, where Mum received magnesium infusions lasting hours. In the mornings she underwent a blood test, we would wait for the results until noon, and in the afternoons the infusions were administered. By January of 2012 we were in and out of hospital three times a week, because the infusions weren't taking effect. Almost as soon as Mum received an infusion, she peed it out. It took weeks for the doctors to understand what was happening, and longer for them to make the adjustments allowing the infusions to remain in Mum's system.

During these day-long stays on the cancer ward, I received something I never had before: my mother's full attention. I was finally granted access to her parallel universe. Indeed I was invited, welcomed, and drawn in. It seemed like Janka was waiting for me. So was my aunt Ania. 'We were there in the worst of times,' they seemed to say. 'Now you are.'

Sometimes I imagined hearing Natalja too. 'I wasn't able to be there for my daughter. I loved her, but I failed her. You will succeed where I failed. You must.'

In order to have access to a private room, Mum and I would arrive on the cancer ward before eight a.m. Mum lay on a cot, and I sat in a reclining chair, pulling out pages from the private memoir, along with a pen and notebook and the mini cassette recorder transported in a schoolbag on wheels. Even before the infusion entered her system Mum seemed revitalised as she narrated the tale of her Dickensian past, knowing it would be preserved. In these recordings, which were her last, Mum emerges fully out of hiding. Having nothing left to lose, she tells the raw, unsanitised, and harrowing truth. That Mum trusted me enough to reveal what heretofore she felt too ashamed to say was a gift and a release. I took breaks outside the room, looking out the seventh-storey picture window onto the twinkling traffic lights and headlights and the roofs of the city blanketed by snow. Seventy years seemed to fall away and I imagined I saw, superimposed onto the modern cityscape, a dark and menacing forest through which a fourteen-year-old girl, stemming the blood from a knife wound at her throat, made a dash for life and freedom through waist-high and blood-soaked snow.

My head ached and so did my heart. If she can stand it, I told myself, then so can I. Receiving an infusion of strength from the spirits of Mum's first caregivers, I returned to the fatally wounded old woman who was once the almost fatally wounded young girl.

When spring came and her condition stabilised, Mum visited my apartment with a handyman in tow. It was the handyman who lugged the paintings and tapestries and portraits of the ancestors.

'My god Mummy, have you stripped your walls?'

'Never mind, sweetheart.' Half to herself, Mum muttered, 'It's going to be a mess After, anyway.' Then, loudly, she declared, 'It will give me pleasure and peace to come here and see that these things are safe with you.'

***

In July of 2012 we sat waiting in the oncologist's office. Generally reticent, Dr Kavan bounded in with a great grin on his face.

'It couldn't be better!' He exulted. He was referring to the results of Mum's latest tests. 'You can go home and celebrate!'

'Dr Kavan.' I was the one who was reticent, now, yet I knew that, at this point, Kavan's opinion was the only opinion which counted. 'If my mother's condition is stable, can she get a new hip?'

Mum gasped.

'That's a wonderful idea! Renata, if you do, it will change your life dramatically for the better!'

Uncharacteristically, Mum kept quiet. Outside Dr Kavan's office she said something to me I rarely heard, coming from her. What Mum said was, 'Thank you.'

This time, scheduling the surgery was tricky, and there was no question but that it would take place in Toronto. It could be scheduled only during the three-month period when Mum was off the drug and the surgeon of choice, along with the right team, was available. Of course Gerry, with his Irish lilt and startling wit, would be there to joke and tease and sing Mum to sleep. Mum had become a patient in two provinces.

In the summer of 2012, Mum did not travel. She stayed with me. She drove on her scooter to my apartment, and rested on my large balcony in the afternoon shade, where I had created a garden. She leaned back in the lounge chair, surveying the tomatoes and herbs and salads and climbing vines and pronounced, 'It's so restful here!' I had to assist her on and off the balcony, because the high step between the balcony and living room floor was difficult for her to navigate. With the air conditioner humming, Mum lay on my sofa and watched me work.

'You just go ahead and do what you have to do. Pretend I'm not here.' Hearing that, I shuddered.

I was writing a column for a newspaper then. I read the material to Mum. She gave me feedback. We worked well together. Mum was a good editor.

As I worked at the computer in my living room, I kept an eye on Mum. She read the library books I brought for her, or listened to library-owned CDs. A recorded Judy Garland concert was a favourite.

Mum began paying attention to the details of my days, particularly to the way I spent summer. I lived in solitary confinement, with swimming my sole form of recreation.

'You don't ask for much.' Mum mused. 'You never complain. Like your father.' Mum smiled, in remembrance. 'That beautiful man left me a beautiful dividend.' By then, I had left my workstation and was sitting on the sofa, stroking the new hair that had grown on Mum's head, as she lay in my lap.

'I made many mistakes in my life,' Mum confessed, gazing up at me as she clasped her hands in mine, 'But your father wasn't one of them.'

When Michael and his children and his friends left on their vacations, whether it was overseas or up north or to cottage country, Mum queried, as if just realising what had been de facto for years, 'Didn't anyone call you?'

I was resigned. 'Oh Mum, you know I'm not part of the In Crowd.'

'You're part of MY In Crowd!' Mum grew reflective. She had time to think, that summer. I don't know whether she accepted responsibility for the part she played in my exclusion by complying with the selfishness of the tribe, but in her heart she recognised the consequences it had, and would have, in the future she wouldn't live to see. Her true feelings began to leak.

'Fuck 'em all.' Mum exhorted. 'Fuck 'em all and build your own life!'

After those with families and well-paying work returned from holidays and vacations, arrangements were made for Mum's long-wished-for and hardly-to-be-believed hip replacement surgery. At first it appeared the surgery would take place close to Christmas. Then the date was moved back, and it appeared it would take place in early December.

'I don't want to leave you before your birthday!' Mum dared to complain.

'Mum.' I was firm. I was also frightened. It had been a four-year battle to reach this point, and it almost didn't happen. I wasn't going to let Mum duck the surgery, now.

'You will go whenever they will take you. Knowing you'll be on your feet again is the best birthday present I can have.'

The date for the surgery settled on 10 December. With a hired driver, two days after my birthday, I accompanied Mum to the train station. While the driver waited, I waited with Mum for the train. We helped her board, and I waved her off. Mum would leave me before my next birthday.

336

With Michael by her side, with Gerry teasing her into sleep, Mum sailed through the surgery. On 13 December, sixty-four years to the day after her arrival in Canada, Mum was sitting up on her new hip. She was racing so quickly down the halls of the rehabilitation residence that Michael and the therapist had to shout at her to slow down.

'Your brother's a slave driver!' Mum bellowed over a long-distance line. 'He's making me do exercise all the time!'

'You listen to Michael, and do what he says.'

Michael went to the rehabilitation residence every evening after work. He also brought in his housekeeper and trained her to supervise Mum's post-operative exercises.

On Christmas Eve, Mum left the rehabilitation residence and moved into Michael's home. She spent New Year's Eve with family friends. I called her cell phone just before midnight, and heard her blowing a party favour into an old man's ear.

'Wake up, Mr Feld! Wake up!' It was the first time, since Daddy died, that Mum and I hadn't been with each other at New Year. We would never again see in a new year together.

While Mum recuperated in Toronto, our long telephone conversations were too often interrupted by attacks of raw, body-rattling coughs. I remained silent while Mum's lungs hacked. When the coughing fits were over we continued our conversation, but we both knew what it meant.

On an intensely frigid and sunny Saturday at the end of January, Michael drove Mum back to Montreal. His housekeeper came with them. She lived in for ten days, to assist Mum.

I waited for the call telling me Mum was on the verge of arrival. The welcome mat was not out. The carpets were rolled up and stored in corners. The surface Mum would walk on had to be level and even.

Before I reached Mum's apartment, she was already there. I let myself in with my set of her keys. I stood in the doorway in hiking boots and a long, heavy, quilted black coat that made me look like the Michelin man. 'Sweetheart!' Mum flung out her arms and flew at me. 'Look! No walker, no cane, no nothing!' Mum fairly danced through the sunlit rooms of her apartment. 'Look at me everybody! I'm walking! It's a miracle! I'm walking!'

Pensively, Michael looked at me. Then he said something he hadn't said since he was a child, and has never said since. Pointedly, he said, 'Thank you.'

'I want to go to the mall! I want to see my friends!' Almost every day between three and five p.m., Mum met with several women at the Mmmmuffin concession in the Cavendish Mall. She rode through the wide glass doors on her scooter. She used her cane to press the electronic sensor that opened the doors automatically. Coasting through the mall, Mum held court at the Mmmmuffin concession, perched on the seat of her scooter, with its protective roof, like a queen on a throne.

Mum's wish was our command. We piled into Michael's SUV. I entered the mall first, and passed the Mmmmuffin concession.

'Hi Sharon!' Mum's buddies hailed. 'How's your mother?'

Mum was hiding behind a wall around the corner, like an actor waiting in the wings. Mum's sense of the dramatic was always finely honed. At this moment, it was impeccable. Hearing her cue, she emerged. 'I'm fine!' She half-skated, half-marched towards her friends.

The calculated entrance had the expected effect.

'Renata! Oh. Look! She's walking!' Michael and his housekeeper stood in the background. Tears welled in the eyes of her friends.

'When did you get back, Renata?'

'Today. Half an hour ago. I wanted to come and see you guys. You're the first people I'm seeing!'

We pulled up chairs, ordered coffees and a tisane for me, and joined the [41]*Klatch*.

---

[41] German term, literally meaning 'gossip' but in this context a gathering over coffee

CHAPTER FORTY-TWO

'Thirty years with him and thirty years without him! Why did he have to leave me so soon?!' It was the thirtieth anniversary of Daddy's death. It was also Passover. Mum did not feel well enough to take a train to Toronto. Locally she received several invitations to Seder suppers, including an invitation from the couple who were Michael's closest friends. After Mum received a new hip, Howard and Lynn resurfaced. Taking their cue from my brother and sister-in-law, Howard and Lynn invited Mum to Seder without inviting me. In this, they miscalculated. Howard wasn't Mum's son, and Lynn wasn't the mother of Mum's grandchildren.

'How dare they invite me without inviting you?! That's what your father's family did to me!!' I could have told Mum how Michael's friends became so daring. But I didn't. That's what my brother and his wife did to me, for years, and Mum never protested, drawing the line only when she was summoned to a Seder on 6 April. 'No Michael. I'm not leaving your sister on April 6. I'll come on the seventh.' Dad's death left Mum emotionally insecure and oddly intimidated by the young and untraumatised. Like her mother before her, my mother sacrificed me to my sibling because she knew she would never lose me. In her milieu, widowed grandmothers are marginalised. Mum feared losing access to her grandchildren. Despite the way I was being treated, I was able to say, 'You don't believe Michael would allow that.' Desperately, Mum confessed, 'I don't know, and I'm afraid to find out!' There are few prospects more frightening to a Holocaust survivor than further loss of family. For my part, being fatherless and husbandless set me up for a shove to the bottom of the heap. I became conditioned to exclusion. I urged Mum to accept the invitation.

'Absolutely not! The nerve!'

'You've received other invitations.'

'You don't get it.' Meaningfully, almost defiantly Mum declared, 'I want to be with YOU!'

It was something I had waited to hear all my life. When Mum finally said it, I sensed the end was near.

***

At Passover of 2013, on the thirtieth anniversary of Dad's death, a call came from a woman who traced Mum through the Holocaust Centre. Zelda Abramson was a sociologist doing research for a book about the post-war lives of Survivors who settled in Montreal. I was lying beside Mum in her bed when the call came.

'Here Sharon.' Wanly, Mum handed me the receiver. 'You talk to her. I don't have the patience.' Nor the strength, Mum might've added, but didn't.

Zelda introduced herself and asked to set up an appointment for an interview. Mum was amenable to the idea until Zelda mentioned that the interview would be filmed.

'The floors are bare.' I confessed. 'Mum recently had hip replacement surgery and the carpets are rolled into corners so she won't risk tripping. The walls are half-bare.' I told Zelda that Mum had tapestries and portraits removed and installed on my walls. I told her why.

There was a pause on the line and then solemnly, Zelda insisted, 'All the more reason not only to record this interview, but to film it.'

Zelda's response punched me in the gut. Just as solemnly I responded, 'You're right.'

On 13 April, Zelda Abramson and her partner John, who would be doing the filming, came to Mum's apartment. I withdrew to a back room until the interviewers invited me to participate. Before their arrival Mum took a codeine tablet in order to subdue her cough. The cancer was in her lungs now. The drug also subdued her effervescent spirit. Encouraged by Mum, I found myself elaborating on her comments and then telling stories of my own. Tacitly, Mum was handing me the reins to her story.

One tale of childhood that seemed to sum up the post-war refugee experience was Mum's comment to her friends on the quality of my diction and speech. For Mum, flawless English was not only mandatory, but considered a tool of survival. Speaking English like a CBC broadcaster would ensure that I'd be able to 'pass'. Indeed, it was the Jew Lorne Greene who, before Going Hollywood, was known as The Voice of Canada.

I was ten years old when I stood before the director of Children's Theatre and announced, 'Moy name is Sharon Zoidman.' Instantly, Dorothy Davis corrected me. In private life Miss Davis was Mrs Stein, but we didn't know that. That is how well SHE passed.

'Your name is NOT Sharon ZOIDMAN.' Haughtily, the elderly director intoned. 'Your name is Sharon Ziiiideman!' Sitting silently in a corner of Miss Davis's drawing room, my mother allowed herself a tiny and satisfied smile.

A year later, Friends of Mum's who had settled in New York spoke admiringly of the way I spoke. Mum's friends spoke like Polish Jews, but their children spoke Brooklynese.

'Sharon speaks The Queen's English!' Mum's friends enthused.

Mum knew better. As a proud member of The British Commonwealth, annually Mum listened to Elizabeth's Christmas broadcasts. Later in life, our Queen seemed to benefit from voice lessons, but at this early stage her voice placement was nasal and irritatingly high.

'My husband and I wont to wish you all a very heppy Christmas!' Elizabeth would chirp, on the CBC's national broadcasts. Mum had heard it, and she remembered.

'Oh no.' Mum protested, to her friends in Brooklyn. 'My daughter speaks much better than the Queen!'

In the middle of Mum's living room, on her bare floors, among her half-bare walls, my satirical impression of a young Queen Elizabeth made such a strong impression on our interviewers that, in the book-to-be, the chapter devoted to Mum is titled *The Queen's English*.

In 2012, I published the short story collection *Bent Branches*. It received respectable reviews. Since the linked stories are Holocaust-related, Mum gave a copy to the director of Montreal's Holocaust Centre.

Every two years the Holocaust Centre holds a book fair which promotes Holocaust memoirs. When its director read *Bent Branches,* she told Mum she would enter it in the upcoming fair.

'But Mum, I'm not a Holocaust survivor and the book isn't a memoir.'

'You be quiet. The book is whatever they want it to be.'

I was certain the book would be disqualified. Instead, the director established a new category called Second Generation Writing. Now the book was eligible.

Twenty-four authors would be represented, and three were asked to give a public reading. I was one of the three. Mum was over the moon. She had the book's best review enlarged and laminated, propped it up on her coffee table, and sold copies from home. At least, that's what she told me. I told her to use the money from copies sold to pay the private drivers who chauffeured her. I suspect she gave away more books than she sold.

Mum's cancer, which now lived in her lungs, kept asserting itself in the form of a virulent cough. One afternoon, coming in to apply ointment and bandages to the cracks on her feet, I discovered soiled pads in the bathroom.

'Mum.' Delicately, I referred to the discovery. Mum's reaction was violent.

'Are you telling me I stink?!' After hurling a volley of abuse, she began to cry. Her cough was so violent that it had depressed her bladder.

'You can have a bladder lift, Mum. Michael can arrange it. Compared to hip replacement surgery, it's simple.'

'I don't want Michael to know. I don't want my grandchildren to know they've got a smelly old grandmother who can't hold her pee!'

After spending the afternoon with a woman who alternately attacked me and then cried in my arms, I returned to my apartment and called my brother.

'Don't tell her you know. Get her to tell you.' He did.

At our next appointment with Dr Kavan Mum tested, 'If I stop treatment, how long have I got?'

Dr Kavan darted a startled glance at me. 'That is not a good idea.'

'Then can I have the bladder lift done in Montreal?' Mum wailed.

'You know what goes on here. You would have to wait months, and there is no guarantee it could be done during the period when you're off the drug. If Michael can arrange it for you, let him.' Dr Kavan said Mum could 'cycle on and off the drug for years.'

Because Mum could not be without cancer treatment for more than three months, and because she had to be off treatment for at least one month before having the bladder lift, and because the surgeon in Toronto willing to do the procedure as a favour to Michael would be on vacation in September, the cancer treatments were extended to last over the course of the summer, and the bladder lift was scheduled for 3 October. Not only was the current course of treatment extended, but Mum was given stronger doses in order to keep her condition stable. As we sat together in a hospital waiting room, she broke down.

'Some people get to die in peace! Why do I have to go through this before! I don't deserve it!' Indeed, she didn't. If doctors had a fraction of the courage their patients demonstrate, they'd get rid of the killers in their midst.

'How I wish I could go to sleep and never wake up again.' Mum moaned. How I wished I could lie down and die with her.

On Sunday, 23 June Mum and I attended a funeral. The husband of Mum's cleaning lady had died. It was a second marriage for both of them. Basia was a Catholic Pole. Her husband was a Romanian Jew. Basia and Boris were together for thirty years. Each had children from previous marriages. Basia's daughter, son-in-law and granddaughter were in attendance. The Polish Catholic son-in-law was one of the pallbearers at the Jewish funeral.

Boris had four sons. One lived in Montreal, and was often with Basia at Jewish Elder Care as she sat, daily, by her husband's side. After cleaning apartments and condos, Basia headed directly to Jewish Elder Care. For five years, she sat by her ailing husband's bedside every day.

The three sons in attendance sat together in the first pew. Basia looked lost. It was her first time in a Jewish funeral home. She didn't know where to sit. That's when Mum stage-whispered directions.

'Basia! You go and sit in the front! Go! You belong there!' Egged on by her employer, Basia took a seat in the front, by herself, off to the side. Her daughter did not sit with her.

In his eulogy, the only reference to Basia made by the rabbi was, 'his devoted companion, Barbara.' Basia was Boris' legal wife. In preparing the eulogy, the rabbi would have received information from Boris's sons.

As Basia's employer, Mum paid her more respect than did her family, and Boris's family. Stretching like a wary eagle, Mum honed in and seemed to vibrationally will Basia strength and support.

When the time came to accompany the coffin out of the funeral home, Basia walked alone. Mum's blue-grey eyes turned steely. Outside the funeral home our hired driver waited for us, his car parked to the side. Mum positioned her cane in front of her, leaning on it with both arms, like a song-

and-dance man. She surveyed the proceedings like a security guard.

Boris's sons got into a car and rode to the cemetery. Basia's daughter was bemoaning the fact that it was too early to go to church. How was she going to fill the time, until then? Mum accosted her and in Polish, commanded, 'You're not going to church this morning. You're going to the Jewish cemetery with your mother. She'll feel better if you're with her.'

Basia's daughter did as she was told. If she hadn't, I knew, without being told, that we'd be accompanying Basia to the cemetery, chauffeured by our driver.

In the privacy of the driver's car Mum erupted, 'It's because of this kind of shit that I've decided not to have a service. I want a pre-war European Jewish funeral. I am to be taken straight to the cemetery and put into the ground. I want you to be spared a circus of hypocrisy!'

Mum's wishes would not be respected, and I would not be spared. That was still to come. On this humid day in June I was proud of my mother. She was proud of me, too.

'I want you to know,' Mum said, suddenly stopping her scooter and coming to park by the food court in the mall. 'I want you to know that if I don't live to see the opening of the museum in Warsaw, I have left instructions with Bieta to make sure *Bent Branches* will be featured in the museum's shop'. Among her many projects, behind the scenes Mum was working as a consultant for the creation of The Museum of the History of Jews in Poland that was being built on the site of the wartime Warsaw Ghetto. Mum trusted the woman she considered her best friend to fulfil this mission for her, in the event she could not.

The museum's opening was repeatedly postponed. It was as if Mum wasn't meant to see it.

'But Mum,' I protested, 'The book is in English.'

Mum was attached to the vision she created, and would not be deterred. 'Tourists will come from all over the world to visit this museum. Many of them will be English-speaking. Imagine, our story, our dead and those still living, in your book, will be there to greet them, on the site of Ghetto.' Mum appreciated the symmetry of the image. 'That is where and how it should be.'

The Museum of the History of Jews in Poland finally opened on the third week of October in 2014, almost to the day of what would have been Mum's 86th birthday. *Bent Branches* wasn't there.

Mum expressed further wishes. To Michael, she commanded, 'I want to be buried in Ontario and I want Daddy's remains exhumed and moved to lie beside me.' To me, she explained, 'I don't want you to feel that you have to sit in Quebec to tend your parents' graves. Michael is established in Ontario and his kids are there, but I WANT YOU TO BE FREE.'

CHAPTER FORTY-THREE

People have a sixth sense about the signals their bodies send them. Mum began going through old photographs and her stash of films; among which were interviews she had given both for Living Testimonies and the Shoah Foundation, inviting me to watch them with her. She showed me old photographs and told me the stories of the few people I didn't recognise. After two years of background research, I began writing Janka's story. Then Mum picked a fight.

'I don't want you coming with me to hospital! I'll go by myself!' I appealed to my brother's friend Howard.

'Would you or Lynn accompany Mum to hospital? She says she doesn't want me with her. No one should be alone on a cancer ward.'

'We're taking her out for dinner next week. We'll have a talk with her.' Howard and Lynn resurfaced after Mum got a new hip.

The upshot of Howard and Lynn's talk with Mum is that she went to see Dr Kavan alone, and was then sent scurrying around the hospital to different departments, on her new hip, with a requisition in hand, because Howard and Lynn decided that I needed psychiatric evaluation.

'Howard and Lynn say you need help for your anxiety and depression.' I agreed that, after standing by for nine years watching my mother being destroyed, I needed support of some kind, and it was clear where it wasn't going to come from.

Shortly after Mum's latest appointment with Dr Kavan, I came home to a message from a secretary who worked for a hospital psychiatrist. I was told I was ineligible for 'help' because the psychiatrist was treating my mother. The psychiatrist was not treating my mother. What he was doing was writing prescriptions for anti-depressants that weren't working. Because the psychiatrist wouldn't see me, Mum dropped the psychiatrist and stopped taking the anti-depressants.

While I was being pinned to the path of an avalanche, preparations for the Holocaust Centre's bookfair were underway. In the summer of 2013, I was invited to come to the centre to be interviewed by local media. Recognising the signs of magnesium loss in Mum, I declined. I didn't dare make commitments nor leave the neighbourhood. I knew we would soon be back in hospital.

Back in hospital, Mum and I worked on preparing my public reading. This time we did not have a private room. Behind the drawn curtains of public cubicles, cancer patients perked up as I rehearsed an excerpt from the short story *A Wedding in Heidelberg*. My theatre training comes back to me when I prepare a public reading. I sensed my unseen audience enjoyed what they heard.

'I think you should listen to Mummy's cough. There's something different about it. It's changed. It's gotten much worse. It racks her whole body. She's choking. She can hardly breathe.' I called Michael on his cell phone. Since the holiday Monday when Mum fainted and we were made to wait, I never called his home.

In response, Michael informed me, 'I'm on my way to the theatre.'

'But it's really bad, Michael. She's in terrible pain.'

'I said I'm on my way to the theatre.' It was six thirty on the evening of Thursday, 26 September.

'The play starts at 7:30. I'll be there for three hours.'

I had no answer. I was stunned.

What Michael didn't tell me was that the next morning, he was flying to New York for a three-day conference. He may have called Mum the next day but if he did, he didn't tell her to go to hospital.

It was a harrowing weekend. The intervals between vicious coughing fits were getting shorter. The oncology ward was closed on weekends. The only alternative was the emergency ward, and Mum didn't want to go there.

On Saturday evening, leaving Mum alone for an hour, I went to the pharmacy and dragged a humidifier to her apartment.

It was a wasted hour. The appliance was useless. I did not yet realise that Mum was dying.

On Monday morning a neighbour drove Mum to hospital, and stayed with her on the oncology ward. I came in the afternoon. Mum could not decipher the message behind the lung specialist's doctorspeak, but I could. I stepped back, and turned to my mother's primary nurse as if, in her, I might find an anchor.

'He's telling her she's dying.'

Instantly an unseen veil descended between Mum's primary nurse and me. A buzz went off through the ward.

Energetically, we were walled off. We had entered The Land of the Dying, and no one had the courage to follow us there.

Mum was receiving oxygen, which relaxed her and eased her cough.

'Do you want to go home tonight, Mrs Zajdman?'

Mum didn't know what to do. I decided for us.

'Absolutely not. We don't have oxygen at home. You will keep her here and keep her comfortable.'

Michael was notified. He flew in the next morning.

A night spent on oxygen seemed to restore Mum. Michael brought her home. She looked fine.

It was Tuesday, 1 October. That evening, an event was scheduled at the Polish consulate. Mum did something that would have been unbelievable in anyone else. She put on a bright yellow and orange dress and adorned herself with amber jewellery. Then she waddled back into the living room, beaming and looking beautiful. I was standing on the balcony, looking at the trees on the front lawn.

Mum seemed like the autumn leaves, bursting into a last glorious blaze before fading and falling to the ground.

Mum linked arms with Michael, and he escorted her to the event at the consulate.

CHAPTER FORTY-FOUR

'I lost only the battle, sweetheart. The war, I won.'

Renata Skotnicka-Zajdman, in the last weeks of her life.

Mum did not see her oncologist before leaving hospital on Tuesday. Dr Kavan was flying in from a conference in Europe. The lung specialist told us that the tumour, considered stable, had turned aggressive and collapsed her right lung. It meant the new drug was no longer working, and she was considered untreatable.

We called Dr Kavan's secretary. Between scheduled appointments she squeezed in a consultation for Wednesday, 2 October. Dr Kavan was surprised and upset by this twist. He refused to accept the lung specialist's interpretation of the x-rays. He said he had never before seen such a development in Mum's form of cancer, and he suspected that what was being interpreted as an aggressive tumour may have been the same stable tumour contaminated by infection from pneumonia. He put Mum on a fourteen-day course of powerful antibiotics. A CT scan, either publicly funded or paid for out of pocket, would be done within days of Mum's next birthday. In the meantime it was arranged that the CLSC would send in extra help at home in order to relieve me, and Michael made arrangements for palliative home care as a precaution, rather than as an immediate necessity.

The bladder lift, scheduled to take place in Toronto a week later, was cancelled. Because Mum was scheduled to be in Toronto, I had arranged to visit a friend in Vermont. On cancelling my plans I was inundated by a barrage of protests, even from Mum.

'Go! Have a good time!' Howard assured me that he would watch over Mum in my absence. I refused to leave.

My mother and I were so enmeshed that we fuelled each other's anguish. I looked at her, and she knew my heart was breaking. She looked at me, and I knew her heart was breaking as we were being inexorably wrenched away from each other. We handled our mutual heartbreak by getting back to work. On Wednesday morning, 2 October, understanding that helpers from the CLSC would now handle some of the grunge work, I returned to writing Janka's story. Outside my living room window, the leaves on a maple tree burst into flames of hot colour. I wrote in the mornings, and then sent the pages to Mum's computer. She was waiting for them. Each evening I entered Mum's apartment, lay down beside her, and she gave me notes.

On Saturday, 5 October, Michael drove in from Toronto with his wife and three children. Howard and Lynn drove in from the West Island with their three children. It would be the one day, for the rest of what remained of her life, that I was not with my mother. Over the phone she said to me, 'You didn't come because Ann was here.'

'Yes.' I admitted. Mum sighed. Late in the evening, after my brother and his tribe left and retired for the night to Howard's West Island mansion, Mum went to her computer, picked up the pages I'd written that morning, and wrote back, 'I missed you today. Not to work. Just to see your face.'

On Saturday, 12 October, Michael came back to Montreal with his family. That is when it happened. With a tank of portable oxygen, in a wheelchair, Michael and his family took Mum to the Cavendish Mall for her three-to-five p.m. coffee klatch. On their return to the apartment, my nephew was pushing Mum's wheelchair. Michael was walking ahead. He went through an exit door first.

It was a lovely Indian summer day. Friends and neighbours were lounging in the raspberry and pistachio-coloured Adirondack chairs in front of YEH!, the frozen yoghurt place. A small man ensconced in one of the long raspberry-coloured chairs basked in the sunshine while spooning frozen yoghurt out of a Styrofoam cup. On recognising Michael he leapt out of the chair and extended his hand. When Michael recognised him he recoiled and thrust out his arm.

'No! Get away from me!' It was Barry Stein, Michael's former medical school classmate and the colorectal specialist who had repeatedly dismissed the early signs of Mum's cancer eight and a half years before. Stein flailed in bewilderment until he saw Mum, hooked to portable oxygen, in a wheelchair, emerge through the large glass doors of the mall. Mum's weary eyes regarded her killer. Then she looked away.

'Poor Michael.' Mum clucked, over the telephone. 'Did he need an encounter like that?'

'Maybe Barry Stein did,' I said. Maybe they both did, I thought, but did not say.

There would be no CT scan. Before the fourteen-day course of antibiotics ended, it became clear that they weren't working. Despite Dr Kavan's investment of time, knowledge, compassion and care, it seemed dark angels had taken over and decided to bring Mum's suffering to an end. Dr Kavan did not call to say goodbye.

As wind and rain lashed at the maple tree outside my window, I continued to write. The leaves on its branches faded and fell. I kept writing. Each morning, its branches grew barer. Driven by the mother of all deadlines, I turned away from the sight of the dying leaves, went to my workstation, and wrote. On the morning of Tuesday, 22 October, I completed the first draft of Janka's story. The branches on the maple tree were now half bare. I didn't wait until the next day before sending the completed story to Mum. It was the best present she could have on a birthday that would be her last.

The week before, Mum received an e-mail from Yad Vashem stating that, because of her medical condition, the Israeli government had fast-tracked her application to have Janka instated as a Righteous Among The Nations. On 15 October 2013, Mum was notified that her childhood nanny Ewa Janina Wocjicka, born on Christmas Eve of 1908 in the slums of Warsaw and murdered before Christmas of 1942 in front of the Warsaw Ghetto gates, was officially recognised and honoured as a heroine among wartime elite.

On Wednesday, 23 October, I hung back while Mum's apartment was inundated with well-wishers. It was her 85th birthday. Her last birthday. Mum was propped up in bed, on a bolster, while people streamed through the apartment. When the well-wishers left, I entered her bedroom and lay down beside her. The telephone for the hearing-impaired, which sat on the nightstand beside her bed, emitted a shrill shriek. My brother's eldest daughter was calling to wish her Nana a happy birthday.

'Thank you sweetheart. Would you speak to your aunt? Forgive me, but I'm tired.' Never before had Mum cut short a conversation with one of her grandchildren. For a few moments I spoke with my niece, and then ended the call. Mum took her nightly dose of codeine, to suppress her cough and help her sleep. She closed her eyes. Before the drug took effect she said, with urgency, 'Hold my hand.' I did so. We lay wordlessly side by side until that damned phone for the hearing-impaired went off again. This time, the call was from my nephew. Mum ended it quickly. She still had enough strength to grip my hand. Then she confessed, 'For a few moments, I felt like I was floating away. I thought I was dying. I thought to myself, if this is what dying feels like, I don't mind. It's my birthday. My daughter is beside me. It's – okay.'

I shuddered. 'Must be the effect of the codeine.' I couldn't convince myself, so how could I fool my mother?

'But I take codeine every night now, and it never had this effect before!'

With my mother's hand in mine, I rolled on my side to face her. My big brown eyes widened, and I questioned Mum like I had questioned Daddy when he lay beside me at bedtime spinning unfinished tales, so very long ago. 'Were you disappointed to come back?'

Mum reflected. 'No. I would like to hang around – a little while longer.' It felt like foreshadowing. 'A little while longer' was all the time Mum had left.

CHAPTER FORTY-FIVE

'Can we still make the trip? It's only a month away.' Mum had been invited to speak at Halifax's King's College in early November, during Holocaust Remembrance Week. The college was sponsoring the event, and the speakers. Mum insisted the college bring me with her. We were going to be joined by Norman Conard, who was being flown in from Kansas. On the afternoon of Sunday, 2 November, there would be a public screening of *The Courageous Heart of Irena Sendler,* followed by a question and answer session.

Mum looked questioningly at Michael. Dr Zajdman considered my proposal. 'Maybe.' He refused to commit to a definitive answer.

When Howard heard of the trip he offered to rent a van, have it stocked with portable oxygen, and take Mum on the day and night ride to Atlantic Canada, since Mum was no longer able to fly. In a phone call no one knew about, Howard told me I needn't come along. No one knew how much and how far my brother's best friend presumed to dare.

'What a guy!' Mum exclaimed. 'Sometimes I wish I could kill him, and then he goes and does a thing like this!'

The Holocaust Studies department at King's College was notified of our revised plans. They proceeded to create posters and promote the event. They also took out insurance.

Around Mum's birthday, Michael announced he was taking us to Halifax and we would be taking the train. Hearing that, I breathed more easily. Mum breathed more easily, metaphorically.

On Hallowe'en Michael, Howard, Mum and I rode to Central Station. We made a strange caravan: a dying woman, her two children, already grieving, and a sidekick.

Michael booked first class tickets. Mum and I bunked together, and a private room, with a day bed, was made available to Mum whenever she felt the need to lie down.

Neither of us had been to Atlantic Canada. Mum was seeing Atlantic Canada last. The dying woman lay in the lower bunk of a sleeping compartment watching, from the window, as bottle-green evergreens and mustard-coloured tamarack trees whizzed past. Gamely she sang, 'O Canada!' Mum knew none of the words to our national anthem except for the first two, and thought the lyrics 'our native land' referred to the Indians. Yet, in the sixty-five years since reaching this lucky land of peace and snow, Mum always teared up at the sight of the Canadian flag.

A kindly black porter catered to us in the dining car. It was then, on her last train ride in Canada, that Mum told Michael and Howard the story of her first train ride in Canada, when a kindly black porter brought her hot, black coffee and a warm, white roll. Hooked to portable oxygen, speaking breathily, Mum held court in the dining car as long as her waning strength allowed. She revealed and reviewed her life as if unravelling a roll of film. Howard listened, mesmerised. Michael broke down.

We arrived at Halifax's intimate train station at four p.m. on the afternoon of Saturday, 1 November. Mum was helped onto an assistance buggy, and we piled in behind her. We were driven along the side of the train tracks, towards the station's entrance. As we rode into view, two friendly figures took recognisable form. Norman Conard and the head of the Holocaust Studies department, a Polish-born professor, stood at the edge of the path and waved in greeting.

Norman Conard had been contacted in advance.

'Living history is passing away.' Norman signalled to the audience, in his public address on Sunday afternoon. In a wheelchair, Mum sat beside him, on stage. She was hooked to portable oxygen, and held a portable microphone in her hand. I had just delivered the speech Mum originally planned to give. She felt too weak to speak for herself. It was four and a half years since *The Courageous Heart's* Hollywood premiere, when I refused to give a speech on Mum's behalf. Now I had become her conduit.

After the event Norman sat with me. 'Do you know this year will see the earliest Hanukkah in recorded history?' The American Protestant history teacher queried. 'Really. It will fall on the same date as the American Thanksgiving. 27 November.' No, I hadn't known, and couldn't have cared less. My sun was about to fall from my sky, and I was about to become a cast-off satellite spinning in the desolation of outer space.

Mum marshalled her formidable psychic forces to gather the strength to make this trip, which she called 'my last hurrah'. A week later, a Halifax newspaper ran the headline, 'Holocaust Survivor Humbles King's Crowd'. Now that it was over, Mum was crumbling.

CHAPTER FORTY-SIX

'Have you got an extra toothbrush?'

'Ah, if I don't, I can get one.' We were back from Halifax. Michael had returned to Toronto. Mum was bedridden, now. I was going to her apartment every day.

'A journalist has come from Poland to interview me. She'll be sleeping here. She needs a toothbrush.'

Anna Bikont, the offspring of a Jewish mother and a Catholic father, was a leading player in Poland's Solidarity movement. As a journalist and a writer focusing on Polish Catholic and Jewish relationships during wartime, Poland's right-wingers considered Bikont traitorous for having unearthed and exposed a wartime atrocity, which she documented in the award-winning and best-selling *The Crime and The Silence*. Bikont was doing research for a book she planned to write on Irena Sendler. As she had done with Harrison and the Hallmark people, Bieta steered Bikont to my mother. When Mum's condition shifted from chronic to terminal Bikont was prepared to fly in almost immediately, but Mum put her on hold because of the trip to Halifax. The day after our return from Atlantic Canada, suitcase in hand, Bikont was at Mum's door. Without a toothbrush.

I showed up with my shopping trolley, and led the internationally recognised author to the Cavendish Mall. We bought food at IGA. I also took Bikont to the pharmacy, where she was able to purchase a toothbrush.

For two days Anna Bikont stayed in Mum's apartment, interviewing her when Mum felt strong enough to give an interview, and retreating when Mum needed to rest. I can't recall whether Bikont slept on the hide-a-bed in the living room or on the open futon in the back room but either way, she must've been uncomfortable. In the back room, an oxygen tank pumped incessantly. The front door was unlocked so members of a palliative care team could enter without having to ring the intercom.

After two days Bikont moved across the city, to the apartment of a friend. For the rest of the week, in relentlessly driving rain, she criss-crossed Montreal by public transport to gather material for her work-in-progress while a primary source was still living and able to supply her with it.

During our long weekend in Atlantic Canada, the clocks were pushed back. Because there is an hour's difference between Atlantic Time and Eastern Standard Time, for us, time stood still. Now that we were back in Quebec darkness fell suddenly, like a final curtain, and the branches of the maple tree outside my living room window were almost bare. A few brown and withered leaves clung tenaciously to blackening branches. The rain fell, like darkness; cold, heavy and hard.

On the evening of Saturday 8 November, Mum looked up from her pillow and plaintively implored, 'I'm afraid to be alone.' Instantly, I went to the back room and called Michael.

'Can you stay overnight?' Michael shouted. It wasn't like Michael to shout.

'Well, yes of course I can, if I have to. But if Mum's afraid to be alone then I'm afraid to be alone with her. I'm not medically trained. What if something happens in the middle of the night?'

'Do I have to call Howard?!' It sounded like a threat. Why was Michael so angry? Did he believe I was attempting to abandon our dying parent?

'I don't know! I just know I can't do this by myself! Do you expect me to?'

Dr Zajdman was displeased. 'I'm on my way.' Several minutes later he called back. 'Howard is on his way.'

Howard stormed into Mum's apartment with a box of pizza, a bottle of wine, and a copy of *The Saturday Gazette*. He was surlier than a government-sponsored caregiver. After greeting Mum and ignoring me he heated his pizza, downed his wine, dined alone at Mum's dining room table, and then moved into the back room. My purse and my scarf, hat and jacket were lying on the futon. Howard thrust out his arm, swooping them off the futon and onto the floor. Then he plunked himself onto the futon with his copy of *The Saturday Gazette*.

I hid in the bedroom, clinging to Mum. She urged me to leave and get some sleep. As if I could.

'I'm alright now, sweetheart. Howard is here. Imagine, he drove in from the country just to be with me. Oh, I feel so loved.'

I wasn't sure what to do. I held Mum until she drifted into a drugged sleep. Then I went into the back room to retrieve my belongings. While Howard remained prone and silent on the futon, supposedly engrossed in *The Saturday Gazette,* I was compelled to crawl on my hands and knees in order to gather the accessories that Howard, an obsessive neat freak in his home and on his person, had scattered across the floor.

As my mother lay dying on the other side of the wall I collected my accessories, got off the floor, straightened up, and offered two words. 'Thank you.' Howard grunted. I left.

At one o'clock in the morning Michael arrived and relieved Howard. The following evening, packing the wheelchair and portable oxygen into his SUV, he took Mum to a local synagogue to attend a commemoration for [42]*Kristallnacht*. On their return Mum noticed that her ankles and calves had swollen. 'Look Michael! See how swollen they are!'

Calmly Michael responded, 'Does it hurt you?'

Mum answered meekly. 'No.'

I looked at my mother's distorted legs and then looked at Michael. 'I don't suppose it would help if I massaged them?'

Michael shook his head. 'No.'

---

[42] The night of broken glass. The one night and two days of terror and violence against Jews in Germany initiated and enacted by the Nazis on 9 and 10 November 1938.

CHAPTER FORTY-SEVEN

On Monday afternoon, Michael wheeled his mother to the mall. On Tuesday afternoon, Michael wheeled his mother to the mall. On Wednesday afternoon, on 12 November, his fifty-fifth birthday, in a downpour, once more Michael wheeled his mother to the mall. I joined them. We sat with her buddies at the Mmmmmuffin concession. Mum was happy to be out and among people. She was particularly happy to watch children play. At a small round table at the Mmmmmuffin concession Michael leaned back in a chair too small for his large, husky frame, joked with and charmed Mum's buddies. They gazed at Dr Zajdman in awe. They envied the dying woman in their midst. When Michael took a break to buy groceries at IGA, the old women at the table nodded and stared. 'No one has a son like this.' They insisted. 'No one.' Then Michael returned, continuing to smile and joke and charm, all the while keeping an eye on the oxygen tank. When it ran low he dropped to his knees behind Mum's wheelchair and quickly replaced the tank with the spare that dangled on its handlebars. When he was satisfied that Mum was receiving the air she needed he sprang up and returned to his seat, as though he had never left it. When the time came to leave, Michael knelt down and bundled up Mum, buttoning her jacket, lifting her hood onto her head, and wrapping a scarf around her neck. Sweetly, Mum smiled at him.

'Payback time! I did this for you, now you're doing this for me!' By then Mum was stoned. Michael had begun administering morphine.

On his birthday, I walked behind my brother as he wheeled our dying mother back from the mall. Pellets of rain struck his bare head and burdened shoulders. My heart ached for the boy Mum had risked her life to bring into the world. The beautiful sweet-hearted brother I grew up with resurfaced. As long as he is beside me, I thought, I can endure this wretchedness and misery.

In the evening Howard came with a box of pizza and a bottle of wine. In the dining room Michael and Howard went through the motions of a desultory birthday celebration, while I lay beside Mum. When Howard left Michael joined us, playing, on his laptop, the 1997 interview Mum recorded on her 69th birthday for the Shoah Foundation. Listening to her strong and steady younger voice Mum, on morphine, referring to herself in the past tense, slurred, 'I was quite a character!' Even this nightmare Mum and Michael managed to transform into a dark victory.

The day after Michael's birthday, I confronted him directly.

'I know a lot of people depend on you, but would you consider taking a leave of absence?'

In his Canada Dry manner, Michael responded, 'I've taken a leave of absence. Haven't you noticed?'

The day after Michael's birthday, a magazine Mum subscribed to, arrived in the mail. Two pieces dealing with the Warsaw Ghetto appeared in the current issue, written by Renata Skotnicka-Zajdman. In the final weeks of her life, in her fourth language, Mum became a published writer. She asked me to read the pieces out loud. As I echoed Mum's words back to her, she nodded with satisfaction. Mum's published pieces were models of memoir writing.

People whose lives Mum had touched continued to visit. A member of Mum's network, a younger child survivor, flew in from New York. Outside Mum's bedroom she said to me, 'I was with her in Warsaw. I knew she was bleeding. I told her she needed to see a doctor. She told me, 'It's nothing serious. I've got haemorrhoids, that's all. I've got a good doctor.' I stared at the woman with a renewed sense of horror.

'Renata led busloads of students on tours twice a day. She was so strong. She had so much passion and energy. She changed my life. She changed many lives.' Echoing my endless regret, my mother's 'child' stated brutally, 'Why did she trust that doctor? Why didn't she go for a second opinion? This is a tragedy.'

In her bedroom, Mum leaned back on her bolster, seemingly resigned. 'Everyone has to go through this. It's my last journey.'

Mum was deteriorating daily. She lost control of her bodily functions. Even more shocking, she was losing the power of speech.

'Pain.' Mum's eyes suddenly opened. 'Pain. Morphine. Need more morphine.'

It was Saturday, again. Those close to Michael came in from Toronto. Michael took a break to go out to dinner with a friend, leaving his wife in charge. I lay in bed with Mum. I lay beside my mother every evening, now. Wordlessly, with waning strength, she would lift her arm and I curled under it, trembling and terrified, clinging to her like a baby bird snuggling under the wing of its mortally wounded mama. When Michael informed me that he was leaving us alone with Ann, I clung to Mum even more fiercely. 'Don't wake up.' I willed her. 'Oh please don't wake up until Michael gets back.' Within moments of Michael's departure, Mum woke and called for morphine. I had no choice but to call Ann.

As Ann prepared the injection, I held up Mum. She was now a glassy-eyed rag doll hovering between life and death.

Ann injected Mum.

'Where's Michael?' Mum tensed.

Blandly, Ann responded, 'He'll be back soon.'

'Where's Michael?!' The one faculty Mum retained to the end, was her mind.

'I'm here now.' Ann authoritatively stated.

'Where's Michael?!' Mum was seized by panic. Ann injected her again.

'He went out for supper with Lawrence, Mum.'

'Shhh!' Ann hissed, darting me a warning glance.

'Want Michael.' Mum whimpered. 'Want Michael!'

Repeatedly Ann injected Mum, but the morphine would not take. Mum was growing frantic. 'Michael! Michael!'

'I'm going to call Michael.' Literally, I left Mum in Ann's hands.

'No!' Ann commanded in a tone that, for almost twenty-five years, always succeeded in cowing me into silence.

'Don't disturb Michael.' Ann's command almost worked this time, too.

Witnessing Mum's terror and inability to accept pain relief from Ann, I had an appalling thought. Did Mum know? Had she woken up on the carpet sooner than I realised, on that harrowing Labour Day Monday, while I was on the phone pleading with Ann?

The spell was broken. Disobeying the attending doctor's orders, I went to the back room and called Michael. Ann did not try to stop me.

During the third week of November Lynn came in to assist Michael. Though long out of practice, she was a trained and registered nurse. Howard flew to Switzerland. Apparently, business couldn't wait. He would be back soon. Lynn and Howard had already scheduled their monthly break in the Bahamas. They booked their flight for 6 December.

As they knew, 6 December was my birthday.

CHAPTER FORTY-EIGHT

The head of the palliative care team 'strongly suggested' that Mum be moved to the neighbourhood Mount Sinai hospice. They felt exhaustion was impairing Michael's judgement.

'Can you give her better care than I can?' He challenged, knowing they could not. Michael promised Mum she would die at home, in her bed. The lengths he went to in order to keep his word were heroic.

Each evening, as I walked into what felt like a chamber of horrors, Michael would update me.

'Mum was babbling in Polish this afternoon. I didn't understand what she was saying.'

As I lay beside her, Mum stared at the ceiling and shouted, 'Janka! Janka!' It seemed she could see her beloved Lilliput. Perhaps she was hallucinating. I hope she was not.

After crying out for her first caregiver, Mum called for her last. 'Michael!'

Each evening, after Mum drifted into a drugged sleep, I returned to my apartment to cry a lot, to sleep a little, if I could, to pull myself together and do it all again the next day. Each evening, as I left my mother's apartment, I saw a car parked in front of the building's entrance. Its licence plate read DAD, and its logo, as with all car plates in Quebec, read *Je me souviens* (I remember). The car with the licence plate that read DAD sat in front of my mother's building each evening for the last three weeks in November.

On Monday evening, 25 November, Mum gazed up from her pillow and strained to communicate.

'Babies!' Her head almost lifted with the effort. 'Babies!' Michael and Lynn did not understand what she was asking. I did. Mum wanted her babies. I went to the back room and retrieved a framed photograph of Michael and me as toddlers. In the decades-old photograph Michael rests trustingly in my arms, gazing up at me with unabashed adoration.

I set the photograph in front of Mum. Her radiant smile, which would soon become a memory, broke through the fog of morphine like sunshine bursting through a cluster of clouds.

On Tuesday evening, 26 November, once more Mum strained to communicate. Michael and Lynn lifted and held her. I was on my knees on the floor in front of Mum, earnestly searching her face.

'What is it, Mum? What are you trying to tell me?'

With a mighty effort, Mum managed to emit one word. 'Money!' She moaned, with urgency. 'Money!'

Once more, Michael and Lynn were mystified. To me, Mum's message was clear.

'Don't worry about me, Mummy!' Tears rolled down my cheeks. 'Don't worry about me! I'll be okay! Michael will look after me. He'll make sure I'm protected. Don't worry, Mummy! I'll be okay! I'll be fine.' Telling Mum what she needed to hear, I could only hope it was true.

'Can you rest now?' Michael didn't seem to realise how much he was saying. Limply, Mum nodded. Michael and Lynn lay Mum back onto her pillow. Mum managed to convey her last request. She had also pronounced her final word.

On Tuesday night, the morphine pump broke. Michael stayed up all night injecting Mum at regular intervals, serving as a human pump. On Wednesday morning he contacted the CLSC and instructed them to deliver not one, but two pumps. When Lynn arrived in the afternoon, Michael allowed himself to sleep. When I came in the early evening, Lynn was making dinner. She was in the kitchen. The monitor was on the dining room table, which was adjacent to the kitchen. Michael was resting in the back room.

At quarter to seven I heard what sounded like static on the monitor. I alerted Lynn. She came out of the kitchen.

'Man, you've got good hearing!' She raced to the back room, alerted Michael, and they both rushed into the bedroom. A few minutes later, they returned to the living room, looking stone-faced.

'Is that what they call 'the death rattle?'' All I knew of expected deaths was what I had seen in movies.

'Oh no!' Lynn insisted. 'We just had to change her position, that's all.'

I still don't understand why we sat down for supper, and I've never been able to forgive myself for it. Michael's judgement was impaired and mine was cloudy, but Lynn?

Ten days after her passing I asked Mum, in a dream, what her last hours were like. She stated clearly, 'I felt like I was burning up. I felt like I was on fire. I thought Michael turned off the oxygen tank. Then the fire went down and I was okay.'

To this day, I cannot eat my evening meal at my dining room table.

I am grateful only that Mum hung on until we finished dinner and didn't leave without me.

Like obedient children, Michael and I came to the table and consumed Lynn's dinner. Between 7:45 and 7:50 Michael stepped outside for much needed air, and I went into our mother's bedroom, clutching a copy of *Bent Branches*. Since it was no longer possible to lie beside Mum, I sat next to her bed and read out loud. I didn't know what passages to read, so I let the soft covers of the book fall open and show me:

'Where's Mummy?'

'You know where she is. She's in the hospital.'

'Then how come I can't see her?'

'Because they don't let children in the hospital.'

'Then bring her here!'

'But *shepsaleh*, *if I could bring her here, she wouldn't be in the hospital!*'

'*I don't care! I wanna see her! Don't lie to me. She's going to die!*'

'What?! Where did you hear such a thing?'

'Never mind, I heard it.'

'But it's not true.'

'Then prove it to me. Bring me Mummy so I can see her. You prove to me she isn't going to die!'

Painfully Adam pressed his eyelids shut. He had been left no choice but to place his cherished child at the mercy of a woman who appeared to be vicious. How had she twisted the information his sister had given her? What had those evil children done to his daughter now?

Fiercely Adam pulled Nehama to him. He cupped her oval-shaped, delicately featured face in his work-worn, crippled hand. The shape of his daughter's face, and its expression of stubbornness and defiance were so like her mother's. Solemnly Adam swore, 'Shepsaleh, *I promise on my life that I will bring Mummy to you. Your mother will be well. You will keep your mother for a very long time.*'

For almost two hours I sat beside my supposedly unresponsive mother, reading from the book I wrote for her, about her, and dedicated to her. Her head tilted toward the sound of my quavering voice. As the words fell from my mouth and tears coursed down my cheeks Mum's features softened, and her laboured breathing eased. She looked like an ill child listening to a bedtime story.

As I looked up from the pages of the book I noticed fat, moist snowflakes dropping from an illuminated sky, lacing the panes of the large picture window behind Mum's bed frame, behind Mum's bed. On the wall directly above Mum perched a portrait of her mother Natalja, an enlargement of the small photograph Aunt Ania hid in her panties throughout the war. The portrait looked so much like me. Mum had placed it there deliberately. At that instant the spirits of three women came together; the grandmother who was dead, the mother who was dying, and their memory keeper, who was being left behind.

It was between 9:40 and 9:45, at Mum's usual bedtime, that I sensed a new and sudden stillness in the air. Is this it? I thought. Softly, I called for Lynn, but she still wasn't paying attention to the monitor.

I was reading the last pages of the last story in *Bent Branches*. Not wanting to disturb Mum, and not wanting to leave her, I read to the end.

Illuminated after dark, the faded jade dome of St. Joseph's Oratory glowed in the Montreal skyline. On the ground, Renata was standing as close as she could get to the passenger exit. Her arms were spread wide apart, with a winter coat for Nehama flung over a bent elbow. It was 22 December. Again. Nehama was home. She had fulfilled her mission. She had made the final instalment. The bill on Alek's life was paid in full.

375

As fellow passengers poured into the terminal and paused in the embrace of those they loved, Nehama moved towards her mother. Satisfied, Adam's spirit receded into the ether. His mission had been accomplished, too.

It was then that I knew. Mum's soul had escaped her tortured body like a bird flitting from a tree.

I sat motionless. It was only when I heard the front door open that I moved. Michael had returned. I went into the hallway. I could not bring myself to look at my sibling, so I looked to Lynn. In a hushed whisper, I managed to speak. 'I think she's gone.'

For a brief moment I returned to the bedroom. Kissing Mum lightly on the forehead I suggested, 'Go be with Daddy now. I'll see you – both – soon enough.'

An hour later, on this remarkably early first night of Hanukkah, I stepped out into an atmosphere illuminated by candle-lit menorahs in neighbours' windows. Moist, doily-like snowflakes dropped rhythmically from a lightened sky. Our corner of the world turned white. The entranceway was clear. The car that kept vigil during the rainy black nights of November was no longer there.

***

The whole of my past is like a film tightly rolled up and hidden in a drawer in the recesses of my memory. Only if you happen to touch this roll, the whole film unwinds and shows individual frames. Some of the images are faded, some are wiped out. But they are still there. Sometimes it seems to me that it is still happening, that I am still living in that time.

The 1st of September 1939. It was my mother's birthday. What began for me as a happy day with my mother turned into a never-to-be-forgotten horror.

The 3rd of September 1989. We'd just celebrated my son Michael's wedding. Fifty years later, in a solemn and hushed sanctuary in Mississauga, Ontario, my friends and I were sharing, in our minds, our flaming past. Fifty years ago in Warsaw, German aircraft relentlessly bombed our city, killing thousands of people. As I watched my son's bride under the [43] chupah I thought of my brother's almost-bride, who was destined to become our family's first victim. Sweet, gentle Marysia Zilberstein, gone two months before she could realise her dream of standing under the chupah with my brother.

My friends are precious jewels. You, who survived our joint and grotesque history, I love you all. You survived the mutilation of the human spirit that can be caused by enduring six years in hell. Where did we get the capacity to keep struggling? Where did we get the strength to survive healthy and whole in such a sick world? We were shaken and bruised and uprooted, and yet determined to retain our humanity. Fifty years later, it has become clear that we will never see a sane world where character and ability matter more than religion, colour, or gender.

Our stories are hard to hear, but as we grow older it becomes more and more important to tell our stories. My story is one of macabre masquerade, in which my name and identity were changed in a crescendo of terror.

Fifty years ago – half a century ago – our world collapsed. In 1939, in one grand stroke, the world as we knew it collapsed. Still, it would be a distortion to see our lives only in terms of horror. My life has been half horror and half success. As I look back to the events of 50 years ago, I can still smell the stink of war and remember the degraded, hungry, beaten and frightened child that I was.

---

[43] Wedding canopy

I wish I could be a real writer. Everyone suffers just as much, but a writer can say it better. Still, I've broken my silence because I cannot bear the thought that the world will not remember. We will be dead and unable to prevent those who try to deny what was done to us, from re-writing history. My problem is time. Time is running out.

How can I evoke, for my children, a childhood buried in ashes? To remember, to forget nothing, has become an obsession for many survivors. We have been subjected to countless analyses. Our psyches have been dissected. We have been placed on exhibition, treated like passive objects, and betrayed, so I plead for the dead, in order to defend their memories. I plead for memory and decency. It is all I can do. And I remember. Remembrance is the marrow of my Jewish identity. I carry Memory like a precious gift and a relentless curse. Memory is at the core of my identity. I have no choice but to carry it with me.

From the private memoir of Renata-Skotnicka Zajdman,
September 1989

THOSE UPON WHOSE SHOULDERS WE STAND

Michal Zajdenman: born 20 February 1875, died 21 February 1933

Joseph Łucjan Skotnicki: born 6 December 1889, died 27 April 1939

Rachel Natalia Młynek Skotnicka: born 1 September 1893, died New Year's Night, 1940

Surah Laja (Sarah Leah) Glat Zajdenman: born 14 June 1881, murdered 24th, 25th, 26th? August 1942

Ewa Janina Wocjicka (also known as Little Janka and Lilliput): born Christmas Eve 1908, murdered (?) December 1942

Aleksander Młynek /Skotnicki (Uncle Alek): born 19 December 1912, died 4 January 1981

Hania Mlynek Hoyos (Auntie Hanka (Ania)): born 13, 30 or 31 March 1918, died November 19th, 1981

Abraham (Abram) Zajdman (Daddy): born 16 April 1917, died 6 April 1983

Renata Skotnicka-Zajdman (Mummy): born 23 October 1928, died 27 November 2013

Renata Skotnicka-Zajdman

23 October 1928-27 November 2013

With gratitude. In memory.

Printed in Great Britain
by Amazon